Rainbow Remedies
for Life's Stormy Times

Rainbow Remedies
for Life's Stormy Times

Joanne K. Hill

foreword by Al Siebert, Ph.D.

MH
Moorhill Communications
South Bend, Indiana

Published by:
Moorhill Communications
P.O. Box 4114
South Bend, Indiana 46634-4114
Printed in the United States of America
First Printing: 2002

Drawings, unless otherwise noted: Pilar de la Torre
Design and production: Joya Helmuth
Hummingbird and flower: Heather Ann Bare
"Little Tramp" illustrations: Janice D. Cowen
Author's photograph: Doris Holik Kelly

Publisher's Cataloging-in-Publication
(Provided by Quality Books, Inc.)

Hill, Joanne K.
    Rainbow Remedies for life's stormy times / by Joanne K. Hill ; foreword by Al Siebert. -- 1st ed.
    p. cm.
    Includes bibliographical references.
    LCCN 2001126171
    ISBN 0-9707032-0-1

    1. Self-help techniques. 2. Life skills guides. 3. Bereavement--Religious aspects--Christianity. 4. Life change events. 5. Stress management. I. Title.

BF632.H55 2001   158
                    QBI01-700470

This book is dedicated
to the Universal Creator
in gratitude
for
life, love, family and friends,
past, present and future.

When the lamp is shattered
The light in the dust lies dead —
When the cloud is scattered
The Rainbow's glory is shed.

Percy Bysshe Shelley

CONTENTS

FOREWORD

Why is it that some people are made stronger by adversities that devastate others? Joanne Hill provides her answers to that question in this amazing account of how she survived years of deep personal anguish and emerged with valuable insights about how to cope with life's worst crises.

Losing a loved one can be deeply distressing, but what if it keeps happening again and again? What if you lose another loved one before you have recovered from the last loss? How well would you hold up if your family kept dying, one after the other? During what Joanne calls her four "Locust Years," she lost her husband, son, mother, father, brother, foster son, aunt and more. Twelve family members in all.

Ironically, Joanne had worked as a Crisis Intervention Specialist for over seven years. She had passed the tests to become a Crisis Specialist when life tested her own crisis coping skills — over and over again.

Rainbow Remedies for Life's Stormy Times is a valuable guide-book on how to weather life's crises, and it is an account of a hero's journey. Heroic survivors have five things in common. First, their challenges and travails are extreme tests of their spirit. Second, they are determined to survive and cope well; they do not become victims. Third, they are transformed by the experiences. Fourth, they make their journey a defining part of their life story and integrate what they went through into their public identity. Fifth, they talk or write about what they discovered and learned in ways that encourage, help and inspire others.

Rainbow Remedies is rich with the kinds of learning that can come only from someone who has made the heroic journey through the fires of anguish, has healed, and emerged wiser. Every chapter contains valuable insights and useful suggestions about how to survive and surmount personal crises. Every chapter contains pearls of wisdom that reassure, heal and inspire.

My experience with survivors of the most extreme human adversities gives me deep respect for Joanne's ability to not only recover from her grief and emotional anguish, but to also have the strength and courage to relive all of her distressing feelings in order to write this book. Only a few of life's best survivors ever make it this far.

The transformational process of recovery after deeply distressing, traumatic experiences takes years and proceeds through these phases:

Reliving the Pain

• You take the courageous step to relive your painful experiences with a friend, a counselor or a support group of people who have been through similar experiences. You may have nightmares. You may feel like you are falling into a bottomless well. You find yourself reliving the memories and feelings during conversations, at movies, when shopping, almost any place. You wish something could make the intrusive memories stop, but nothing works. Not even medications, drugs or alcohol can stop the feelings and memories from intruding at unwelcome times.

Taking Control

• You relive and talk about the experiences again and again with good listeners.

• You gradually gain control over the feelings and memories of your experiences; they no longer control you. You can stop thinking about the painful past when you want to.

Transition Phase

• You experiment with talking about your experiences to others outside your support group and circle of closest friends. A sign that you have healed is when you can talk about what you've been through in ways that do not distress your listeners.

• From Post-Traumatic Stress to Post-Traumatic Growth, you find gifts, learning and blessings in your experience. You discover that your struggle to regain emotional peace and happiness has strengthened you, has made you a better person than before.

Publicly Declare and Validate Your New Identity

• You make your story and your healing journey a part of your identity. You avoid letting your experience become your primary identity in your own mind, even though it may be how others refer to you.

• You discover at times that you've gone many days without thinking of the traumatic experiences or your long healing journey. You appreciate that your emotional wounds have healed, that you are emotionally free from what happened.

Helping Others

• You offer your strength and insights to others who are struggling with their pain, anguish, traumas and crises. You can stay calm and keep your attention on others in distress without having your painful memories stirred up. Your presence is helpful to others who see you as a role model and as proof that a person can heal and be happy again.

• You have the courage and strength to relive all your experiences to write a book like this that can inspire and help others.

Al Siebert, Ph.D.
Author of *The Survivor Personality*
web site: www.THRIVEnet.com

*I believe you can't have a rainbow
without going through a storm.*

John Bryant
Operation Hope

PREFACE

This too shall pass...

In my younger days, I hated it when Grandma said to me, "This too shall pass." I knew the trouble would pass, but the hurt lingered. Or so I thought. Ah, how sweet it is to look back and understand. You're right, Grandma, "This too shall pass." Today the words bring a promise of peace, not anger. That doesn't mean I don't feel the pain. I do. I have. I will again. The difference is that now I know the pain won't last forever — provided I take charge of my thoughts — my life. Grief hurts. Sorrow cuts deep wounds. Painful wounds. Why let it linger any longer than necessary? I know it's necessary to grieve — but not forever.

Many years ago, my friend Margie, an only child, took her mother to the doctor for a routine checkup. While her mother got her annual physical, Margie ran a few errands. When she returned, Margie learned her mother had died of a heart attack in the doctor's office.

This was in the days when tranquilizers were liberally prescribed. For a year, Margie killed her emotional pain with the prescribed medicine. Then on the anniversary of the death, the pills no longer worked. Now Margie had to face the grief.

Another friend and I stayed with Margie through a midnight visit to her mother's grave where she let out all the pain and sorrow in a torrent of tears and stormy anger. I vowed then that if ever I had to face that kind of pain, it would be without chemicals. Bottled-up emotions are like a bottled tornado.

It's normal to feel the pain. We can learn much from it. But to stay there is dangerous. Sooner or later, we must get out of the storm and seek shelter. We must clean up the debris and rebuild. Life goes on and so must we.

Palm Sunday, April 11, 1965, tornadoes ripped through Indiana and other states. As in most of nature's disasters, incredible stories came forth of strength, courage, incredible kindnesses and serendipitous happenings.

Judy's grandparents were caught in one of the tornadoes. They ran from the living room toward the basement door, but in the darkness her grandfather grabbed the wrong door knob. When he opened the door, all he saw was a flight of stairs going up to nothing but a dangling toilet. He grabbed his wife and they ran out of the kitchen door into the yard. Their house, barn and every other building had been swept away. Incredibly, they were spared.

When the family came to help pick up whatever pieces were left, the grandmother's cherished porcelain figurine of a couple embracing was found in the hollow of a cement block. "It looked like a giant hand had carefully placed this delicate object into the center of the foundation stone," she said, hugging the anniversary gift to her heart. Amid the rubble, protected and unscathed, they found a reminder of the beginning. Like the rainbow which stands as a promise that God is always with me, the little figurine became an icon for this family.

When our daughter Cindy's house burned to the ground, she and her family escaped into the freezing early morning with only the clothes on their bodies. Barefoot mother. Pajama clad babies. A snow drifted fire hydrant.

Neighbors quickly took them in and bundled them up. The Red Cross gave vouchers for free clothing from St. Vincent de Paul. Friends, neighbors and co-workers donated furnishings. Thankfully, Cindy and her children were alive and unhurt. The heirloom youth bed made by her great-grandmother, the Noah's Ark crewelwork from her mother and treasured photographs were ashes.

Then came Christmas time with the family, a time for the sharing of gifts. Cindy's sister, Brenda waited until last to distribute her gifts. Beaming a mischievous smile, she passed around identical packages to her parents and siblings, leaving

Cindy's gift for last. Cindy watched as the others opened their gifts, suspecting what they would find.

Brenda worked for a photo laboratory. Her gifts that year were photo albums — empty albums for holding memorabilia of the good times. Cindy forced a smile of gratitude and slowly began to open hers.

The room grew still, for everyone but Cindy knew what was inside. Together the family had gathered photos and negatives for reproduction. They couldn't completely replace her albums, but they came close. Laughter and tears filled the room. The rainbow sparkled on the golden treasure of love.

As I've reviewed my four Locust Years, when twelve family members died, and the years before, to write this book, I've recalled these stories and others like them. Stories of strange and mysterious happenings, miraculous coincidences and wondrous people who came to us out of chaos, troubles and sorrow. The journey down memory lane has not been an easy one. To relive some of the moments drew fresh blood, but also new insights. Many times I wanted to quit. I thought, *I can't do this! What good will it do?*

Soon answers would come. A new book to give me support. A friend would come calling for help.

"You're the only person I know who would understand what I feel. I don't think I can take it anymore. I feel like I just want to curl up and die." We talked, we laughed, we cried. I gave her paper and pencil to begin her journal of this adventure.

I encouraged her to find the treasure within, turned on the music and left the room. An hour later I returned. There were fewer tissues in the box. My friend's eyes were red, yet she was smiling. "Thanks," she said. As she started to leave for home, she turned and said, "Now, when are you going to finish that book?"

Here it is, dear friend. I pray you find it helpful.

My divine sign indicates the future to me.

Socrates

Prologue

And the bow shall be in the cloud;
and I will look upon it, that I may remember the everlasting covenant between God
and every living creature of all flesh
that is upon the earth.

Genesis 9:14 KJV

The Rainbow Promise

The March Sunday in 1985 burst forth with bright sunlight and unseasonal warmth. As my husband Ken and I walked into St. Mary's for 7 o'clock Mass, Ken said, "It's going to be a great day." I looked up, smiling hopefully.

But inside me, there was no "great day" feeling. My stomach twisted into knots. Through the stained glass windows, the sun cast rainbows on the pews, but I didn't notice. As we knelt in prayer, my eyes squeezed tight so tears couldn't betray my thoughts.

Oh, God, I prayed. *I thank you for helping Ken make his decision, but I'm so scared. I hate the reason for his decision to go on disability leave. I know he needs to leave that stress-filled sales job if he wants to live, but what will he do to fill his days? What will I do if money runs short?*

I've sometimes thought that one advantage of the Catholic Mass is that I can follow the crowd in participation, even as I drift off into my own thoughts and prayers. No one ever yells out "Hallelujah!" or "Amen, Brother!" to interrupt my musings, as worshipers did in the church of my childhood. On this sunny, sad morning, instead of worshiping with others in the church, I drifted into worry, terrified at not knowing what might lie ahead for us.

No matter how I tried, I could never put Ken's heart condition totally out of my mind. From the day of his first heart attack, at age thirty-eight, Ken's health was a constant concern to me. For thirteen long years, I lived on the edge of a precipice.

I guess it's his toughness that keeps him going, God, I pondered while bobbing up and down with other parishioners attending the Mass. *How long can he keep doing this? How long can I hold on?*

Ken was a tough guy. Even as a teenager, he stood his ground against teachers, parents and anyone else who told him he couldn't do what he wanted to do. Early in our relationship he told me, "If it's something I really want to do, I will find a way to make it right." Over the years, especially after becoming a father, he mellowed enough to realize that particular philosophy didn't always serve him well. Now it did. The strong will that often caused trouble in his youth now helped Ken fight this disease called "congenital heart failure." Even as he experienced his first heart attack, Ken did his chores. The man simply would not quit!

After seventeen years of marriage, we moved on to twenty-two acres in the country. Ken, a city boy, fulfilled a dream. He fenced a piece of land and purchased two calves. Several times each day, Ken carried buckets of water 500 feet from the house to the calves because we didn't have water in the barn.

One gray, Friday evening in early November, when the calves were about six months old, I watched Ken fill the water buckets and head for the barn. He looked tired, so I offered to help. "I can do it!" he barked. "You take care of what you have to do."

Swallowing my hurt and fighting tears, I turned back toward the house, but before going inside, I looked back at him. He had stopped to rest, setting the buckets down. He did this a couple more times before reaching the barn. I thought maybe he had a touch of the flu, so I said a little prayer that he'd take care of himself.

After supper, he went straight to bed but refused to acknowledge any discomfort. I tried to shrug off my concern but spent an uneasy night. Early the next morning, I asked the children to help me feed and water the calves before Ken woke up. To my surprise, he showed no anger as he slowly poured himself a cup of coffee. I waited for an outburst. I hoped for an outburst. None came.

He watched the Saturday football games as usual, but the armchair coach was silent. On Sunday, I learned that Ken, an avid Notre Dame fan, had turned down an opportunity the previous day to watch his favorite team play at the stadium a few miles away, and he had asked the kids to feed and water the animals again.

Something was seriously wrong. As badly as I wanted to deny the possibility, I forced myself to confront him. Sitting dejectedly on the bed, he finally admitted to having pains in his jaw and down his arm along with experiencing some breathing problems. "Just a bug," he insisted. "I'll be fine."

I couldn't believe my ears! I was furious.

"You're not fine and it's not just a bug. Since your dad has a heart condition, I want you to see a doctor. Shall I take you to the emergency room or call an ambulance?"

He sat up straighter. "I'm fine. You worry too much," he insisted, giving me one of those charming, dimpled grins.

I didn't want to cry. Ken hated crying. His father had told him that was how a woman got her way: "She'll cry and make you feel sorry for her. Don't give in." I knew the advantage was in meeting him head on. Yet, I couldn't quash my fear. "I don't *want to lose you,"* I managed, choking back the tears.

"Aw, you'll be better off if I die, anyway. I got a big insurance policy, remember?" His laugh was weak.

For a moment, I thought I would explode with anger. Words flew out of their own accord. *"I don't want any damn insurance money, Ken Hill,"* I said, choking back the tears. *"If you die, I'll take all that money and give it to the church. I swear I will!"*

"You probably would," he grinned. *"Yeah. I'll just bet you would. But I'm not going to die. If I'm not better tomorrow, I'll go see the doctor. I promise."* Then he reached out and pulled me down on the bed and kissed me. Suddenly, he looked fine — except for a thin white line around his lips. I wanted to believe my eyes, but my heart said otherwise. *"I'll fix us some hot chocolate,"* I said pulling away and hurrying to the kitchen. I wanted to hide my persistent fear for this man I loved.

The next morning Ken was up and gone by seven. He stumbled in the door a couple hours later, tears streaming down his face. *"I've had a heart attack. I have to go to the hospital right away,"* he murmured through a film of pain. With unsteady legs and shaking hands, I reached out to my husband. Only later did I learn that he'd driven himself to the doctor's office after having breakfast with his buddies. The doctor confirmed he'd had a heart attack. *"Do you have someone to drive you to the hospital?"* Ken answered, *"Yes,"* then got into his car and drove the five miles home to ask me to take him there!

Ringing bells jolted me from the memory and into the church service once again. I watched as the priest lifted the bread and wine in the reenactment of the Last Supper. Father blessed the bread and wine for Holy Communion, and I responded "Amen" with the rest of the congregation. As we walked to the altar to take communion, I finally noticed the rainbows dancing on the walls. I smiled, remembering our good times together.

"Thank you, God, for the gift of these years."

As I knelt and waited while others received communion, my mind began to drift again, back to the doctor's prognosis after that first heart attack, thirteen years earlier.

> *Ken's veins were so small it was impossible to do open-heart surgery. His main arteries were clogged and a third of his heart damaged because he delayed treatment so long. Not one to be put off, Ken insisted the doctor tell him everything about his condition. (This was before doctors' fears of lawsuits forced them to reveal all the horrible possibilities of any disease or treatment.) His doctor reluctantly admitted that Ken probably had one to two years to live. "However," the doctor said, "if you give up smoking and change your eating and drinking habits, you might extend that time some."*
>
> *Although I desperately wanted Ken to change those habits, I also thought this was not the only solution and urged him to get a second opinion. Finally he agreed, and I called the Cleveland Clinic. "Send all his paperwork and we'll decide if we can help him," the doctors said. Although the original paperwork went from Ken's doctor to the clinic, the report came back to our house. Ken was alone at home when the letter arrived.*

When I returned home, Ken's car was in the drive, the door hanging open. My heart thudded in my chest as I raced to the house. On the dining-room table, I found the letter from the clinic. My eyes filled with tears as I read, "If the patient is still alive in a year, we'd like to examine him." I struggled to control waves of nausea threatening to engulf me. Having worked in crisis intervention for ten years, I knew what desperate people could do. I hurried to look for Ken's hunting guns. All were in place. I let out an enormous sigh of relief. Maybe he'd just gone for a walk.

I ran into the woods yelling his name. After tramping five acres of trees, I searched the barn and pasture, then returned to the house and grimly called a neighbor across the road. Yes, she'd seen him heading north on foot. I jumped in my car, threw it into gear and drove rapidly up and down the nearby roads for an hour, trying to find him. "Please, Lord," I pleaded over and over, "let him be okay." Finally, through a cascade of tears, I returned home.

Holding my breath, I stepped into the house, hoping he was there. He wasn't. I should do something constructive, I thought, but instead, paced the house crying and praying. Another hour passed. Then the telephone rang. My heart stopped as I grabbed the receiver. To my relief it was another neighbor a mile down the road with happy news. "We've got your husband," she said laughing. "Maybe you ought to come get him."

In his despondency, Ken had walked aimlessly, ending up at their house. Through grief-clouded eyes, Ken noticed his buddy's car in the driveway *and decided to stop. This was Ken's friend, a man he trusted. He had encouraged Ken to go into an auto-parts business for himself, offering to help Ken financially. They drank a few beers and soon were in a merry mood. I was so relieved that I forgot my anger and went to retrieve him. By the time I arrived, I barely noticed the hard knot of fear in my stomach.*

As time passed, we held our fragile lives together with humor, prayer and hard work. Two years later, his health had somewhat improved, and Ken was working as an auto-parts salesman, traveling three states. He had a new doctor who finally convinced him it was possible to gain more time if he changed his lifestyle. Ken listened.

He sold his small auto-parts business, took a year off, joined the doctor's early morning jogging group, lost weight and cut back on health-robbing habits. He had one minor heart attack two years after the first, but went straight to the hospital, and no further damage was done. It looked like his life was turning down a sunny path. I began to relax, forgetting there are often stormy times on the horizon.

"The Mass is ended, go in peace," said the priest. Ken and I stood up to leave. I looked at this robust looking man walking beside me and marveled. How often had I heard people who knew about his condition ask, "Why does he look so healthy? How can he do all that he does?" Most never knew the extent of the miracle they were seeing. Many others never even suspected he had a health challenge.

We stepped out of the church and scurried to the parking lot. The sun now hid behind ominous black clouds and a chilling north wind blew in. I buried my face in my coat collar.

"Let's go to breakfast," Ken suggested. We headed for our favorite family restaurant where we met several friends. For a while my spirits lifted.

By the time we finished hearty plates of apple pancakes, the weather changed again. Like siblings, the seasons were squabbling over who would be in control. Leaving the restaurant, we strolled to the car in bright, warm sunshine, waved goodbye to our friends and headed for home. Once there, Ken stretched out in his lounge chair to read the Sunday paper.

I changed into an old sweat suit, grabbed the rake, and headed for the lawn. *It might be a little early,* I thought, *but the weather is so nice, I'll do some spring clean up.* The exercise and sun quickly heated my body. I took off my sweatshirt, letting the sun on my back brighten my spirits.

Good, now maybe I can think about what I should do, rather than worry about what's happened. I thought Ken's decision to apply for disability payments probably meant he was feeling worse than he let on. He became efficient at acting as though he were completely healthy and had the physique that belied his real condition. *He'll be fine,* I told myself.

As I worked in the yard, I tried to put Ken's health problems aside and focus on the good times we could share when he wasn't working every day. Still, the nagging doubts would not go away. Ken's disability payments would bring in only two-thirds of his normal income, plus there would be no bonuses or opportunities for increased sales commissions. There would be no more company car with paid insurance and repairs.

Splat! A wet maple leaf hit me in the face. I was shivering from another change in weather. I glared at the menacing clouds. Why did they cover the sun and make me uncomfortable? Why was there no certainty in life? Where was the joy and peace? I scrambled to find my sweatshirt. As the thermometer registered the ups and downs of nature, my sunny disposition dropped behind gloomy patches of the week just past.

When Ken told me about his decision to apply for disability payments, my emotions jumbled. I felt relief because he wouldn't be fighting daily traffic, ever-increasing sales quotas and irritated customers, but I also felt anger because he had kept his plans from me.

Although Ken was advised years before to stop working, he chose to continue. I grew accustomed to his being at work and having the house free for personal projects from breakfast to dinner. There would be no time to get adjusted to the idea he would be home all day. His leave was effective immediately.

Guilt reared up to remind me that I had recently opted to start a business, rather than bring in a regular paycheck working for someone else. However, unlike Ken's auto-parts business, mine did not show immediate profits. In fact, it cost us money. Still, I passionately didn't want to give it up. Did I have to? Should I? I feared not being able to find a job. With a sinking heart, I realized that if Ken was ready to accept disability, he must be feeling that he didn't have much time left.

Why didn't I see that probability before? When Ken reached his goal of paying off the mortgage, he kept working. As I now contemplated why, I felt ashamed. Maybe Ken had hoped I would relieve the financial burden, and, instead, I chose otherwise. Rather than earning money, my decision to publish a newsletter for craftpersons cost money.

Nevertheless, Ken had encouraged me to follow my dream. He helped convert our children's former bedrooms into office space, putting together shelves and a table in the basement for warehousing and shipping of a greeting card line I acquired to publish and market. If I worked a full-time job for someone else, I would have to give up my writing and publishing business. I wouldn't have much time for Ken. Icy fear added to my discomfort from the weather. *How will we make ends meet with his income cut by a third?*

As I raked the lawn, my warm, salty tears mixed with the cold drizzling rain. Gloomy memories whirled inside my head, taking me back to Ken's forty-ninth birthday, two years before.

> *I was working full time as marketing manager for a local retirement community close to our home. I loved the convenience of going home for lunch. On this day, however, I was an hour late leaving the office due to a long discussion with my boss. Normally, I would have been home, eaten my lunch and returned.*
>
> *Ken was on a sales trip to Ohio for a few days, so I was concerned when a car pulled into our driveway behind me. Looking in the rearview mirror, I grinned seeing my husband's car. Ken so disliked being away from home overnight that he often worked marathon days to get home early. This being his birthday, I chuckled. "Thought he didn't like cele-brating birthdays," I said to myself.*
>
> *When we reached the house, I jumped out of my car first and ran to greet him with a big "Happy Birthday." As I flung open his car door, the greeting caught in my throat. Ken's face was ashen and etched in pain. Oh God, no. Not again!*
>
> *"Do you want me to drive you or should I call the ambulance?"*
>
> *"You drive," he gasped, painfully moving over to the passenger seat.*
>
> *Please, God, please help, I prayed silently as we sped down the streets toward the hospital. Each red light allowed me a glimpse of the agony on Ken's*

face. Halfway to the hospital, I saw a fire and ambulance station, swerved into the drive and jumped out. "Help! Please help!" I screamed as I ran inside the station. Nobody was there!

Looking frantically around, I spotted the telephone and dialed 911. Firefighters and paramedics came running and quickly moved Ken into the ambulance to begin their work. One firefighter stayed with me, calmly reassuring me that my husband would be just fine. When he heard Ken's history, he hurried into the ambulance.

I felt suspended in time until they were ready to transport. When a firefighter offered to drive me to the hospital, I came out of limbo and declined the offer, certain I could manage the drive. I did and functioned well through admission procedures and the doctor's initial examination of Ken. The paramedics did a good job keeping Ken alive and talking, so I relaxed a bit. Shortly after arriving at the hospital, Ken was taken to intensive care.

"Do you have family?" The intensive care unit nurse asked.

"Yes."

"It would probably be best if you called them," she said kindly. My heart plummeted. The nurse showed me to the waiting room and a telephone.

"May I help?" asked the lady at the desk, looking efficient in her pink jacket. I stood immobile staring at her.

"Would you like me to dial the numbers for you?" she offered. I swallowed hard.

"I don't remember the numbers," I responded. She appeared to be far, far away. I felt suspended in foggy space.

"Why don't you give me the names? I'll look them up for you," she suggested.

I stared. "I can't remember their names," I croaked. I felt lost. Deserted. So numb I couldn't even think, let alone cry.

The hospital volunteer appeared to float out from behind her desk with opened arms. Feeling the human touch, I snapped back into reality and burst into tears. As a swift river washes away the debris of a storm, the tears washed away the memory blocks. I drew in a deep breath, squared my shoulders, wiped my eyes and dialed the telephone.

Ken made it through the night. The doctor and nurses urged the family to go home and rest. When I returned later that afternoon, Ken looked better. Maybe we'd get to have a birthday celebration after all. He was grumpy, which I took as a good sign, an indication that he was fighting back. He became so grumpy, in fact, that I decided to leave again. The nurse intercepted me outside the intensive care cubicle. "Don't go," she whispered.

"Well, it's obvious he doesn't want me here," I said. "I'll just upset him more."

She stood firm. I went back in and stood at the foot of his bed for several minutes. Neither Ken nor I spoke. In the past when he was sick and crabby, he wanted me out of the way. I came to understand the feeling after going through a few hospital stays and energy-draining illnesses myself. Sometimes we just want to be alone.

Standing there motionless, weighing the situation, I prayed silently. Well, should I stay or should I go? What will help him the most?

"Before you go," Ken said, without opening his eyes, "would you get me fresh water?"

"Sure," I said. The nurse winked at me and left the room. I went out to the desk and asked for fresh water, then returned to the room, took off my coat and sat beside the bed. Ken was no longer grumpy. He was quiet. Too quiet.

The nurse returned and pulled up a chair on the other side of the bed. When I saw a tear leak down her cheek, fear gripped my heart. Oh, no. He's still in trouble. Oh, God, please don't take him yet. I don't want to let him go. We've just begun to have a good life together. Please.

The long night vigil had begun. The nurse never left his side. Others came and went, with soft whispers at the door. For a long time, Ken just lay still. The sound of his breathing mixed with the sounds of the machines and monitors that were feeding the medications into his veins. I continued praying that his life be spared.

Somewhere in the middle of the night, Ken began to talk to someone. His nurse asked if Ken's words made any sense to me. Our eyes met. "Yes," is all I said. Although I didn't tell her, Ken was talking to his father who had died a few years earlier. I think she understood. The tears flowed unchecked down her cheeks.

Until that moment I had been pleading with God to let Ken live, pleading my case with appeals for his children and grandchildren. Now came the full realization of what Ken's life might be like if he did live with a severely damaged heart. I reluctantly, determinedly, changed my prayer.

*Father, I know Ken wouldn't want to be handi-
capped. He loves life too much to be held down. I
don't want him to go, but if it is best..., it's okay. I
know you'll help me get through it. All I ask is that
if he lives, he enjoys life. If not, please don't let him
suffer a long time.*

Yanking me back to the present moment, cold water splattered on my forehead and nose and trickled down my neck.
Shaking off the memory of that terrifying day two years before
was as impossible as stopping the rain drops from falling on
my head. An invisible giant hand picked up the leaves raked
into a pile and flung them back across the lawn. Frustrated, I
grabbed my shirt and stalked into the house.

Ken was enjoying a nap in his favorite lounge chair with
Boots, our miniature Yorkshire Terrier, curled up on his legs.
Their soft snoring mellowed my mood. As the room darkened
from the storm clouds moving in, I curled up on the couch for
my own nap. But not for long.

CRACK!

We all bolted upright.

"That was close. Wonder what it hit," Ken said as he
punched the television remote. No response. The wind
whipped the storm closer, plunging our house into darkness.
Ken lit the kerosene lamp waiting on the fireplace mantle for
such an emergency. A few minutes later, Ken had a fire roaring
in the fireplace to take the chill out of the room.

"The storm will be over soon," he said, watching the mes-
merizing flames leap upward. Boots stood on Ken's feet for
reassurance as the storm raged outside. I wanted some reassurance also, some comfort from the turmoil inside my head.
Once again the inner questions sent me in a downward spiral.

*Should I quit my business? Does it make any sense to go on, espe-
cially when I feel so financially insecure? Where are the answers*

when I so desperately need them? How much time does Ken have left? Up and down. Over and under. I was becoming unutterably weary, creeping my way up an emotional mountain, then hurtling down again with indecision. *Why can't life be smooth and easy?*

Then, as Ken had predicted, the rain slowed to a light drizzle. The sun came timidly out of hiding.

"Let's go out and eat," said Ken. "I'm sure someone has electricity."

We found a restaurant where the pizza was hot and delicious. I burned my tongue in my haste to eat. Ken shook his head in amusement. *Will I ever learn to be patient?*

As we emerged from the windowless restaurant, we squinted in the bright sunlight. The storm was over, leaving behind the clean scent of freshly washed earth. Ken winked at me as if to say, "Feeling better?" Eating did make me feel better.

We drove westward toward home, watching the sky change colors with the setting sun. As we rounded the curve where city meets country, a glorious sunset greeted us.

In the deep blue velvet sky hung a giant 14-karat sun medallion. Ken pulled to the side of the road. We got out of the car to stand together in silent wonder. In slow motion, the sun moved gently downward, transforming the sky with gold spikes radiating across the horizon like reflections of angels' wings.

Oh, God, how beautiful. Thank you, my soul whispered. *No matter how bad things seem, You are always there... shining... warming... loving.*

Ken gently touched my shoulder, his words barely above a whisper. "Look," he said, pointing behind us.

In the east, a rainbow was forming. The biggest, brightest rainbow I ever saw. We gazed from rainbow to sunset... east to west... west to east... watching as the golden sun ball dipped deeper into the earth and brilliant rainbow colors splashed across the sky. Soon the sky was aflame with color as a second perfect, bright rainbow formed across the sky on top of the first. "Oh! How beautiful!" I exclaimed with misty eyes. Ken smiled.

When we looked back at the sunset, the ball was nearly gone. The western sky had become a giant jewelry case, piled high with variegated chains of gold. (Now I know why the Irish believe there is a pot of gold at the end of a rainbow.) Another peek at the double rainbow brought a gasp.

Joyous tears overflowed my cheeks, running down into my neck. A *third* rainbow was forming! I reached out my hand and Ken folded his over mine. His eyes, too, were bright with moisture. As we watched the new rainbow quickly expand the sky, neatly atop the other two, I thought my heart would burst with the awesome, joyful feeling inside.

Ken slipped his arm around my waist. I leaned against him as we watched the last golden sliver of sunlight slip beneath the earth and the rainbows fade away.

We never forgot that day, for in the golden sunset and the triple rainbow, we found a promise. A promise that no matter how bad the storms, God is still there and His glory is magnificent.

There was another message in the rainbows that day — a message about choice.

Shortly after the third rainbow formed, a car came screeching to an abrupt stop next to us. "Is something wrong?" yelled the driver.

Ken and I looked at him in silence, then back to the sky, our heads moving from east to west and west to east.

"Is there something wrong?" he yelled again. "Do you need help?" The poor man did look worried.

"No," said Ken firmly. "We're enjoying the sunset... and the rainbows," he said as he gestured toward the sky.

The driver looked puzzled. He glanced quickly at the sky, shrugged his shoulders and sped away. The man in the passing automobile chose to stop to see if there was a problem. Finding none, he drove off, choosing not to enjoy the rainbow moment. Was he so focused on problems that he couldn't see the miracle that was as big as the sky? Could he take time out only for problems, but not for pleasure? These are the questions we need to keep in mind if we are to see rainbow blessings in stormy times.

My Darkest Hour   1

And God smiled again,
And the rainbow appeared.
And curled itself around his shoulder.

James Weldon Johnson
God's Trombones [1927]
The Creation, st. 7

"**I**t's your son. He's dead." *NO! I won't hear it!* I felt myself sinking, my knees touching the floor. "Catch her," someone yelled.

I stood shaking and quivering on the edge of a precipice in that moment of learning of my son's death. A vice-like grip squeezed the air from my lungs as I sank into darkness. I longed to join my son in the oblivion of death, so I wouldn't have to feel the horrid pain of yet another loss.

Release did not come. Instead, I felt strong arms holding me up. Then the other part of myself — that observer part, which is strangely able to step outside my emotions — pulled me back into the moment. It was 1994, and I was thousands of miles from home at a professional speakers convention, being led down a hallway into a tiny room where someone handed me a telephone.

When my 20-year-old granddaughter, Melanie, came on the line and said, "Heart attack," the room grew dim. I willed myself to stay conscious. "A delivery man found him early this morning," she added.

Kenny, the only son I had given birth to, had died at work. "They said he had a smile on his face," relayed Melanie's shaking voice. That was little comfort to me. Nor was it comforting to hear that someone back home in Indiana was making reservations for my return. I didn't want to go home — not for this. I couldn't bring myself to even think "funeral." How could life be so unfair?

From Melanie, I learned that Ken's wife, Lynn, was in shock. After seventeen years of marriage, Lynn was finally pregnant with their first child. Crushed under my own anguish, I could not bear to imagine how much greater her pain might be.

Slowly I hung up the telephone and turned to the familiar strangers beside me. Naomi Rhode was the president of the National Speakers Association (NSA). She and her husband, Jim, who had come to get me when the devastating telephone call reached convention headquarters, were there to comfort me. I knew who the Rhodes were. All the conventioneers knew. But they hadn't known me. And now they were about to see the worst I could offer.

"NO! NO! NO! I won't accept it, God. I can't take anymore, do you hear me? You're asking too much!" I screamed and ranted, thrashing around the room, banging my fists on anything and anyone available.

Though she was next to me, Naomi's soft voice seemed to come from far away. "I'm sorry, so sorry." I knew she wanted to calm me, but I could only flail about in rage. "It's too much! No one can bear this load."

For four grievous years, death robbed me of loved ones. Less than six weeks earlier, my foster son, Henry, had died of AIDS. My husband had died in 1990. My father, my mother, my brother, on and on. Now Kenny's death made it an even dozen family members. Gone. Forever. I felt crushed under a mountain of cemetery plots.

I thought I could bear no more. With eyes closed, I thrashed, trying to beat the pain away, but it only intensified. I wanted my rage to banish the hopelessness lurking with the grim reaper in the corners of that hotel room.

"What can we do?" asked Naomi gently. I opened my eyes to glimpse this beautiful woman in her well-tailored, colorful suit. She had left her duties at the convention to be with me, and I was acting like an ungrateful, spoiled child.

I don't care. It hurts too much. I squeezed my eyes shut. Tight.
"I don't know what to do," she prodded. The pain and concern in her voice pricked my senses.
*Am I losing my mind? Will they take me to a mental ward? No! I
must stop this. Now!*
Willing control of my emotions and body, I sucked in a deep
gulp of air. Then another. My body shuddered, then calmed.
"I don't know what you can do," I forced myself to say. I felt
panic returning. Another deep intake of breath brought calming oxygen, and a firm resolution.
"I don't know what you can do," I repeated. "But I know
what I don't want you to do. Please don't call a doctor and
have me sedated. *I have to go through this.* It's the only way. I
can handle it."
"I understand, my friend," whispered Naomi. "Do what you
have to do."
Naomi's trusting words confirmed my ability to handle the
situation responsibly. The sense of being overwhelmed lifted
enough for me to start thinking a little more rationally.
Although stunned by this searing pain, I knew that copping
out through drugs or crazy behavior would not work for me. I
had done that in the past. Strangely, even in my deepest distress, I knew, *positively knew,* I would make it through this, my
darkest hour. What I didn't know was how or why. But God did.
"Is there someone we can get for you?" Naomi asked. For a
moment I fumbled, then Mitchell's theme came to mind: "It's
not what happens to you in life, it's what you do about it."
"Mitchell," I cried, "get Mitchell."
I don't know how he got through all the crowd that had just
come out of the breakout rooms, but there he was by my side.
He held my hand in quiet support until I calmed. Once I
stopped the ranting, had my cry and became focused on positive choices, I caught glimpses of the miracles that were happening, even in the midst of this tragedy. The biggest miracle

was my recognition of an incredible support system already in place beginning with Naomi and Mitchell. As we sat together holding hands, my mind rolled back to the day Mitchell and I met four years earlier.

The Meeting

My file cabinet bulges with newspaper and magazine articles about ordinary people overcoming extraordinary obstacles. In the file is a *Parade*[1] magazine story about W Mitchell who triumphed over two horrible accidents which left him badly scarred from burns suffered in a motorcycle accident and in a wheelchair due to a plane crash.

Before putting the article into the file, I said a prayer. "Lord, it helps a lot to read about positive people like Mitchell, but I sure would like to meet one in person sometime." Once said, I forgot about the request.

Six months later, my husband, Ken Sr. died, followed six weeks later by my brother. The same year, the NSA convention was to be held on July 21 and 22. Normally, we would have celebrated birthdays on those two dates: my brother Richard's on the twenty-first and Ken's on the twenty-second.

For several years, I had wanted to attend the convention but had found excuses not to go. Considering this a good possibility for taking my mind off birthday anniversaries, I sent for the information. When I saw that my favorite author, Norman Vincent Peale, was a featured speaker, my decision was cinched.

That year, for the first and only time, newcomers were paired with old timers for a special introductory session. More than a thousand people attended the convention, but by the time I got through the crowd to find my partner, most were paired and gone. Disappointed, I turned to leave the room.

---

1 November 26, 1989.

"Would you like to be my partner?"

I turned to face the person who spoke and my mouth dropped open in silent amazement.

"I'm Mitchell," said the man, grinning broadly. "Would you like to join me and get acquainted? I see some chairs over there," he added, turning his wheelchair toward the wall.

"Sure... love to." I hoped my voice sounded calm, because my heart was beating out a bongo tune of "Thank you! Thank you! Thank you!"

Mitchell and I had a wonderful chat and he was a faithful partner for the convention. He waved to me from the hallways and invited me to meet his friends, some of whom were the biggest names in the public speaking business: People whose books I had read and whose tapes I had listened to for insight, strength and courage to get through life's challenges.

Now, four years later, Mitchell and I were at another NSA convention, only our meeting was not as delightful as the first. But it was comforting. Enlightening. Even in my deep shock and grief, I knew miracles were happening... again. Little miracles to assure me that Someone does indeed watch over us.

Noticing that I had settled down, Naomi asked, "Do you have a roommate?" Had she asked the question earlier, while I was erupting like a volcano, I might not have remembered, for my roommate and I had just met at the convention, although she lived in my home town.

Jim Rhode stepped into the hall, now jammed with conventioneers getting out of their sessions. "Does anyone know Barbara Steele?"

While I was in the tiny room venting my grief and anger, Barbara was trying to get through the crowds of people in the large convention center. At the moment Jim called out, Barbara emerged from the crowd right in front of the him. Hearing my plight, she insisted on leaving the convention to accompany me home.

In my darkest hour, I was surrounded by people who had chosen to use the privilege of the platform to make a better world. In the spirit of service, they gave their all, as did the personnel of the Hilton Hotel and American Airlines, who went out of their way to make my travel home for my son's funeral a bit easier.

As word spread of the devastating news, some of the speakers came to my room to hug me and give me an encouraging word. In the days and months to come, many messages of support, hope and love came from NSA members all over the continent and from a new friend in the United Kingdom. Strangers became friends, adding their support to those most dear to me at home, my family and long-time friends.

Still, I feared what lay ahead. I didn't know that in the coming days, weeks and months, I would move in a spiritually automated state, through God's grace, managing to take care of the essentials. The rest of the time, I would fumble my way through each challenging day, wandering and wondering. The wandering took me on short walks around my home, and long soul-searching journeys far beyond. The wondering took form on paper... and in strange, revealing dreams.

Rainbow Talisman

As a small child, before I learned to read or write, I pretended I could do both. The stories in books helped me find happiness in a family situation filled with strife. As an adult, most of my writing went into journals, particularly during the stormy times. Writing down my feelings of grief and confusion helped relieve the pressure that built inside. Coupled with workshops and self-help books, my writing helped me form an understanding of how I was able to get through loss after loss, storm after storm. In the search I found many rainbows, the first one being most significant.

When I was seven years old, my family fell apart. My parents separated. My younger brother and sister, Richard and
Vicki, were sent to a foster home in a neighboring state, and I
was sent to my grandparents' dairy farm. Besides being a
farmer, Grandpa was a strict Nazarene minister.

Two hired hands also lived in the farm house — a young
woman to help Grandma and a man to help Grandpa. The
woman's little brother, Nate[1], was seven years old, like me, and
also staying on the farm for the summer.

One day, while all the adults were busy with chores, Nate
and I disobeyed my grandparents and went to a neighbor's
house to play. That childish mistake became a nightmare that
would haunt me for years.

The neighbor's fifteen-year-old son sexually molested Nate
and me. Although I received a minor cut from a stone used on
me, it wasn't the bit of blood, nor the pain that frightened me;
it was facing my grandmother.

I knew that I would have to show her. I wasn't sure how
badly I was hurt, and I was frightened to keep it hidden. I
understood enough to know that once she saw my injury, she
would consider what happened to us a sin of the worst kind.

To cheer me on our dismal trudge home through the fields,
Nate suggested we play "Wizard of Oz," a popular movie at the
time. Although I was forbidden to go to movies, my mother
had given me the book, and I listened to the music on the juke-
box in her restaurant.

To hide my guilt and terror of facing my grandmother, I
jumped on a pile of fence posts and began to sing Dorothy's
song as loudly as I could. "Somewhere over the rainbow... "[2]
The words floated across the misty meadow and into the barn-
yard, filling me with courage.

---

1 Name Change
2 "Over The Rainbow" — Words and music by E.Y. Harburg and Harold Arlen

Something else happened during my performance to the cows. A sense of love and peace flooded over me. I suppressed a niggling fear that Grandpa might hear and chastise me for singing popular songs. Only "Christian" music was allowed in our family.

By the time supper was ready, I still hadn't told Grandma. When I went to the bathroom and once again saw the blood and felt a burning pain, I knew I couldn't put off confessing. In spite of my fear and embarrassment, I called Grandma into the bathroom.

She listened without comment. She saw the blood, but wouldn't look at the wound. When I finished telling my story, she turned and walked to the telephone and called my other grandmother, Mom's mother. Then Grandma packed my clothes while I waited in the darkening living room in terror of the devil that I was sure was coming to take me straight to hell.

But it was Grandma Gladys who came. Laying my head in her lap, her hand gently caressing my hair, I cried my relief all the way to her house. Grandma gently cleansed and treated the wound, waiting patiently for me to speak. Afterward she listened to my story as she hugged me close to her side. Her love and understanding helped me recover from that terrible day.

Rainbow Remedies

Although I never forgot the violation, the rainbow scene faded into the background until my Locust Years. To find new ways of growing, and to fill the void left by the deaths of my loved ones, I began a storytelling quest. The night before a storytelling retreat, I had a dream. "Tell the story of your first rainbow," it said. So I told my story of the abused seven-year-old self buried deep inside. When it bubbled out, I knew I had set that child free and found my talisman for getting through the stormy times of life. From that point on, all the coping processes discovered and developed during my stormy times became "Rainbow Remedies."

Remedy 1: Stop, Look, Listen and Learn

This remedy calms, balances and encourages healthy emotional growth. When we stop the emotions long enough to look and listen, we learn what we can do for positive results. Failure to apply this remedy will put us in jeopardy, for hasty decisions made from fear and panic are seldom the best ones.

A positive side effect of this remedy is that when used faithfully, it increases sensory perceptions. We become tuned into God-incidences, serendipitous opportunities and wonder-filled surprises that appear in even the worst storms.

Remedy 2: Praise and Thanksgiving

Giving thanks in all situations is a powerful treatment for dealing with the fear and heartache that accompany stormy times. Thankfulness draws out the hurt and fear and injects the power of inner peace and assurance; it attracts more God-incidences. Even if we don't directly pray to God, we pray indirectly, for our Creator hears every thought and spoken word. Praise and Thanksgiving are the strongest prescriptions for bringing good back into our lives. Used as a treatment for the PLUM (Poor Little Unfortunate Me) disease, Praise and Thanksgiving are awesome soul healers.

Remedy 3: Accentuate the Positive

Accentuating the positive and eliminating the negative are the supplemental basics for optimum emotional well-being. Cleaning the mind of negatives is as crucial to good health as cleaning the body of impurities. The same is true of putting back healthy substances: wholesome foods for the body and positive concepts for the mind. The PMA (Positive Mental Attitude) supplement for the soul eases tension, increases joy and attracts positive friends and supporters to help us weather the stormy times and enjoy the good times.

Remedy 4 : Power of Choice

Choice is a physical exercise, a preventive medicine. We are born with the Power of Choice. Like our breathing, we do it constantly and frequently, unconsciously. And we do not always choose wisely. Combined with the first three remedies, our choices are enhanced.

Many people hire trainers to teach them how to exercise their bodies properly for maximum benefit and minimum damage. They are often amazed at the awesome physical power and strength they develop. The same is true when we train ourselves to make wise choices and find that we have power over our environment. Well thought out choices bring happier, healthier, more productive and prosperous results.

Remedy 5: Forgiveness

For many, the Forgiveness prescription is a bitter pill to swallow, particularly if the person we need to forgive is still hurting us. However, with a spoonful of love, forgiveness brings miraculous healing. The first sign that we are indeed forgiving someone is a lifting of the dark fog of bitterness so we can see life's rainbows.

Forgiveness brings freedom. We are no longer trapped by the past or a difficult present. The most amazing part of this remedy is that it also works on other people, diluting difficult relationships as it diffuses someone else's meanness. The mysterious workings of this treatment obviously come from a Source greater than ourselves.

Remedy 6: Helping Others Help Themselves

This remedy is similar to the Forgiveness one in many ways. Both are essential for happiness; both only work when the heart is right. Many of us do forgive and do help others in what appears to be a PMA mind set. Often, however, we fool ourselves, shoving aside secret feelings of being "used" and "abused." And since we may well be used or abused, correct "Helping Others" involves learning to help with the focus on helping someone to help oneself. The antidote here opens the door to a shared adventure. Helping someone help himself is like creating a double rainbow — one for you, one for him.

Remedy 7: Support Systems

Remedy seven is actually a therapy that works from the inside. Not everyone benefits from the Support System treatment, as it is ineffective unless we unlock our hearts, minds and souls. This therapy is also one that works best with other remedies.

We begin with the Stop, Look, Listen and Learn antidote. As we increase the dosage, using the remedy often throughout each day, we develop an alertness to the positive side of life: people, places and perceptions. This makes it easier to increase our intake and output of Praise and Thanksgiving.

As we grow emotionally and spiritually stronger, our Choices improve. We are attracted to positive supportive people as they are attracted to us. The more we Forgive, the more we receive. I like to think of this remedy as the pot of gold, for it brings great joy and many rewards as we become interconnected with all God's children. The remedy also takes away loneliness and eases depression.

At the time of my son's death, I was unaware of these remedies, yet they were working wonders throughout that day, bringing shafts of light into my pit of despair. Thirty years of reading self-improvement books and attending personal growth workshops, coupled with ten years in crisis-intervention work, had made me a fertile base for the remedies. They were working even when I wasn't. Caught in chalking up my losses, I was only vaguely aware of the possibility that a new life was dawning for me.

Even in the worst storms, my joy and positive attitude could be revived, if only momentarily. The briefest break in a storm can let the sunshine in. With the sun comes the rainbow. And with the rainbow, often comes laughter. That's where we'll find the pot of gold at the end of the rainbow.

Life Goes On

"Everything is taken care of," I was told that day of my darkest hour. "Your daughters have contacted the airlines, and the hotel manager has made arrangements to get your ticket and provide a limousine to take you to the airport." Someone else was in charge, a new experience for me. Although my world had stopped, life went on.

As the oldest in our family, I was the primary caregiver, particularly during the previous four years. It was up to me to make, or at least help make, necessary arrangements when my loved ones died, and in several cases, to take care of the estates as well.

At my aunt's funeral, my brother-in-law, Julius, quipped, "I'm not sure I like being related to you."

"Better not make me executrix of your will then," I countered.

Now I was on the receiving end, simply taking in the tender loving care of those around me while others did what needed to be done. It felt strange, but comforting.

"They're ready for boarding," Barbara said gently as she took my arm. I let myself be led to my assigned seat, grateful that Barbara was with me. She says I curled up in a little ball, like a baby. Once in a while I whimpered. Not much else. For a long time, I wasn't aware of much around me until I heard Barbara call to the attendant.

"Miss," Barbara said, "I have a candy bar if that will help."

The flight attendant thanked her and hurried to take it to a passenger a few seats in front of us.

"What was that for?" I asked.

Barbara turned to me and smiled. "Oh, the passenger up there is diabetic. She needed some sugar, probably to counteract hypoglycemia. We had a long wait for take off, you know."

I didn't know. Time had stopped for me.

"Are you okay?" she asked. I seemed to rise up from a deep sleep.

My body is all in one piece. I'm calm. Getting collected. I'll make it.

"Yes, I'm okay." *But I'm not sure why,* I thought.

Saying the words, "I'm okay," was like dropping fresh rain on dormant roots. A few minutes later, I giggled. Barbara looked at me with concern (probably thinking I'd lost it entirely).

"Barb," I said. "I just had the strangest thought. I remember sobbing so hard that my nose began to run. Then I realized my face was buried in the top of Naomi's head. I didn't know what to do, and I couldn't figure out how I grew taller than she was. How could that be?"

Barbara grinned. "Well, Naomi was kneeling on the floor so she could hold you as you sat in the chair. You leaned over and, yes, you cried in her hair."

"Oh no! It's true. I must have made a mess in her hair!" I laughed in embarrassment.

Yet Naomi knew I had to do what I had to do. No judgment, no flinching, not even when those tears went into her perfectly coiffed hair and down on her beautiful suit! (I later apologized to Naomi. She laughed and hugged me. It truly hadn't bothered her.)

Then I recalled another hilarious part of the scene. "Oh, no, there's more," I said. Now I was barely able to talk for the laughter.

"I fainted when they told me. And I remember hearing, 'Catch her.' Then I remember feeling cold air on my behind." More laughter spurted out. I had worn only panty hose as underwear, because the convention center was overheated.

"Apparently whoever caught me, grabbed hold of my skirt and… I must have mooned all those people coming out of the sessions!"

Laughter helps the healing process, and I settled back into my seat and actually dozed a bit. I'm sure Kenny — from his Heavenly view — was tickled about my reaction. He loved practical jokes and would appreciate that a couple of doozies had been played on me.

When I awoke, the reality of why I was on a plane flying home came flooding in. Anger welled up, and I knew that I would have to deal with it for some time. I also knew I had to forgive, but at that moment, I was not in a forgiving mood. Nor was I willing to explore the subject further. So when a little voice inside my head started spouting messages like, "You know that holding onto anger can destroy you," and "Forgiveness heals the mind and body as well as the soul," I told it to *"Shut up!"* Like Scarlett O'Hara, I would think about it tomorrow.

Primary Ingredients
for
Creating Rainbows

- Stop, Look, Listen and Learn.

- Give Praise and Thanksgiving.

- Accentuate the Positive.

- Power of Choice.

- Forgive.

- Helping Others Help Themselves.

- Support Systems.

A God-incident

After Ken Jr.'s funeral, a rainbow encircled the airplane carrying his oldest sister, Debbie, back to Florida.

A Golden Nugget

*Katelyn Marie Hill, my son's only child,
was born prematurely on December 13, 1994.
Although she had two operations before
she was a month old, Katelyn bubbles
with health and vitality today.*

Crisis Dynamics 2

Every cloud engenders not a storm.

William Shakespeare
Henry VI

Throughout Kenny's funeral, I did very little. Although I felt deeply sorry for my daughter-in-law, Lynn, and her family, who shouldered the burden of arrangements, I was glad I didn't have be in charge at this funeral, as I had been at so many others.

As the days accumulated into weeks, the weeks into months, I became more aware of my life and more curious about my ability to cope. In the aftermath of my husband's death four years before, and all that followed that year, people often asked me, "How do you do it?"

"Do what?"

"Manage to keep smiling, to keep on with all that happens to you and your family."

"Oh, I just put one foot in front of the other," I'd say, sometimes feeling my right foot swing out a bit in affirmation. Most of the time my accompanying smile was heartfelt. Other times, I pushed the smile out. Fortunately, good feelings followed, as the effort to smile reminded me that I was indeed "making it."

After Kenny Jr.'s death, I often asked myself that question. "Just *how* am I making it?" Sometimes insightful answers came and I'd feel good. At other times a disturbing question haunted me: *"Am* I making it?"

The Locust Years

There had been so many deaths in the previous four years that I found myself frequently reciting a litany of them: first my husband Ken, then my brother Richard, followed by Dad (my dear stepfather), Mom, Aunt Becky (my second mom), Uncles Richard and Merrill, cousin Tom, Henry (foster-son), Hector (Henry's partner), Jonnie (beloved stepmother) and finally the son I gave birth to, Kenny Jr.

Multiple family crises plagued us through those four years: Mom's Alzheimer's and her two years in a nursing home, her breast cancer operation and two broken hips (separate falls); brother Richard's six-month bout with lung cancer; Aunt Becky's struggle with liver cancer; the deteriorating health of my beloved mother-in-law, Gladys; the frequent intensive care hospitalizations for my sister's husband, Julius. It seemed the hospital had become my hangout. I prayed for them and helped as best I could.

All my children faced their own crises: Laura's thyroid cancer; Cindy's mysterious disease that took her to the Cleveland Clinic (discovered to be chronic dehydration); Brenda's injuries and challenges as a UPS driver; Debbie's prolonged bout with chronic fatigue and bipolar-depression; Ken Jr's struggles with ever-increasing pressures from his boss; Henry's and Hector's AIDS. Everyone I loved seemed to need help.

Debbie lived in Florida, Henry in California and Richard in Texas. The others lived within a thirty-mile radius of my home. In addition to car mileage, I chalked up thousands of frequent flyer miles in those years!

Some people compared me to the Biblical Job, tested like Job who lost his whole family. But unlike him, I didn't lose everyone and it didn't happen all at once. It kept happening year after year, along with a myriad of other problems, like the invasion of the locust in Egypt that destroyed the source of sustenance.

I watched anxiously as the next generation, my teenage grandchildren, wrestled with the temptations of modern-day youth: rebellion, slipping grades, drug and alcohol experimentation. Having been a crisis intervention counselor for ten years, specializing in teenage problems, I was terrified and frustrated. Terrified at how far they might go, frustrated in my attempts to help them. Troubles swarmed over and around me, nibbling at my life, like locusts on a wheat field.

I often shared with friends who were burdened with their own problems. Along with a sense of sharing the load, we helped each other find answers. Stormy times exclude no one. But sometimes the sharing added to my concerns. Most nights I fell asleep while naming people in my prayers. Thankfully, God heard the prayers, giving us all strength and courage to get through those stormy times, growing in wisdom and strength.

Shortly after my husband's death, I lost my job as a weekly columnist due to the sale of the newspaper. Six months later, I discontinued publication of *Crafters' Link,* my national monthly newsletter and gave up my freelance writing. My previously enjoyable projects had become burdensome deadlines I could not meet.

A friend, John Thurin, offered me a job writing grants for a foundation he administered. "You may need something to get up for," he said. Having lost his own loved ones, he knew the void I was facing. The job provided a lifeline in that first year as the locusts of despair began to eat away my life.

John, as my supervisor, was flexible, allowing me to work out my own schedule so that I could take care of family matters. But the juggling left me exhausted and frustrated. I had trouble focusing on the job and at times fell asleep at the computer. Finally, I quit, disappointed that I wasn't Wonder Woman, yet grateful for the year to "tread water" while I caught a second wind.

Writing this chapter brought back some of the suffocating feelings that nagged me throughout my Locust Years. So strong were the feelings recently that I took a fifteen-minute break/brake from my writing to catch my breath and become centered. (I prefer to use "brake," as the word signals a complete stop, whereas "break" symbolizes something broken. When we are troubled, we already feel broken. Words have power to heal or hurt. Braking stops the hurt for a while and allows us time to find solutions and healing.)

My mother had a wonderful word I used to describe my world at that time: *discombobulated.* Grandma Gladys, however, had her own metaphor: "I can't tell if I'm on foot or horseback." My sentiments exactly.

The oddity of those confusing, frustrating days, riding an emotional see-saw, was that most of the time *I felt in control.* While my world crumbled, I felt as though I were making progress. Amazingly, I actually was. During stormy times, major personal and spiritual growth happens — particularly when we stay alert and tuned into God's love.

During that time, I clung to my affirmations like a shipwrecked sailor to his life raft:

"I can do all things through Christ who strengthens me."[1]
"All things work together for good."[2]
"It can be done and I can do it!"[3]

I dug out the training manuals I wrote as administrator of Hotline, a telephone crisis intervention program I founded in the early seventies. I dug out self-help books I had used to free myself from deep depression and irresponsible behavior. I sought new sources for self-help in books, tapes, workshops, music and lectures.

Until the time of the Hotline experience so many years before, I reacted to personal crises in ways that made matters worse. Unknowingly, I also made crises happen where there

---

1 Philippians 4:13
2 Romans 8:28
3 Song written by Carmen H. Moshier

might have been only slight problems. Had I known the elements of a crisis, I could have developed better responses for resolution, even prevention. During the Locust Years, had I still been a young wife and mother, I might have lost my sanity. But after so often experiencing the fascinating dynamics of crises and the "rules" for crisis intervention, those four years took on the aura of a mystical sojourn.

Crisis Specialist

I received the title "Crisis Specialist" near the end of seven years' service in the telephone crisis intervention organization. As with most other social services, Hotline frequently experienced financial crisis. Then, one year, a major fund-raising organization decided to take on the county-wide service. In the process, they wanted one of their staff to run the program and I had to step down as administrator.

In the Hotline agency reorganization, my title became Crisis Specialist, because I'd founded the Hotline and been involved in the formation of nearly every crisis-intervention service in the community.

I felt the title was a misnomer. I had learned to deal with all that life threw at me and no longer experienced daily crises. Before the Hotline experience, however, the title would have fit perfectly. I had lived my very own soap opera, specializing in crisis living.

Crisis Living: I came from a broken home, lived in foster homes as a young child, was sexually molested and experienced emotional abuse. As a child with a hormonal deficiency, I got shots twice a week for two years just to grow. The doctor told my mother I'd be normal size, but probably never have children. Boy, did he miss that call!

I married at eighteen, two weeks after graduating from high school and was pregnant seven times in seven years, giving birth to five healthy children: four daughters and a son. (Two were born in the same year — *not* twins.)

In addition to the physical and emotional drain of so many little ones, there were financial difficulties. Like many couples, especially those who marry young, my husband and I were emotionally supercharged and experience deficient. We operated from crisis to crisis.

I immersed myself in self-improvement articles, particularly those in women's magazines and found a counselor I trusted. And prayed. I managed to stay emotionally afloat most of the time, but didn't understand how the puzzle pieces of my life were supposed to fit together. I couldn't get the big picture.

How was I able to deal with some problems and not others? Why did little things become monumental? Why did I feel continually inept? I didn't even know what I did right. To me, it seemed that whatever I did was wrong. With maturity, however, came perspective.

Now I see that no matter how badly a situation is being handled, if I take time out to *look* and *listen,* I learn. First I learn what I'm doing *right;* then I build on that. Sadly, I see people around me taking the opposite stance. Forcing themselves to stop while staying focused only on the negative increases the frustration.

As a teenager, I took piano lessons from a teacher who made me stop every time I made a mistake and start over. I finally quit because I rarely managed to get through a piece of music, often making the same mistake every time. As an adult, I learned that it helps to *play through the mistakes,* then stop and practice later, correcting the difficult places. Once perfected, they can be easily incorporated into the full piece.

Along with reading books and articles, Hotline training taught me how to focus on the positive (right) in my life, rather than what I saw as negative (wrong). (Not everything that I saw as wrong was wrong. Nor was what I thought was right always right. My perceptions can be quite biased.)

To become proficient in a positive, constructive and productive reaction to crisis, it helps to know the nature of crisis: how it happens, what can be done about it, when, where, how and why to take action. Once I learned that, life became a joy rather than a burden.

Soap Opera Syndrome: Using a soap opera as a metaphor for my former life makes it easier to look back and find the joy. It allows the observer in me to see those days (and current ones that might be moving in that direction again) in a different light.

Watch any soap opera or sitcom and observe how people make most of their own troubles. Those of us in constant crisis take the same action over and over again, while expecting different, more positive results. Common sense tells us that when one action doesn't work, try a different action. Unfortunately, we don't always listen to our common sense.

In my newly-married days, I literally blocked the living-room door with my body to keep my husband from going out with his buddies. Then I wondered why I ended up getting shoved out of the way. Only when I understood there might be a better way did my life change for the better. There were two abusers in our marriage (husband *and* wife), but at first I refused to see that.

Our creations of reality come from our own attitudes and our belief systems. I believed married life should be lived only one way; my husband believed it could be lived another way. Fortunately, we both came to understand the need for attitude adjustments and new beliefs, which allowed us to end up in a happy, healthy relationship. We actually became best friends, for which I am deeply grateful.

Treating the Dis-ease: A doctor cannot treat an ailment until finding out what the ailment is. Before treating a problem, we must learn what the problem is. Some problems are simple: "What outfit shall I wear?" "What school shall I attend?" Then we have the problem of a crisis: "Should I get a divorce?" "Should I quit my job?" "My best friend just died. How will I go on without him?"

Modern researchers know the relationship between the emotions and the body. While we feel the emotions in our body, those emotions actually originate in our head. Few human fears are instinctive; most are learned. Emotional conflict imposed upon the mind and body is called "stress." Some call it "dis-ease," signifying stress makes our life harder. We are bombarded with messages of stress as a negative part of life. In reality we need some stress in our lives to strengthen us.

Some crises bring good into our lives. We get fired, revealing to us that we were in the wrong job. We then find employment that feeds our soul as it fills our wallet.

The Chinese character for crisis is a combination of two characters, *Wei* (danger) and *Qi* (hope or opportunity). Webster's[4] dictionary gives six definitions of "crisis." All refer to the crisis as a point of change. The first calls it a turning point "for better or worse." I agree. A medical crisis, as we know, is the point "leading either to recovery or to death." A crisis can take us to higher ground or bury us in the muck of destructive habits.

Even though it's the ups and downs that make life interesting, meaningful and rewarding (and make great movies), we would be healthier and happier by keeping them in balance, making them as constructive as possible. Just as we can become addicted to chemicals, food, shopping or television, we can become addicted to crisis. In "reel" life, actors thrive on chaos; otherwise, the story won't sell. However, when *our* lives are in constant turmoil, we destroy ourselves and each other, physically and emotionally. For healthy and happy living we must learn to deal with crisis in constructive ways.

---

4 Webster's Encyclopedic Unabridged Dictionary, Random House, 1996

Crisis Manager

A crisis is not an emergency. That is the first lesson we learned in crisis intervention and crisis management. Understanding that a crisis is *not* an emergency puts sanity back into living. Our Hotline training manual quoted from training information I received at Children's Hospital in Los Angeles, California.

> Crisis is the **inner state** of a person **reacting to stress** when **normal coping methods have broken down**.
>
> A crisis is **different from an emergency**, a situation which requires **immediate external action** on the part of someone to **prevent injury or death**.
>
> *"Hotline Training Manual"*

By creating arguments with people because we don't like what they do, we create a crisis. When we push to escalate the argument, we risk turning a crisis into an emergency, especially when we know that the other person is volatile. Now the crisis becomes an emergency, needing quick intervention.

We are *not powerless* in crises, although we often feel that way, particularly when we cannot control another's behavior. What we feel is a threat to our relationship, the possibility of permanent loss. If we're willing to be patient, wait until emotions are not so high to deal with the situation, we have a better chance of a positive resolution. There is more than one option for resolution. The tricky part comes in pushing aside the feelings of urgency as a life is **not** in danger.

Whether we are aware of it or not, within a short time the crisis will be resolved, either *constructively* or *destructively.* The difference depends on whether the *action* comes from a *conscious decision* or an *unconscious reaction.*

A *conscious decision for action* focuses on what will help, rather than hinder, the situation. An *unconscious reaction* latches onto the desire to escape the pain, whatever the cost. The unconscious reaction leads to fruitless decisions, such as drug and alcohol abuse or forcing senseless arguments that get us nowhere. Once we learn this, we understand how critical it is for us to calm ourselves before taking action.

Anger has escalated in today's society. Fist fights on the playground are passé. Today's children shoot it out in the cafeteria. Rudeness is in, politeness out.

"We're a nation whose collective mood has gone sour," says C. Leslie Charles in her book, *Why is Everyone So Cranky?* "It's America's 'anger epidemic.' *Never have so many, with so much, been so unhappy."*

In my crisis-intervention work, and through the years of observing my own and other's reactions to crises, it became apparent that many people see their crises as emergencies — a threat to their lives. In fear and retaliation, they lash out in an "I'll-get-you-before-you-get-me" attitude. If we are to stop creating these horrible scenarios from our crises, we must first accept the fact that *a crisis is not an emergency.* Remember: *an emergency requires immediate external action to prevent injury or death.* That means someone *already* is in a life-threatening situation. We don't put them there.

A domineering and unreasonable boss, cursing at me in front of customers and co-workers, is only threatening my pride, not my life. People who hurl insults and look at me with disdain are showing their own ignorance and shallowness. Their words may sting, but I do not bleed. The driver who cuts me off on the freeway may indeed threaten my safety, but does it make sense for me to do the same in retaliation? We must stop the escalating emotions. *Now!*

Calming down is obviously the first step when we realize that a crisis comes from the inner *emotional* part of oneself.

Maybe Mom was right after all: "Count to ten and you'll feel better." Taking time out to think about what is happening and considering options to deal with it gives us better odds for finding positive, workable solutions.

CRISES CAN WAIT. EMERGENCIES CANNOT.

Crisis Characteristics

Sitcoms and soap operas thrive on crisis situations. That's what makes the action happen, the program riveting. Perhaps many of us become addicted to crisis living because it's exciting and stimulating. Hey, things happen. We always have something to talk about. For years my bridge club supplied a private comedy club in which I entertained with funny stories about daily crises with a brood of six. But constant crisis takes its toll in broken homes, harmful relationships, damaged bodies and addictions.

The characters in the sitcoms take less than an hour to resolve their crises; soap operas drag them on for years. In real life, a crisis is dissipated in about six weeks, whether we actively work toward resolution or not. Dissipated but not always resolved. That does not mean we can just sit back and wait for the crisis to go away. The problem is not gone: it's just taking a nap. The upsetting situation will come back another time, slightly disguised, making us think it's a new problem. Don't be fooled. Sooner or later we have to listen to the music and sing it.

The crisis intervention training course taught that a crisis has identifiable characteristics, is time limited and comes in stages which can be classified.

The following characteristics make up a crisis:
- A crisis begins with a *hazardous event* or issue happening to a *person(s) in a vulnerable state.*

- Something precipitates *(triggers)* the event, pushes it out in front so the person(s) involved has to face the event or issue.

- *Emotions rise up causing cognitive and perceptive distur-bances.*

- *Coping methods fail. POW! You have a full blown crisis on your hands.*

In my workshops, I use a drawing of a tornado to illustrate the way a crisis develops.

POW!
Full blown crisis
Failed coping methods

Rising emotions

Precipitating event

Vulnerable state

Hazardous event

Because of the emotional pain involved, many people today react as though their problem is one of life or death and push for an immediate resolution, regardless of the consequences. This erroneous thinking might be averted if a Crisis Intervention Specialist (CIS) can be called. A well-trained CIS can put a "tourniquet" on the flowing emotions long enough to apply some calming "first aid." However, unlike the EMT

(Emergency Medical Technician), they are not reached by dialing 911. Although there are some general Hotline services available (the one in our county is still going strong), many crisis lines specialize in a particular problem. They provide a valuable service and I recommend them. However, the first step to self-control is self-awareness. We don't see the solutions because we're caught up in the problems, like not seeing the forest for the trees.

To illustrate, let's look at a situation common in many homes across the nation.

The Report Card: Jean, a single parent, is trying her best to care for a family, work full time, maintain her house, care for her car and meet a myriad of other demands on her time.

Her crisis begins with a **hazardous event** (son Billy is failing in school) occurring in the life of someone in a **vulnerable state** (single parent, overworked, tired and lonely).

If the parent never finds out that her child failed in school, life would probably roll along as usual. However, the arrival of the report card acts as a **precipitating event,** stirring up emotions in both parent and child.

The rising emotions cause **cognitive and perceptive disturbances.** [The student sees parent as harsh, nitpicking and uncaring about his feelings. The parent sees child as stupid, lazy and uncaring about her feelings.] In reality, both are feeling scared, confused and helpless.

At this point, due to emotional pressure for a resolution, the parties will push toward an outcome. Guaranteed. What is *not* guaranteed is that it will be a productive resolution.

If one or both are aware of how a crisis works and stops to assess the state of affairs, it will give them time to cool down. With a cooling-off period, they increase the odds for resolving the issue in an affirming and helpful manner.

Obviously, this is not a life or death matter, although it may *feel* that way to the parent. Jean may think that others will see her as a failure. She might be concerned about her ex-husband's reaction. And she probably envisions her son as a future homeless bum because he's failing in school. (We blow our crises out of proportion by projecting future possibilities as if the situation were guaranteed to continue.)

Take Ten: Of all the processes I've learned and the understanding of crises I've gained, the awareness that a crisis is more or less time-limited or self-liquidating has proven the most useful. For me, it is comforting to know that my sense of crisis (the emotions that I feel and am reacting to) will change in a short time, whether I do anything or not. While there is comfort in that knowledge, there is also a danger. Doing nothing leaves me vulnerable to other people's choices, and it does not keep the negative feelings from coming back.

The *Hotline Training Manual* gave the time frame of a crisis as generally six weeks. Critical points occur in three places, the first occurring at impact (precipitating situation). This is when emotions are highest and the need for resolution the greatest.

Where there is a lack of coping methods or when normal coping methods break down, the second critical point will come about midway (about the third week). Here depression, a dip in emotions, is common, although emotions will sometimes rise again (anger and frustration). This again triggers a strong desire toward resolution, which can be constructive or destructive, depending upon coping methods.

For example, binge drinking may temporarily take away the pain of a loss, but it will only create another crisis with negative consequences — lower productivity on the job, illness, accidents, alienation of friends and family. A positive reaction to crisis will reduce the emotional residue of a crisis, but may not always eliminate the depression or anger.

Although I've been aware of this factor for nearly thirty years, I often wonder why I'm feeling down when several weeks have passed after a major crisis. Then I figure back to the event and realize I'm in the phase referred to as "recoil." This minor "setback" is like a rubber band that's stretched to its limit, then snaps back. Knowing this time factor balances me, for I know that the feelings are temporary. Soon I'll be emotionally "on top" again.

The third critical point comes at the end of the six-week period, when we've dropped our guard or our support systems have left us, thinking we've made our adjustments. Once again, we feel the emotions of our crisis.

The Challenge: Once the Hotline was established, other social service administrators invited me to teach crisis intervention procedures to their staffs. In a training session for probation officers, a participant challenged the time-factor subject.

The officer was adamant about the "impossibility" of a six-week time span. The concerned officer cited the fact that some people *feel* the urgency of crisis over long periods of time. Confused, as are many people in the beginning (including myself), he thought their feelings stemmed from only one crisis unfolding.

Usually a destructive resolution or lack of a resolution (ignoring the matter) creates more crises. This leads to a feeling of a long-term crisis, but in reality, several crises are overlapping each other. Let's look again at our example of the mother dealing with her son Billy's poor report card.

Perhaps the mother overreacts and takes a belt to the boy. He runs away from home the next day. Now we have three crises: bad report card, beating, runaway. Each will probably have its six-week emotional run, which makes those involved feel like the original crisis (poor report card) lasts forever.

Beating the boy adds to the tension in the relationship, putting both mother and child into extremely vulnerable states, ripe for another crisis, which Billy then creates. And so the cycle continues.

I remember that due to the energy with which the probation officer took exception to this theory, I decided to "brake" from my speaking. While the men enjoyed their coffee, I took a brief walk in the soft, warm, summer evening. As I walked, I prayed for guidance. When I came back, the atmosphere had changed.

The participants told me of their discussion during the recess. Apparently, the discussion became heated. Then one officer reminded the others that he could prove the theory with their own statistics. In their training, they were taught that if a convict messed up and was returned to prison, it would most likely occur within *the first six weeks* after release. Even some things we want can be a crisis as changes are happening and choices need to be made.

While it may appear at first that the emotional upheaval surrounding a death is only one crisis, the dynamics remain the same. Losses produce other crises: funeral arrangements, disposal of personal items and property, notifying the proper agencies. Each one presents *another* crisis. Yet, we need not look at it as endless lines of crises to deal with, but simply a process of life that we must go through.

Knowing how a crisis develops and plays out has empowered me. Often, just knowing that the emotional ups and downs are contained within a limited time span helps dissipate the helplessness and uncertainty. Caught in the tangled emotions of crisis, I sometimes forget the theory and envision the awful feelings lasting forever. Or I think that something is wrong with me. Then I notice the time frame. "Oh, that's why," I tell myself, and relax.

Just like learning to be alert to weather changes in order to be prepared for or avoid dangerous situations, we can learn to read our own (and others') "emotional weather maps." Understanding the dynamics needed to create a full-blown crisis helps to prevent many crises, particularly in relationships.

Prevention also demands that we get plenty of rest, eat properly and exercise our bodies so that we are not physically run down and vulnerable. The same holds true for our mental and emotional health.

A continual feeding of mind and body through new ideas and positive alternatives for dispelling negative feelings, such as fear, doubt and worry, all help to maintain a strong, positive and alert attitude. Such an attitude often nips a crisis in the budding stage. Avoiding negative people, places and situations prevents many crises. People who continually go where they know there will be trouble for them are a puzzle to me (although I used to do the same).

Familiarity with the elements of a crisis is akin to knowing what symptoms mean trouble in the body. Most people will not ignore the warning signs of a heart attack: crushing pain in chest, arm or jaw, shortness of breath, dizziness, fatigue, numbness. Yet, they will approach someone who is obviously in a vulnerable state — tense, short tempered, depressed, fatigued or worried — and then wonder why that person explodes in anger.

We laugh at adages, but many have endured the test of time. My grandmother often reminded me, "A stitch in time saves nine." While few people sew these days, the warning stands. By taking steps to keep ourselves calm and alert, we take that stitch that prevents the tears in our lives that leave painful holes in hearts.

Obviously, no matter how prepared or aware we are, we can't prevent the crises through loss of loved ones, homes or jobs. However, awareness of how crisis works can help us to hang on just a little longer while our minds and bodies adjust to the changes in our lives. Instead of raging at the storm, we can take sanctuary in a quiet respite, giving ourselves the same loving care we would give to someone else.

Rainbow Ingredients
for
Crisis Situations

- Take a cool-down break.

- Pray.

- Be gentle with yourself and others.

- Take your time.

- Learn from the past.

- Prepare for the future.

- Live in the now.

- Find the rainbows.

A God-incident

We might think we're prepared to lose a loved one, but we never are. After Ken Sr.'s death, followed six weeks later by my oldest brother, Richard, my spirit sank into grief's muddy bog.

I had just returned from Richard's funeral, where I had helped his children with funeral arrangements, sort through his belongings and pack them for distribution. Now I was working in the lower level of our house, cleaning out my husband Ken's things, my mind a fog of indecision. What to save, what to give away? To whom? I was on the verge of tears when something caught my eye.

Fluttering outside the bedroom window was a large radiant hummingbird. He hovered close to the windowpane like a Peeping Tom. I had to laugh. Hummingbirds were Ken's favorite and he always kept their feeder full.

"Okay, okay. I'm sorry. I'll get you something right now," I said.

I dug out the feeder, filled it and hung it out. Although I never let the feeder get empty again that summer, I noticed a curious thing as the weeks went by. No matter which room I might be working in, the hummingbird peeked through that room's window.

One day, as I was sitting on the deck looking at the pond Ken had dug, I began to cry.

"I'm sorry, God," I said. "I just miss him so."

At that moment, I heard a loud buzzing noise. Opening my eyes, I saw the hummingbird in front of me, not six inches from my nose. I stared in disbelief.

For a few moments I held my breath, then I burst into laughter. I couldn't help myself. The bird continued to hover in front of me.

"Okay, I'm better now. Thank you," I said.

The bird flew away, but for the rest of the summer he continued to make frequent visits to my windows or deck. The second year following Ken Sr.'s death, the hummingbirds stayed at their feeders or out among the flowers. It was time for all of us to get on with our normal lives.

A Golden Nugget

A crisis is not an emergency.
A crisis is a turning point.
We have time to stop, look, listen and learn.

Stop, Look, Listen and Learn 3

*Learn to get in touch
with the silence within yourself and know
that everything in this life has a purpose.
There are no mistakes, no coincidences,
all events are blessings given to us
to learn from.*

Elisabeth Kübler-Ross

In my early years, I allowed myself to be so caught up in busyness that I ignored the signals for time-out. Meanwhile resentment, anger, frustration, fear, doubt and worry built up inside me like steam in a volcano. In my hurry to do everything, help everyone, I neglected my own needs, collapsing exhausted into bed each night. Fatigue works like a magnifying glass, increasing the intensity of negative feelings. Pushing through the warning signs, I set myself up for disaster.

True, there were times I pushed my way through trouble's warning signals with no major problems. Eventually, however, an accident, illness or emotional breakdown forced me to stop whatever out-of-control reactions or emotions were sapping my energy.

Many self-help teachers and scientists have proved the cause and effect relationship between mind, body and spirit. Even thoughts play a role in attracting to us that which we don't want.

"Stop. Count to ten," Grandma said when I was angry or frustrated. My child mind thought, *Humph! How does counting to ten change anything?* "Oh, why does it take so long to get smart?" asks my adult mind.

Stopping the emotional reactions long enough to look and listen increases our ability to find what we can and should do for positive results. Failure to apply this remedy puts us in jeopardy, as decisions made are apt to come from fear and panic, rather than love and wisdom. Halting the action or reaction by choice, rather than force, is a safer, healthier choice.

Too Young To Know?

As a young homemaker and mother, I was ill almost every week. At the time, my chronic ailments appeared a natural outgrowth of life as a "sickly" child. Because I was very small for my age, most adults saw me as puny, frail and susceptible to contagious diseases. Also, I lived in foster homes for three years due to a broken family, receiving little TLC (Tender Loving Care) except when ill. Between the need for TLC and the expectancy of illness, I was sick a lot.

When I became an adult, my illnesses took on a new meaning. The only extra rest came when I was too sick to get out of bed or went to the hospital to give birth. In those days, new mothers stayed in the hospital for a week and the nurses took care of the baby. Clean sheets every day, prepared meals served in bed. Flowers. Ah!

Eventually I was battling two or three bouts of bronchitis a year, which sometimes progressed into pneumonia. Each illness presented a crisis for me and the family. I'd be in bed for a week or two and feel tired and cranky for weeks afterward.

With six children in the house (my own five and a foster child), there were no coffee breaks or leisurely luncheons. I was lucky to get three hours sleep a night. In addition to the care of the children, an eight-room house, assorted animals and my husband, I committed time to Cub Scouts, Girls Scouts, PTA, car pooling, a monthly bridge club and church activities. I couldn't say, "No."

I loved all the activities, but lacked the time, energy or stamina to do everything I was committing to. Invariably I got sick and had to bow out of something temporarily to get some rest (such as it is in a houseful of children).

One year I volunteered to chair the decorations committee for our church's main fundraiser: a style show and luncheon. For several years, Jane,[1] a well-known businesswoman in our city, had organized the event for St. Mary's Church. She bypassed my offer, drafting Todd,[2] a talented art teacher, to supervise the decorations committee. I volunteered to help Todd.

Once we decided on a plan, Todd left me to implement it. I didn't mind. He liked my ambitious ideas to use tiny twinkle Christmas lights (new that year) for stars in our simulated American flags. I knew the results would be stunning for the "Miss America" theme. I persuaded a local business owner to let us borrow his decorative lights. *This will make a great impression on Jane,* I thought.

Somehow I managed to keep up with all the meetings and preparations and continue with my other activities. Then shortly before the event, Jane called (as she frequently did) to check on progress. I was in bed with bronchitis. Jane heard my raspy voice and said, "I knew you were too young to handle this job." I was flabbergasted! What did being young have to do with it? I was sick. Anyone can get sick.

As Jane berated my ability to handle the job, I was speechless. When she finally drew a breath, I jumped in with every bit of voice I could muster.

"I am twenty-nine years old, but I don't see what my age has to do with this."

Now she was confounded. "But you look like a teenager."

I was not complimented. (Oh, to hear those words again!)

"How I look has nothing to do with my competency." I rasped into a list of all the preparations that were in place. Hearing about the coup with the lights, that I was saving as a surprise, she begrudgingly apologized, said "good-bye" and hung up.

---

1 Name Change
2 Name Change

I lay back on the pillow to think, really think, about my chronic illnesses.

Am I immature as she intimated? Incapable? Why do I always get sick at critical times when I can least "afford" it? Was my husband (and sometimes even my doctor) right about my growing list of aches and pains?

My list of symptoms grew, often with no obvious physical cause. The medical bills grew proportionately. Ken's frustration erupted as well.

"It's all in your head. Just work through it."

Although my doctor never used those words, I felt the inference in his comment, "Well, it's only normal to have those symptoms... with all those children... but I can't find anything *physically* wrong." Then he'd prescribe a tranquilizer or muscle relaxant. Only when I had bronchitis did I get "real" medicine for a "real" disease.

Several days after the phone call, while still sick in bed, my questioning thoughts led me to a fascinating insight.

As with a close friend, I talk over my problems with God. Unlike some of my friends, my Creator never interrupts me, or tells me to "get over it" or "don't worry about it." What's more, He never commiserates. In fact, I never hear a voice with distinct messages. But when I really listen, something happens that touches my soul deeply. Peace comes. That's when I know that my prayers and questions are answered and life improves.

Prior to this particular time, my prayers were acts of pleading. "Please, please, *please* heal me fast. I need to get back to work."

Sometimes the answer came back "yes" and sometimes it was an obvious "no." When the bronchitis progressed into pneumonia, I felt like the answer was "NO! And another thing, young lady... ," as if I were being punished for something. Learning more about the relationship of mind to body, and body to spirit, brought an understanding that it is I who does the punishing. And it has nothing to do with maturity either. It's about listening to the inner spirit.

For the first time, my forced bed rest brought healing to my spirit as well as to my body. I asked the right questions and looked for answers from within myself, not from outside. Instead of asking for healing for my body, I asked for insight into what I might be doing to cause chronic health problems. Initially I resisted the nagging thought, "It's all in your head." Finally, in frustration, I took out pad and paper and wrote an argumentative letter to God.

"I don't see how a disease in my body comes from my head. I don't go around saying, 'I want to be sick.' You know that. In fact, I'm always begging you to heal my body."

Once I'd vented my anger, I fell into a sound sleep. Several hours later as I was waking, an often spoken phrase came to mind. "I just want some rest!" Sitting bolt upright in bed, the truth poured into my mind.

That's it! Only through an illness that restricts my breathing can I find "breathing space" to hear myself think. Although Jane had caught me off balance with her remarks, she touched something inside that caused me to look at my choices. How fortuitous!

This evaluation became a time of balance as I looked at what was really happening in my life. From the reflection came an inner wisdom I didn't know was there — a valuable lesson. I owe Jane a big thank you.

"Change negative thoughts to affirmative thoughts and you change negative, unpleasant experiences to affirmative, pleasant experiences," writes G. Eric Pace in *Don't Just Sit There — LIVE!*

Seeking Optimum Health

After "B-day"(bronchitis) — that great turning point — I opted for health and happiness, rather than sickness and sadness. I went to the library in search of books on the mind-body-soul connection for creating optimum health. In addition to G. Eric Pace, I found Joan Borysenko, Gerald G. Jampolsky, Louise L. Hay, Norman Cousins, Deepak Chopra, Paul Pearsall, Larry Dossey, Bernie S. Siegel and Wayne Dyer.

Recently, the following passage from *The Seat of the Soul* by Gary Zukav caused me to sit up and take notice.

> *Is it chance that one person develops heart disease, while another develops cancer? Even though disease states have correlations to factors of diet, exercise, lifestyle, and heredity, these correlations cannot mask the fact that life, for some people, is a heartbreak, while others allow themselves to be consumed, to be eaten alive, by the negative experiences of their lives. Can by-pass surgery or chemotherapy heal that?*

With my decision to go for optimum health, I read extensively about the mind's influence and practiced the psychological exercises I discovered. The reading sent me searching deeper into my spiritual life.

Coming from a deeply fundamentalist religious background, I was knowledgeable in dogma, able to recite many Bible verses. When it came to finding the truth, soul deep, I had a lot to learn. Digging deeper into my Bible and the stories of others' quests for spiritual truth, I found the tools to gain and keep a healthy body and strong mind.

But my stops to look and listen only focused on the mind and spirit aspects. Since I saw amazing results from the mind/spirit work, I forgot about the needs of my body. Or maybe I thought that positive thinking overruled lazy activity and poor eating habits.

When minor ailments once again led to a cycle of bed-rest sickness, I found suggestions for better nutrition, exercise and dietary supplements. I also became keenly aware of that incredible, powerful word: "NO." Although I haven't perfected "saying no," I am more conscious of filling my own cup before trying to fill that of others.

When the Locust Years started, I was in good shape, with a strong mind, body and spirit. Still, I knew that with all the trauma, I was statistically considered "at risk" for a major health challenge.

Although I refused to listen to anyone with statistical "evidence" that many people encounter catastrophic illnesses about one year after traumatic losses, I remained cognizant of the fact. So I increased my exercises and nutritional supplements and looked for healthier ways to eat. I cut back on all but the most essential outside projects and focused on this renewed quest for ways to strengthen mind and body.

Proper rest is a priority. However, there are times when we must search our inner wisdom and listen to others for signals of escapism, disguised as fatigue. That's why proper exercise is important. An energetic workout can refresh both the body and the spirit. Doing something physical often results in a "good" tired feeling. When life becomes too hectic, mini-respites help maintain mind-body-spirit balance. The key word here is *balance.*

I find that when we choose our timeouts, the results are sometimes outstanding. We lessen the risk of making mistakes, having regrets. We make wiser decisions, prevent many problems and prepare ourselves for those stormy times we cannot avoid. That is why it is critical to take a breather when in crisis or as a preventative, at the H.A.L.T. (Hungry. Angry. Lonely. Tired.) points.

The H.A.L.T. System

When troubles and temptations threaten our peace and joy, it's time to call a HALT. "HALT stands for the trigger points for trouble," says a friend who is in a twelve-step program. "You stop the action when you're hungry, angry, lonely or tired."

The most successful recovery programs for addictions of all kinds grew out of A.A. (Alcoholics Anonymous), the original twelve-step organization. A.A. teaches recovering alcoholics to take life "one day at a time." When we stop to look, listen and learn, we take life one *moment* at a time.

We can use the H.A.L.T. system to teach our children as well as ourselves. Had my family been fully aware of this method, we might have prevented many arguments, accidents and illnesses. Looking back, I realize I knew that fatigue, hunger and anger played a major role in the children's dispositions, and I often insisted they stop to rest, eat or take a breather and cool off.

As they grew older, my awareness diminished. I didn't have an authoritative tool like the H.A.L.T. system to remind me. I didn't set an example either, too busy being a busy person. I realize that much of my busyness, and perhaps some of my family's needs, came from my loneliness. Does it seem strange that in a family of eight persons, one could be lonely? Yet I recall times when I felt left out. So why wouldn't my children and husband also feel like that at times?

The happy news is that we can always learn and improve, no matter what our age or situation, and live more fulfilling lives. Rest stops get us back in sync with our bodies, minds and spirits, making the world look a lot brighter.

Stopping to eat an apple or banana when I'm hungry prevents my binges and sugar highs. Taking twelve deep breaths, going for a 10-minute walk or slowly drinking a glass of water when I'm angry or frustrated changes the picture, and improves my responses.

"Water carries nutrients and oxygen to cells through the blood," say Phyllis A. Balch, C.N.C., and James F. Balch, M.D. According to these authors of *Prescription for Cooking & Dietary Wellness,* drinking plenty of water (at least eight glasses daily), helps relieve anxiety attacks, headaches and extreme fatigue, which often affect our ability to think straight.

"Happiness is self-generated, something we set in motion for ourselves," says Douglas M. Lawson, author of *Give to Live.* The next time you feel lonely and left out, why not HALT the feeling? Visit a shut in, another lonely person or volunteer for a service organization.

"Giving is one of the nine choices made by extremely happy people," says Rick Foster and Greg Hicks, authors of *How We Choose to Be Happy.* However, giving of one's time and energy needs to be kept in balance. Wearing ourselves out by giving ourselves totally away is counter-productive to happiness and health.

Going to bed before exhaustion sets in is a smart idea. A short nap can revitalize a tired body. Sometimes fatigue isn't of the body, but the mind. Then some peppy or relaxing diversion is needed, perhaps roller blading or working an hour on a hobby. My favorite energizing activity is solving intricate jigsaw puzzles. As I focus on the shapes and colors, my body rests and my mind forgets my troubles. It often takes only twenty minutes to become refreshed.

I do not recommend television as a "braking" period, for it seldom provides the quiet atmosphere necessary to look, listen and learn. In fact, it may compound the problem. Commercials whet one's appetite for food, drink and shopping, which may lead to addictions. Much of the news and many programs consist of violence and negativity, often producing anger and depression. The little box of celluloid people won't take the place of the real human touch.

My recommendation is to record positive-focused programs with sound lessons, such as *Oprah* and *Touched By An Angel,* so you can fast forward through the commercials. But the little box of videotaped people won't take the place of real human touch, either, so I recommend rejuvenating your spirit and energy through conversations with positive people. Sharing experiences, ideas and humor are great energy boosters.

Learning From Experience

A new friend I'll call Gloria recently told me about her healing experiences with the Stop, Look, Listen and Learn remedy.

A "nervous breakdown" put her into a psychiatric hospital ward. Although this was a difficult time for Gloria and her family, she says, "It was the best experience of my life. In there, I healed spiritually, mentally and physically. I focused all my attention on myself. I learned that I couldn't be truly helpful to anyone else, not even my children, when I was running on empty."

Today Gloria is a successful, self-employed business owner with a full schedule. Still, she makes it a priority to schedule regular stops for R & R (rest and renewal).

> IN RETURNING AND REST YOU SHALL
> BE SAVED; IN QUIETNESS AND IN TRUST
> SHALL BE YOUR STRENGTH.
> ISAIAH 30.15, REVISED STANDARD VERSION

Establishing regular quiet times for reflection, preparation and maintenance strengthens us, as it helps put problems into perspective. Regular stops in our daily lives acquaint us with the language in our heads and emotions in our hearts that cause us grief. Brief intermissions from daily activities help us recognize secrets within: judgment, anger, fear, doubt and worry. All these stand in the way of our peace, happiness and healthy living.

Not until we get quiet enough to discover the truth of our thoughts, can we change them. "You can learn from wisdom, or you can learn from woe," said the angel Tess in *Touched By An Angel*. Being stuck in bed with bronchitis is learning through woe. Not fun!

Building mini-respites into our daily routines creates a life maintenance plan that lessens the risk of making mistakes and having regrets. We make wiser, stronger decisions. Pauses prepare us. Pauses prevent problems. Pauses allow us to return to the source of our strength while in good health, rather than to be catapulted there through sickness.

Finding the time and place for stops can be challenging. I remember the first time I "escaped" my problems in a positive way and got in touch with my inner self.

The Kneipp Springs Experience

As a young, naive, exhausted mother of three little ones, I was desperate for help. Ken and I married in 1952, two weeks after my high school graduation. Deborah, our first child, was born in 1953. We began and ended 1955 with a newborn: Cynthia in January, Kenneth Jr. in December. (Try and explain that to teachers who must have information cards filled out each year.) My body was stretched to the max. So were my emotions. I was running out of dishes to smash against the wall.

Ken's boss, Bob, and his wife had nine children, so Ken sought his counsel. Bob told Ken that he occasionally tended the entire family so his wife could go to a health spa. Kneipp Springs was owned by a Catholic religious order and was located in central Indiana. In addition to tending to the needs of the health spa's clients, the sisters had a secondary mission: to provide a quiet, healing place for overworked mothers. For a donation (or nothing if funds were limited), tired mothers could go there for a rest.

Although it was a three-hour drive and took lots of preparation before leaving home, I decided to give myself a weekend at Kneipp Springs where I found heavenly restoration.

I ate delicious, nutritious meals prepared (and cleaned up) by someone else, slept through entire nights undisturbed, walked along restive tree-lined lanes by bubbling springs and wrote at length (and with honesty) in my journal.

Sometimes, in the evening, one special sister and I talked. Two adults. No interruptions. Sister Mary Teresa was an excellent listener. The visits were healing and spiritually expanding. I treasure those times in that holy place with the kind, loving sisters.

Going to Kneipp Springs rejuvenated me and convinced me that I needed short, daily quiet times. How could I find such moments with a growing, busy family? Was there a way to bring home some of the peace I felt at Kneipp Springs?

My first experience in slicing out a bit of quiet time each day was rather bumpy. To find silence in a house full of active people, I had to rise earlier than anyone else. Sometimes, even the birds can't beat the babies. I decided to get up thirty minutes before our earliest riser. But when the alarm went off, I couldn't force myself out of bed.

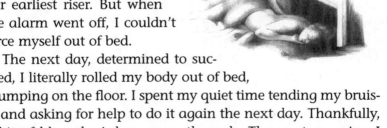

The next day, determined to succeed, I literally rolled my body out of bed, thumping on the floor. I spent my quiet time tending my bruises and asking for help to do it again the next day. Thankfully, a bit of blessed wisdom came through. The next morning I rolled myself out of bed onto a pile of soft pillows.

It took a week to adjust. The thirty minutes spent each morning in prayerful meditation, journaling or Bible and inspirational reading, brought me self-confidence and a desire for more. I looked for niches where I might plug in quiet time, either in prayer and meditation, journaling or just for reading self-help books.

In the stillness, my mind was free to ask questions. Often, within seconds of writing questions in my journal, I found answers in books, audiotapes, newspapers or magazine articles, songs on the radio, even through casual conversations with friends. This "magic" continues today. Many times I feel led to a perfect resource for the immediate need in my life.

I believe that once we start looking for something, we find it in many places. For years I carried two small magazines in my purse to read while waiting for my children to finish activities or doctors' appointments: *Guideposts,* a small magazine filled with positive stories of people dealing with life's difficult times, and *Plus, The Magazine of Positive Thinking.*® Through these magazines, countless insights sparked my searching mind. I am continually amazed at how many times the story I am reading is a direct answer to a current concern. (Today, *Plus* is still carried in my purse, but *Guideposts,* and a companion magazine, *Angels on Earth,*® go on my bedside table for uplifting bedtime stories to inspire sweet dreams.)

Waiting for trains or lingering in traffic provide bonus prayer times to give thanks or ask questions. (Don't expect immediate answers, although sometimes it happens. Be patient. Sometimes delivery is slow.)

When the children grew older and I worked full-time, I found lunch-time sanctuaries: a community greenhouse, chapels, cemeteries and parks. A fifteen-minute walk, particularly during seasonal changes, refreshed my body and renewed my spirit. I always accomplished more after one of those brief intermissions.

Now my children are grown. Living alone, I have plenty of quiet time. My dilemma is how to put that solitude into *focused* use. I often take for granted that once I learn a valuable technique, there is no need for further change. Not so. Change is the challenge that recharges my spirit.

Timeouts can vary from quiet times for contemplation to crazy, off-beat changes of pace. A timeout can be as brief as a two-minute breathing space, when I close my eyes, draw my breath deep into my abdomen, hold a few seconds, and exhale slowly and thoughtfully through my mouth. This brief interlude quiets the mind and body as it wakes up the brain.

Breath, The Life Connector

One of my greatest blessings during visiting hours before Ken Jr.'s funeral came from two friends who stood nearby. When they saw me tense up, they moved into the receiving line, put their arms around me and breathed deeply. As they held me close, I heard and felt their calm, centered breathing. When my breathing matched theirs, they stepped back. I was renewed.

Like many people, I hold my breath during tense and troubling moments. We can live without food for a few weeks, without water for a few days, but without oxygen for only a few minutes. To deal quickly with stress and muscle tension: *breathe deeply.*

Breathing balances us. Operating on emotional energy knocks us off balance. We don't think clearly. We react irrationally, rather than acting purposefully. We're like blowup punching dolls, bobbing here, there, getting nowhere. When we stop to breathe deeply, we ground ourselves in natural energy given to us at birth.

Controlled breathing calms the nervous system, making it easier to take charge of our minds. This increases the chance of getting a true reading of the situation and seeing possible outcomes. This moment of breathing is like the fresh air that sweeps in after a good rain, clearing the clouds and letting the sunlight through so rainbows can shine.

Sometimes a simple change in activity helps us reestablish our body-mind balance. Walking, running, listening to music often help. Music can be soft and soothing or upbeat and rhythmic. Word associations that are *positive and uplifting,* can lead to regaining balance.

I remember an aerobics teacher whose favorite music provided a good beat for the exercise. However, the words (once I learned to understand them) were about someone committing suicide. That was *not* a helpful message. We needed something to *renew* our spirits, not destroy them.

Some workshop leaders I know use loud, resonating music with a solid beat and uplifting words to stimulate their audiences between segments. Participants dance, jump up and down, holler and sing along. Their blood circulates; they are happy, refreshed and open to new ideas. Amazingly, they can go longer in session than participants without music. (What a difference this style of teaching would make in our children's schools, particularly at the junior and high school levels where there are no recesses.)

Other positive time-outs include movies, dance, sports, exercise, housecleaning, gardening or carpentry. There is one caveat, however. Look for activities of enjoyment, not frustration. If a golfer gets upset every time his ball doesn't go where he wants, golf is a chore, not a refreshing respite from life's problems.

In addition to renewing the spirit and increasing energy, pauses to listen to an inner voice can bring important corrections on life's journey. "By facing a subject that usually depresses and terrifies us, we feel lighter, freer, more perceptually and cognitively alive in all our encounters," writes Rabbi Zalman Schachter-Shalomi in *From Age-ing to Sage-ing.*

If I'm still, I will come to know that other self, my observer, that part which stands apart and sees the wonder to be found even in the stormiest times.

Stops to Listen

Ninety percent of communication comes from listening. We must make frequent stops to listen to others as well as to our own hearts. And there are times when we can increase our power of listening by tuning into the silence together.

Listening to Others: When we deliberately stop our own thoughts and comments to sincerely listen to another, we may be amazed at what we hear. Surprisingly, some people actually argue in agreement. They don't know it because they aren't listening to each other. Doubt it? Try intensive listening and find out.

When we close our mouths and open our ears, we can hear truths and eliminate false judgments. Listening, not just hearing, allows possibilities, probabilities and new ideas to float into the mind.

Quiet times can also lead to wisdom. Wisdom can lead to answers and solutions that work. This is how eminent people of the world come to their place of greatness. They embrace the quiet time. They listen.

Listening with the Heart: Going into the quiet, we find our inner spirit. Listening with the heart puts us in rhythm with true life, not the phony shell of daily activities.

Our hearts tell us the truth with love — the self-love we can trust. Once upon a time we called this a "conscience" and relied on it to motivate us into right actions. Whenever I asked my beloved grandmother about matters of conscience, she always replied, "Your heart knows."

Listening from the inside also helps us in decision making. It is a powerful tool for developing discernment and happy results. When used faithfully, this remedy increases sensory perceptions. We become tuned into God-incidences, wonder-filled opportunities and joy we experience when making difficult choices.

Listening Together: Dr. Norman Vincent Peale, author of many positive-living books, and his wife, Ruth, used quiet time in a unique way. Whenever they had a major decision to make, such as deciding between two job offers, they sat quietly together in a secluded room. There they stayed in prayerful listening until an answer came to each one separately.

Although each stayed in a private silence, writing down any thoughts that came to mind, they did not discuss and did not leave until both felt they had an answer. Amazingly, their answers were always the same. Wouldn't it be great if all married couples used this quiet listening for major decisions? Think of the marriages that would be saved, the stability for hosts of families.

Astute business leaders recognize the benefits of quiet time. Ian D. Percy, a Certified Speaking Professional, helps leaders restore their spirit through the power of listening. Percy has corporate managers sit in silence to listen to their own thoughts. When he calls "time to speak," his participants are amazed at how quickly and easily they communicate the real problems and viable solutions. As with Dr. and Mrs. Peale, the managers often come together with the same or similar answers. By gathering together in silence, they renew the spirit of the corporation.

Sometimes, however, we go separate ways to look and listen in our own quiet times. This process also proves to be an amazing learning experience.

The Novena Prayer

Once the children were all in school, and we were financially comfortable, my husband, Ken, decided to fulfill his dream of living in the South. His goal was to buy a tavern in Florida.

While the idea of living in the sunny south year round appealed to me, the idea of owning a tavern did not. I wanted something our whole family could actively participate in. A tavern would not provide the positive, healthy atmosphere I wanted for my children. However, I was practicing "letting go and letting God," so I didn't protest.

In preparation for the move south, I cleared out the house, throwing away everything frivolous to lighten the moving load. My husband and I cleaned, painted and refreshed our home to attract a buyer. I resigned from my outside activities: scouts, PTA, church committees, clubs.

Getting rid of "stuff" was the easy part, even though I'm a professional pack rat. The expense of moving extras (junk) outweighed the compulsion to keep everything "just in case." Shedding extracurricular activities was also freeing. I was tired of running around "like a chicken with its head cut off," as Grandma would say. But giving up my ideas of what Ken *should* do for a living was difficult. To help me in my commitment to let go and let God (trust), a friend gave me a novena prayer.

A novena is a devotion consisting of nine separate days of prayers or services. I became a Catholic (Ken's religion), when our youngest daughter, Laura, was born. As I prepared to move, it felt appropriate to use the formalized set of prayers for a special intention. With the house cleaned, kids in school and volunteer activities resigned, I had nothing else to do but pray. (Even my mending was done!)

At first, I found the ritual difficult. A former Protestant, I was not used to saying a litany of prayers, and I felt uncertain of what my "special intention" should be. I knew what I wanted. I also knew what Ken wanted. The two wants were not the same.

The set prayers kept me focused on positive possibilities, rather than worried about possible problems. The daily prayers became a ceremony of acceptance and expectation. When it came time to proclaim my special intention, I left it in God's hands. "Your way, Lord," I said.

My nine days of prayers spanned the same amount of time that Ken had allotted to search for the right tavern to purchase. By the third day I was in total peace. In fact, I was thoroughly enjoying the extra prayer and reflection time that my busy life had not allowed before. I knew God was at work.

On the seventh day, Ken stopped his daily telephone calls to me from our prospective new home state. What was wrong? Had he been in an accident? Was he unconscious or terribly sick?

Now my letting go and letting God took on new meaning. I not only trusted that we'd come to the right answer, I had to trust that Ken was all right and being guided (wherever he was). When I wavered, I prayed, "Thank you for guiding us and keeping Ken safe."

Two long days went by with no word from my husband. Then Ken arrived safely at our door late Saturday night, still undecided about our move. His "lost" time was a quiet drive back to Indiana, reflecting on all his options. He had found one tavern he especially liked. At my request to look at other business opportunities, he also located a root beer drive-in and an ice cream stand that showed promise. They were located in the area where Mr. Disney was planning to build.

As Ken ate a late supper, he shared the highlights of the search, giving location, prices, pros and cons of each business opportunity.

"So, what did you decide?"

"I'm tired. I'll decide in the morning," he said and went to bed.

When morning came, he wanted to go to early Mass, saying, "Then I'll decide." After church, he wanted breakfast. Finally, at the dinner table, he said, "I'm going to buy the tavern I found down there."

The long prayer vigil didn't dilute my disappointment. Still, I said, *"Thank you, God,"* willing myself to believe it was right for us, especially since two couples were interested in buying our house. After lunch, Ken called the tavern owner to make his offer. The owner had just sold the business to someone else.

The biggest surprise to me was Ken's reaction. He didn't seem too disappointed. In fact, he immediately went to work on a plan to go into an auto parts business in our home town. One month later, he was driving his newly purchased used truck and selling auto parts. Ken turned a profit from the first day.

Without my decision to set aside quiet reflection and prayer time, I might well have become an obstacle to God's plan, rather than an instrument of acceptance. My family ended up in the place that was right for us to grow and blossom.

One week after Ken started his business, a rainstorm hit our area. Although it was brief, there were high winds, so when the storm subsided, I went outside to look for damage. Seeing nothing serious, I turned to go inside when something caught my eye and I looked up. Forming in the heavens was a double rainbow that took my breath away.

As I gazed at the rainbows, I realized that Ken's decision brought us two blessings: his prospering business and the beginning of an incredible personal growth journey for me.

Getting my house in order and putting my faith on the line with nine days of worshipful praise and listening, rather than pleading and demanding, brought a better solution than either of us imagined. Freed from clutter, endless activity and indecision, I was now able to fulfill a long-held dream of my own: becoming a college student.

During the next four months, I immersed myself in a creative writing class at the University of Notre Dame. To my surprise, this class became a catalyst for a series of God-incidences that took me out of my crisis-addicted life into Rainbow Living. The professor's suggestion to offer the use of our writing talents to not-for-profit organizations took me to the Y.W.C.A.'s drug abuse study, which in turn led to the founding of Hotline, one of my most satisfying endeavors.

Pausing and Reflecting

The Stop, Look, Listen and Learn remedy is best when used as a preventative to save us a lot of heart- and headaches. However, it is also a potent prescription for treating crisis situations.

From the crisis chapter, we learned the key times for quieting our emotions and stopping the activity that causes discomfort:

   a) point of impact of crisis,

   b) mid-point of six-week period,

   c) end of six-week period.

In addition to the major crisis of the loss of a loved one, there are other times we may need to pause and reflect. Anniversaries of the death, birthdays and holidays we celebrated together, special events or times meaningful to our relationship. There are other times, known only to our subconscious, which may cause us discomfort and knock us off balance. Because the subconscious self knows, we can consider pushing the pause button at these times to find out what is going on and put harmony back into our lives.

Two such times in my life come to mind: the first spring after Kenny Jr.'s childhood burn episode and the first New Year's Day after my husband's death.

The Burn: In the spring of Kenny Jr.'s sixth summer, his dad was burning the grass off a field on our property. The children stayed in their play area until I went into the house to prepare lunch. Then Kenny walked to the edge of a smoldering area and knelt down to play in the ashes with a stick.

Kenny's pants caught fire, severely burning his left leg. I was taught to put butter on a burn, so the first thing we did was slap a quarter pound of cold butter on his leg. The only good part of that remedy was that it was cold. As we know now, the butter turned to fat, continuing the burn process.

For four months, my job was to tend to the leg, pulling off the old bandages each day, replacing them with ointment and new dressings. Each day I had to psych myself up to the task. My stomach churned and my head ached from holding back the tears as Kenny screamed through the process, but he kept his body still "like a man." His leg healed, although badly scarred.

Except when I tore off old bandages, Kenny never complained, and the burns did not stand in the way of his activities, including pony riding. Once the daily treatments were finished, I thought the ordeal was over. I was wrong. The following spring, nightmares terrified Kenny nightly.

In his sleep, my seven-year-old son screamed, "No, Mommy. NOOOO!" I tried to comfort him, but Kenny was so frightened of me that he tried to crawl out an open window to get away. Helpless and afraid for my suffering child, I stayed out of sight, praying, as his father comforted him.

Kenny didn't remember the dreams on awakening. One night after getting him calmed, his dad and I pieced the puzzle together. Almost simultaneously, we came to the same conclusion. The spring season must have triggered Kenny's memory of that awful experience. Since I was the one who hurt him each day by changing the bandages, he was subconsciously terrified of me.

The next day we asked little Kenny if the dreams were about getting burned. He couldn't remember. We encouraged him to talk about his memories of that time anyway. As he talked, his inner healing began. Because Ken Sr. and I stopped to think about the problem, rather than dismiss it as a mere childhood nuisance, Kenny was freed from his nightmare.

The Game: I experienced a similar freeing experience twenty-eight years later when a friend helped me understand a strange depression on New Year's Day, eight months after my husband's death.

I made it through all the holidays without feeling down, even though my family was going through numerous crises at the time. Then, on New Year's Day, my spirit plummeted. All my family and friends had plans for the day. Most were watching the University of Notre Dame in a playoff for number one gridiron position in the country. Football was Ken's favorite pastime, not mine. I like movies, so I chose a movie over the game hoping to lift my spirits.

When I got home from the movie, there was a message on my answering machine from my friend, Marty.

"I was thinking about you because of the Notre Dame game," her message said. *Strange. Ken was the football fan. Notre Dame his team.* I willingly faded into the background on football weekends. Since Marty's voice sounded concerned, I returned her call.

She asked if I was depressed. "I was earlier, but I went to a funny movie. Feel better. How did you know?"

Marty shared her memory of the first New Year's holiday following her husband's death. He was also an avid Notre Dame fan and that New Year's Day the team was in a playoff game for the number one spot. She remembered feeling her loss most on that day, thinking how much he would have enjoyed watching the game. Although I thought I ignored the Notre Dame football hoopla, my subconscious self tuned in.

For Ken Sr., this New Year's game would have been a high point of his year, just as it would have been for Marty's husband. Since it was a championship game, I probably would have watched parts of it with him, chuckling to myself as he coached from his lounge chair. But I could not do that, and the feeling of loss had unconsciously overwhelmed me. The place in my life I had given my husband was still a raw, gaping hole.

When I now feel depression "for no reason," I take a look at the calendar to see if there may be a loss I need to remember and consciously release. Remembering and releasing pay huge emotional dividends.

Just as we do at unprotected railway crossings, we stop the action, look in all directions and listen for warning signals before proceeding. In the process we learn many productive and interesting ways to handle difficult situations.

Rainbow Ingredients
for
Effective Self-Awareness

- *Stop*: Take time out to be in silence.

- *Look*: View your situation, your life from different angles.

- *Listen*: To God's voice, to the wisdom He has placed within you.

- *Listen*: To other voices for truth and understanding.

- *Learn*: Make each situation a growth experience.

- *Enjoy* the experience.

A God-incident

Journal entry: Ft. Myers, FL

Visiting [daughter] Debbie and [her husband] Bartolo. In my house on wheels, the Hummingbird. My plan is to stay a month here, then move up the coast to Carrabelle. While here, I want to visit friends on the other coast. Will rent a car.

"Mom, you don't have to rent a car," Debbie happily informs me on arrival. "Bartolo just bought a used Cadillac from his boss. You can use that for free."

Debbie and I hop into the car the next day to go shopping. The Cadillac coughs and sputters. We take it to a garage. "This was supposed to be fixed," she says. More work is done. No charge. I don't want to offend Debbie or Bartolo, but I'm uneasy about using the car for a 300-mile trip.

A week goes by. Bartolo drives the car every day. No problems. I feel better. Visit a friend in Ft. Lauderdale, then up the coast to Ft. Pierce and back to my temporary home. As I exit Interstate 75, the Cracker Barrel restaurant sign beckons. Long past lunch time. I think I'll stop for my favorite catfish dinner.

Leaving the restaurant, I sit at the stop light, motor purring. The light turns green. I step on the gas. The Cadillac sputters, coughs and chokes. Then stalls — just long enough for a speeding semi-truck to run the crossing street's red light. The motor catches. I move smoothly onto the highway. The semi is barely visible up ahead.

Praise and Thanksgiving

4

*Look upon the rainbow,
and praise Him that made it.*

Ecclesiasticus, XLIII, 11

For a powerful treatment of the fear and heartache that accompanies stormy times, try praise and thanksgiving. This remedy works like muscle-building programs: it stretches and strengthens what we already have inside. Used regularly, the remedy builds assurance and attracts peace, pleasure and prosperity.

Praise and thanksgiving is a strong prescription for restoring good health and positive relationships. Used as a treatment for the PLUM (Poor Little Unfortunate Me) disease, praise and thanksgiving become stirring soul healers.

Gratitude Seed is Prepackaged

Praise is prepacked within us at birth. Most little children express this natural instinct to be joyful and grateful for simple things. Notice how babies respond to loving touches, toys, attention. Their eyes light up; they coo and babble; their arms and legs wave in delight as if applauding whatever or whoever is making them feel good.

The Bible teaches us to praise and give thanks *in all* things! Children have little problem with that. Watch a toddler go after a spider or an ant. Until she gets stung (or is taught otherwise) what she sees is a wonderful little creature she'd like to get to know better — maybe eat!

---

1 Rejoice always, pray constantly, give thanks in all circumstance. (Paraphrased: 1Thes. 5:18)

So what happens to this wonder-filled attitude for appreciating all of life and finding joy-filled discovery in everything? As our little girl grows older, she learns distrust. She falls off her bike. She gets painfully bit by an insect. Her parents promise a trip to the zoo and it doesn't happen. In a short time, our wide-eyed, trusting toddler goes from looking at the world as "awe full" to "awful."

From today's culture, children hear confusing viewpoints. In an effort to protect our children from hurts, disappointments and sorrows, we teach them to be on the defensive or offensive side of life. Some religions help foster the "awful" by focusing more on sins, rather than the love in the world. What is sown, is reaped.

When Academy Awards go to actors playing ruthless killers, how do impressionable young people differentiate between the actor and the villain? The good guys don't wear white hats anymore.

What we see and hear through the media gets slanted. In *A Journey of One's Own*, Thalia Zepatos shares an experience she and her friend, Mary, had while visiting students in China. The students were studying English, so Zepatos invited them to ask questions about the United States. The students asked questions such as:

"What do Americans do on dates? How does divorce work in America? Is it true that after divorce, the father usually raises the children? Are all soldiers homosexuals?"

"Most of these questions arose from generalizations created from a single news story or American film," says Zepatos.

We wonder why so many young people (and adults) have low self-esteem. Instead of honest love, respect and gratitude, we have a selection process fostered by advertisers. Media mania leaves us confused and deficient in spirit. A deficient spirit is a dying spirit. So what are we to do?

Give thanks and praise *in*, not for. The young American women traveling in China were grateful for the opportunity to set the record straight. The Chinese had a similar opportunity to answer the Americans' questions. They took delight in each other's company, experiencing bits of each culture. Together they recognized and rejoiced in the great gift of sharing information and ideas.

The act of acknowledging that which is truly good and constructive renews a weary spirit. Instead of getting stuck in "how awful," we can see the wonder.

> *Prayer is a state of continual gratitude. If I do not feel a sense of joy in God's creation, if I forget to offer the world back to God with thankfulness, I have advanced very little upon the way. I have not yet learnt to be truly human. For it is only in thanksgiving that I can become myself.*
>
> St. John Kronstadt
> Russian Orthodox Priest
> Late 19th or early 20th Century

Webster's dictionary describes praise as "the offering of grateful homage in words or song" and "the act of expressing approval or admiration." A synonym for praise is "boost" and for thanksgiving, "appreciation." When considering "appreciation," think like a banker who sees appreciation as an increase in value.

Cultivating the Seeds

An appreciation for life produces a life filled with love and fun. My mother was a fun-lovin' person who enjoyed life and wanted the same for her family. She played music, sang and danced. She told funny stories, loved meeting new people.

Mom played the piano, organ and trumpet. Sometimes I sat beside her on the piano bench when she played. Other times I sat on the floor, back against the piano, the melodic vibrations keeping time up and down my spine.

Much of Mom's praise and gratitude came through her music, planting a seed deep inside my soul. That seed sprang to life when the song "Over The Rainbow" came to mind as I crossed the corn field that long ago day. The music lifted me above the pain and shame of violation. The dreadful experience of being molested turned into an awe-filled afternoon of turquoise skies, cotton ball clouds, contented cows and a rainbow-filled heart. Through Mom, God gave me a healing song, not just for the moment, but for my eternal soul. Rainbows juice my spirit, produce electrical currents within that activate an aura of pure joy.

Music, like poetry, covers the gamut of emotions, putting us in touch with sorrow and joy, anger and remorse, love and gratitude. Each musical note connects us in mind, body and soul to our Creator. Songs of praise and thanksgiving lift our spirits and heal our bodies in ways no doctor or medicine can. They are beautiful tools for cultivating our gardens of praise. We touch the rainbow life through joyful music.

When I was a young child, Mom taught me to swim, play games, bake cookies and iron smartly-creased white shirts in "double quick time." Mom had other ways to teach appreciation: encouraging experimentation and experiences. She taught me how to read, write and do mathematics even before I was school age.

Mom appreciated my made-up stories, never discounting them. Her encouragement formed the foundation for my writing. Appreciation of a talent, even in its infancy, brings awareness for self-actualization. Mom's appreciation of my meager efforts brought dividends beyond either of our dreams.

"You can learn anything you want to," Mom said. "All you have to do is try." She praised my efforts. When I was frustrated, Mom showed me how to experiment, to search for new ways to work for better results. She did her best to help me overcome fears. Mom showed me how to find joy in the smallest things, the scariest things. Joy is the highest form of gratitude.

Great Balls of Fire: As little children, my brother Richard and I were terrified of lightning. During one particularly fierce electrical storm, Mom pulled a chair to a large window and sat us both on her lap. She "ohhhed" and "ahhhed" over each flash of lightning, giggled at every boom as though we were watching a July 4th fireworks display. Soon we joined in the excitement of watching nature's magnificence in action.

Suddenly, two balls of fire came streaking through the sky. One from our right and one from our left, colliding just on the other side of the glass, in front of us. I felt a tightening of Mom's arm and a slight hesitation before her enthusiastic, "Wow! Wasn't that exciting?" Mom's excitement and delight chased away the strangling fear that clutched my throat as the fireballs collided.

Mom's lessons included etiquette, particularly saying "please" and "thank you." What I remember most vividly about the lessons are not the rules, but the way Mom presented them. "Please" seemed more than just a polite way to say, "I want." Somehow Mom conveyed the idea that asking politely made the granting of the request something worthy of a "thank you." Subsequently, "thank you" became a felt appreciation for what was received.

I marvel now at Mom's cheerful attitude about life in those days, for hers was not an easy one. She had little encouragement, such as she gave me. I was an adult before I fully appreciated what it took for Mom to show me life's happy side while going through her personal hell.

Beauty Queen Meets Preacher's Son: Shortly after winning a beauty pageant, my mother met my father. Mom was preparing for a Hollywood screen test when my father persuaded her to marry him. The marriage was not a happy one. Her broken dreams and subsequent emotional problems eventually led to divorce. She endured a painful three-year separation from her children. Maybe that was why she later seemed impelled to instill in us a sense of gratitude for what we had, rather than allowing us to complain about what we lacked.

When my parents first separated, I was thrown into a world of constant upheaval. From first grade through fourth, I moved from foster home to foster home, each in a different school district (seven in the first year). Although I worked hard at being a "good girl," someone always found my faults rather than my strengths. The only times I felt truly appreciated came during rare visits with my mother or her mother, Grandma Gladys. The rest of the time I felt like a nuisance and a burden.

I was not a ward of the court, but a stray, who ended up in a variety of homes until Mom or my father "got back on their feet." In the meantime, my self-esteem dipped lower than stocks in a bear market.

In an effort to emulate Mom's happy spirit, I turned on a pleasant smile and used my best manners, pretending the words and attitudes I heard didn't hurt. Sometimes it worked, sometimes it didn't.

I am reminded of those times when my own children first learned to play peek-a-boo. They covered their faces with their hands thinking they couldn't be seen. Sometimes the naivete of children carries into adulthood. Some adults seem to cover their ears so they can't hear critical words that come out of their mouths or berating thoughts that run through their heads. Why do we think if our ears can't hear the criticism, our minds won't either? If we are to change our world, we must recognize the significance and magnitude of words.

Weeds in the Garden

Condemning language pops up like weeds in a garden. It comes in many varieties: put-down humor, "just teasing," curses, slams, "helpful" evaluations, judgment. We can curse someone, devalue them and never use gutter language.

"You dummy!"

"I hate you!"

"I wish you were dead!"

"You're so stupid!"

"Well, duh!"

Spoken in the heat of an argument or as a reprimand, the words cut deep into the spirit. Even in jest, the words bruise and batter. Something inside each person cringes, the one speaking, the one receiving and the ones within earshot. Our bodies and minds take our own messages personally, although we intended them for someone else. Over time relationships crumble, individual dreams and aspirations are crushed under the onslaught like vegetation and wildlife in a mud slide. Self-esteem grows dim. Like the farmer says, "You can't slop the hogs without getting some on yourself."

My grandmother tried to help offset childhood slurs with an old saying: "Sticks and stones may break my bones, but words can never hurt me." In essence, Grandma was saying, "Don't let those sticks and stones kill the wonder within you." Through Grandma's advice, I avoided damage from some of the childhood onslaughts, but not all.

Studies now conclude that words do hurt us, psychologically, physically and spiritually. Like crochet thread, words connect mind, body and spirit into beautiful patterns of health and wholeness or knot us into frustrating patterns of pain and suffering.

For better and for worse, words affect our bodies. When we "hate" our bodies, they become ill, filled with pain. They become deformed and drained of energy, old and worn-out. Loving and appreciating our bodies brings new life. Praise for our bodies appreciates like interest on a certificate of deposit.

When you wonder why low self-esteem is so prevalent, remember that it's not just the critical words others spit at us. Most harm comes from within our own heads because we accept the hurtful words as truth. No one else has to do it. We do it... *with our own self-talk.* We choose to incorporate hurtful words into our language.

"I'm so stupid."

"I'm so ugly."

"I'm too fat, too thin, too tall... " and on it goes.

Each derogatory phrase we swallow into our belief system is ingested into our spirit. With them we stick knives into our self-esteem. By allowing negative words to become a part of our thoughts and speech, we devalue the incredible gifts God gave to us — our minds and our bodies.

"[T]he Divine infused us with the power to conceive, express and enjoy the fruits of our creative power," says Iyanla Vanzant.[2] She advises affirming your body with, "I am made in the image and likeness of the Divine."

"Everything created by God is good, and nothing is to be rejected if it is received with thanksgiving," taught Jesus. We are good. Our families are good. Our neighbors are good. Our enemies are good. So bless them.

"As he thinketh in his heart, so is he," confirms the Proverb. When our minds take to heart the berating messages to "have and to hold," we are wedded to that which we may not want.

---

2 Author of *Faith in the Valley*

"I'm fat" overpowers every diet one tries. "I'm such a ditz, I can't do anything right" overrules all efforts to change self-defeating habits.

My favorite mind-body connection book is Louise L. Hay's *"You Can Heal Your Life,"* because it has "THE LIST." Yet, much to my chagrin, I often forget about it until some dis-ease in my life creates a health challenge. In my misery, I go to Hay's book and look up my problem, shake my head in wonder and sigh. Right on target. Again!

The list covers a multitude of physical problems from "abdominal cramps" to "wrist," each accompanied by a "probable cause" and "new thought pattern." I look for the negative thought process that caused my problem: I seek to change my thoughts for better health.

The Accident: When I suffered a whiplash injury in a rear-end collision caused by a speeding driver, I looked up "neck" in Hay's book and found: "Represents flexibility. The ability to see what's back there." At the time I was on an unrealistic, self-imposed deadline. I could feel the stress building and my energies waning, but remained determined to finish the job, no matter what it took. (To do it properly required additional time and research.) The accident derailed me. (I now had time, but was temporarily incapacitated).

What caused the accident? The foggy, rainy day? The slick and hazardous street? The other driver's youth and inexperience? All contributing factors, but not the *root cause.* If there weren't so many past experiences that coincided with Hay's "probable cause," I would have sloughed off the incident as simple chance.

The Blister: Going back in memory to my grandmother with the "sticks and stones" adage, I found she, too, was a victim of her words. Grandma Gladys didn't swear, but she did favor a word to express anger with someone. "Blister!"

Slamming on the brakes when someone pulled out in front of her, she'd spit out the word, "Blister!" If someone said something she didn't like, Grandma related the comment prefaced with, "That blister said.... " Cold sores plagued Grandma all her life.

The Turned Stomach: When my normally positive stepfather underwent emergency surgery, another example of the mind-body connection came to light. Dad endured surgery on the day before Thanksgiving, his favorite holiday, since he loved to eat. After retrieving Dad's twisted stomach from a hiatal hernia, the surgeon said, "One of the worst cases I've seen. His stomach had slipped through the hiatus and had turned upside down." With his food supply cut off, Dad was starving.

A couple of days after the surgery, Dad and I sat together in the hospital room watching a television newscast of anti-war demonstrators burning the American flag.

"That just turns my stomach," said Dad, a World War II veteran.

My ears perked up. "What did you just say?"

"That just turns my stomach. I don't understand how people can do those things."

I gulped, said a little prayer and ventured into new territory.

"Ah... Dad, I've done some reading about how our words can affect our bodies. Sometimes our bodies take literally what our minds and mouths say to us. Do you suppose there is any connection between what you just said and your stomach problem?"

We looked at each other for a long moment. There was no more discussion, but I never again heard him say "turns my stomach."

Weed Eradication: Good Words

Like Louise Hay, my friend Amalie Frank, author of *Amalie's Good Words, Signposts for the Journey,* advocates daily rituals of affirmations and praise prayer bits. Amalie says her "Good Words" before getting up, while in the shower, eating, driving, waiting and as she prepares for sleep. A wise person always has a large assortment of good words ready for those times when there is a lull in thinking — or the thinkin' is stinkin'.

A former English teacher, Amalie stands ready to correct grammar or grimmer speech. If Amalie catches someone saying something derogatory about herself or someone else, she responds with, "Is that what you want in your life?" The person usually stops to reflect on what she said. "Ah... no," she'll reply.

"Then don't give it power with your words."

In my family three generations of women suffered Alzheimer's disease, each the oldest daughter. "Senile jokes" in my direction began long before my fortieth birthday. In a "good sport" mood, I joined in. But when the jokes frightened me, I lashed out in anger, or shrank into silent terror that the relatives might realize something I didn't comprehend. Seeing my discomfort, they sometimes commented, "Only kidding. Why do you have to be so sensitive?"

My sensitivity germinated because I couldn't forget Mom's fortieth birthday. She cried most of the day. With the celebration we gave her, Mom's spirit lightened temporarily, but from that day forward her mantra was, "It's hell to get old."

Determined to change the pattern, I prepared for my big 40 by affirming, "Life *begins* at forty." Boy did it! I give thanks for every day, and every new way I find to be happy. Life itself hasn't always been better, particularly those Locust Years, but I'm better equipped to handle the hailstones and find the rainbow's golden nuggets. Looking for things to be grateful for has quadrupled life's pleasures.

My fortieth milestone came at the same time Amalie came to my hometown to teach a class on psycho-cybernetics.[3] For two years Amalie taught classes one night a week, driving 100 miles each way from Livonia, Michigan. During those years Amalie also took her first solo flight as a pilot and became an ordained minister of Unity Church.[4] Amalie was the same age as my mother, 65, yet she seemed much younger. She became my mentor for aging.

I was fertile ground for Amalie's effervescent "attitude of gratitude" elixir for what ails us. I grabbed onto her joyful messages, vowing to change my negative language to positive. (I'm still working on it, Amalie.) Watching Amalie live each day fully convinced me it was time to give my adult children an ultimatum.

So I have issued the challenge: "I intend to break the cycle in this family. I choose to keep my wits about me right up to the moment I leave this world. So I will not accept anymore comments about senility, not even in jest. Is that clear?" No one "kids" me about senility anymore. They watch me for words that might lean in that direction and give me firm reminders, "That's not what you want, Mom, remember?"

Now my affirmations or "brain stimulators," as I prefer to call them, include: "Good job, Joanne." "Good reflexes." "Great memory!" (I've occasionally high-fived myself, even in public.) My favorite line for those times when I do happen to forget a word or fact *(just like everyone else from time to time):* "It will come in a minute or two. My computer (mind) has to do a search." When the message shows up, I say "Thank you" to my incredible brain.

The more we praise and give thanks to ourselves and others, the more quickly we recognize life's abundance of good. Reflexes improve considerably, and "lost" messages pop quick-

---

3 From the book, *Psycho-Cybernetics*, by Maxwell Maltz.
4 Church of the *Daily Word*

ly into consciousness. When we drop our guard, let the "bad word" messages slip into our garden of thoughts, then fear, doubt and worry plague us.

Many of us are taught to pray in praise and thanksgiving: memorized prayers prayed during designated times or spontaneous prayers whenever we feel the need. According to Amalie, "Prayer time is all the time."

When I first heard Amalie say, "We are always praying," I thought, "No way!" Until then, I hadn't associated everyday conversations and my innermost thoughts as "constant prayers." *If Amalie is right, I better find out what I'm praying for,* I thought (forgetting it was now a prayer). The answer came a few days later.

On the next class day, I awoke with a severe bladder infection. I thought about skipping that week's lesson, but I didn't want to miss anything. Besides, Amalie is as entertaining as she is wise, and I needed some laughs.

Amalie is four feet, ten inches of dynamic energy. She stands and bounces as she plays the piano, getting even the laziest of participants involved. This night she emphasized the connection between health and words. According to Amalie, blessing and thanking one's body for what it is supposed to do brings healing if one is sick and maintains good health if one is not.

Well, it's pretty hard to bless a body that's giving you so much pain, Amalie, I thought, wincing as my body again informed me something was wrong. *I can't see what my words have to do with this!* I looked up. Amalie's eyes fastened on mine.

"Watch what you think! Remember, you create with your thinking."

Another idea crossed my mind. Amalie's eyes never left my face, so she caught the twitch of my cheeks trying to suppress a chuckle.

"What were you thinking?"

My face turned red. "Oh... ah... well, I wasn't feeling good tonight and almost didn't come."

"So what did you create with your thinking?"

My face flamed as everyone's eyes turn toward me.

"Ah... well... I have a bladder infection."

"Who are you mad at?"

That did it. I knew from the look on her face that she knew exactly what I had thought about for several days, and even voiced a few times. I laughed and shared a phrase I used frequently in those days. Yes, I was "pissed off."

Through subsequent bladder infections, I learned how habitual my use of the phrase "pissed off" had become. Once in a while, I'll catch myself thinking it and immediately call out loud, "Cancel! Cancel! I *really* don't mean it." Then I tell my body how grateful I am for its efficiency and good health. I'm aware that words cannot be seen under a microscope to pinpoint as cause (or cure) for illness, but since becoming word conscious, bladder infections are rare.

Another phrase I used a lot then was "AFGE." I changed one word to give it the power for what I *wanted* in my life. Today, AFGE stands for Another *Fantastic* Growth Experience. *Words do have power. Choose them wisely.*

Word Power

God created the world with *The Word.* Jesus had only to speak *The Word* and the sick were healed. He also said, "Whatever I can do, you can do also."

When we use our words to praise and appreciate, we draw praise and appreciation back to us. This is true in health, wealth, food, smooth-running automobiles or loving relationships. Yes, even automobiles.

My husband and I once owned a car I hated. Ken loved it. When the car refused to start for me, Ken got inside. Turning the switch, he turned to me and said, "I don't know what your problem is. There's nothing wrong with this car," as the car roared to life.

One day, as I prepared to leave my parents' house after a visit, the car wouldn't start. Dad stuck his head in the passenger window and said, "What's the matter, Honey?"

"I don't know," I replied.

"Well, try again," he said, not moving from the window.

The motor purred. That's when I was sure the car liked only men. *Fine, I don't like you either,* I fumed.

The final straw for me came one day at a busy intersection. I was in the left-hand turn lane, my car brimming with children and groceries. The light was red, and a string of cars quickly lined up behind me, factory workers just let off work. The car stalled. The light changed — several times.

Angry, tired workers honked their horns repeatedly until one got out and ambled up to my car. "Can I do something to help, lady?" he asked.

"I think you just did," I said, and turned the key once more. The engine roared to life.

"Thanks," I said. "She loves the sound of a man's voice." I smiled and drove off.

In her book *Something More,* Catherine Marshall says, "Months, even years, of praying for something does little as compared to moments of praise for something."

Praising our bodies for getting us out of bed and to work on time, our children for doing their homework without prompting or our Creator for providing another safe and beautiful day, is easy. It feels good too. So why do we berate our children, ourselves or the weather because "everyone else does it"?

When will we stop living on automatic pilot and take charge of our personal destiny, beginning with every word we speak, every thought we think? Perhaps uncertainty and fear stand in our way. Will I look foolish praising someone who is obviously lacking in manners? Maybe. Maybe not. I could take a chance. I might find something to compliment them for and throw them off their guard.

We can teach through praise and get the kind of treatment we want in return. "But I'm afraid if I praise my ____ (child, spouse, employee, student, you fill in the blank), he will think I like poor behavior." We don't praise the poor behavior, *we praise the person.* He or she is a child of God deserving to be recognized as such. We can praise good behavior. When we look for good, we'll find it.

My Son: Zig Ziglar, author of *See You At The Top,* tells an insightful story[5] about how his mother corrected her children. Once, when Zig was pulling weeds in the garden, he sloughed off. When he went to his mother expecting praise, she looked at his work and replied, "For most boys this would be all right. But you're not most boys — you're my son and my son can do better than that."

She had "criticized the performance," but she had praised the performer because he needed the praise. Zig's mother knew how to praise her children's assets, not their liabilities. Mama Ziglar was fully aware of her son's need to improve, yet sensitive to his vulnerability as a child. She looked at the situation through eyes of love and appreciation.

When the sun's rays shine into drops of water, they form a prism that reflects a rainbow. Mama Ziglar's words to her son were like the rays of the sun shining on raindrops. Through her words, she gave Zig an opportunity to see who he was and how his work reflected upon that awareness. The words gave him the opportunity to do something he could be proud of, turning a chore into a rainbow blessing and a golden memory.

Nurturing Gratitude Attitudes

An attitude of gratitude consists of two kinds of thanksgiving. The first comes easily as it is given spontaneously for that

---

5 Used with permission of Zig Ziglar, author and motivational teacher.

which makes us happy. A gift. A hug. A new life being born, an old one being saved. The other kind of thanksgiving demands work. It is given purposefully for that which is not seen, for that which may not yet be, and for that about which we aren't sure. This gratitude comes from trust. Faith. Sometimes that means giving thanks even in the pits of hell.

Through his writing and teaching, Dr. Norman Vincent Peale taught me a lot about the "attitude of gratitude." My favorite illustration is Dr. Peale's search for people with no problems and finding them.

"They were all in the cemetery," he told his audience. With a gentle smile, he added, "I went home and got down on my knees and asked God to give me some problems." If you're not ready for the cemetery either, I suggest giving thanks for the problems as well as the good times.

In his book, *Real Magic*, Wayne Dyer says "You'll see it when you believe it." Jesus told the centurion, "Go; be it done for you as you have believed." If you believe, you only have to ask once. All the rest of your prayers then become praise and thanksgiving for what you are *about to receive*.

A word of caution: Amalie Frank says it's always best to add, "this or something better" to your request. We don't want to limit ourselves. We're also covered in case we ask for something that isn't quite right for us. Remember, God's stalls are not God's stop signs, so we don't keep an eye on the calendar while giving thanks. Some requests need longer incubation time.

The Bible says to give thanks *in* all things, not *for* all things. While I could not bring myself to give thanks *for* Kenny Jr.'s death, I could find many ways to give thanks *in* the various events surrounding the ordeal:

- The love and support from strangers as well as family and friends.

- The new life growing inside my daughter-in-law.

- Kenny's life. His dimpled smiles. His optimism. His spirit.
- The many wonderful memories we shared.

We can make our own pot of golden memories through our appreciation and adoration. All it takes is a change of perspective.

Gathering Golden Memories

Willingness to plant, tend and nurture our gratitude garden brings a harvest of golden memories. An Attitude of gratitude gets Creativity to flow to the Truth that sets us free. That's called "Getting your ACT together."

Once we get our act together, nothing can stop us. Even as our bodies and minds go through the "normal" reactions to stormy times, the simple act of giving thanks and praise chases away the darkness and brings back the light. The light comes through many channels.

Remember the Happy Hours: My stepfather, Ralph Ackenhusen, was a person determined to find warmth in his days. When he married my mother, a divorcee with three children, World War II was raging.

My new dad had no children of his own, so he took on quite a job, especially since the three of us suspected his motives. The recent three-year separation from our parents and each other made us wary. But Dad (my stepfather) had one basic rule, his and mother's epitaph: "Remember Only The Happy Hours." Dad made sure we had many happy hours to remember.

Every morning of his life, Dad got up whistling, even during the years he was sole caregiver for Mom during her final illness, a choice he made from deep love. He complimented and thanked people. He appreciated everything he had, everyone he met. As a policeman for more than thirty years, Dad saw the bitter side of life, but he never soured on people.

Two years prior to Dad's death, I was privileged to type his short autobiography, *The Way It Was, As I Recall.* He insisted that only happy memories go into the book, even though he'd encountered his share of trouble. One example, his first wife, Alice, died of heart failure just four years after their marriage. They had no children.

Dad and I shared a lot in his last couple of years. His legacy lives on. Whenever any of our family starts feeling down about who is no longer with us, we'll pull ourselves up with, "Remember the happy hours."

Collecting Rainbows: When I first heard about using praise and thanksgiving to ward off the "evil spirits" of uncertainty and fear, my skepticism reared up. Then reason moved in. *Why not give it a try? Can't feel any worse than I already do.*

So I carried a small notebook in my purse, writing down situations that caught my attention for which to praise or give thanks. The first day I wrote down three things in my notebook. Determined to do better, the next day I looked for more to be grateful for.

Each day the list grew and I found myself on a mammoth treasure hunt. As my notebook filled, my spirits lifted and so did the atmosphere around me. Clerks were friendlier, my children happier, my husband easier to get along with. I was amazed at how much *they* changed in that short time.

Writing about my day was not new. Previously, I spent hours journaling about the bad stuff in my life. The more I complained in my journal and aloud, the more I found to complain about. What you see is what you get.

My friend, Marie Leddy, calls these notebooks "Joy Books." Because of my affinity for rainbows, I call them my "Rainbow Books." Anyone can start a Rainbow Book, Joy Book or a journal. We might consider redoing photo albums from our past to include only happy times. If we already made the photo albums, we might write the stories behind the pictures. Our families will treasure them. If we don't have photos, or can't find any with happy faces, we can make them up.

We can cut pictures from magazines or greeting cards, and make ourselves see a happy childhood. Anthony Robbins says, "It's never too late to have a happy childhood." Decide that you are being reborn this minute. Go fly kites, play ball or tramp through the zoo with fun-loving friends. Take lots of pictures for your collection of the happy moments you are creating and install them in your book. No matter what you call it, make sure what you put in it is what you want more of in your life. "Leave it out in plain sight," says Marie. "That way you can enjoy it every day and so can your friends when they come to visit."

My books include stories of real rainbows that I've seen. Some are funny moments like the time I was driving down the street on a frigid winter day and saw a woman walking her St. Bernard. The dog had on a stocking cap and muffler! Once a year, usually on New Year's eve, or the eve of my birthday anniversary, I like to review my Rainbow Book. When I'm finished, I can say, "My, that was one mighty fine year."

Pass It On: Giving thanks and praise enriches our entire universe. Let's make everyday a rainbow day filled with promise and positive purpose by complimenting a clerk, leaving a little extra in our tip or including a blessing. My friend Jan leaves small "You are special" cards, with space for writing in what the person did. George folds dollar bills into elephants to leave as his tip for service. Bev gets the names of clerks and writes thank you notes to store managers for good service. Judy takes special delight in driving through run-down neighborhoods to find a place that is obviously loved and appreciated and then dropping complimentary postcards to the "Gardener at 123 Main Street."

Every day is a rainbow day filled with golden nuggets. All
we have to do is gather them up.

Rainbow Ingredients
for
Praise and Thanksgiving

- Sing a Song: Make a joyful noise unto the Lord.

- Courtesy: Honor the spirit within each person.

- Rainbow Book: Use it often. Fill it up.

- Happy Hours: Rejoice in the good times.

- Happy Hours: Consciously make more.

- Believe It: Give thanks before as well as after.

- Find praise, not fault.

- Make it a Rainbow Day for yourself and others.

A God-incident

Super Bowl Sunday, 1987. I am in Chicago exhibiting the "Little Tramp" greeting card line. Ken Sr. left early today for a visit with our daughter Debbie in Florida. Back in South Bend, some interesting events are taking shape.

Yesterday, Kenny Jr. visited his sister Laura. She tried to persuade him to "house sit" while I am in Chicago.

"She's only going to be gone a few days," said Kenny Jr. "You go there every day to feed your horses, why does anyone need to be there overnight?"

"I just think it would be better if someone were there," replied Laura, but she couldn't persuade her brother. He has plans to go skiing. She tries again today, with a telephone call.

"Impossible," says Kenny. "My car broke down. I have to get it towed. I don't even know how I'm getting to work tomorrow. Besides, I'm exhausted."

"Mom's car is in the garage. She'll be gone most of the week. I'm sure she won't mind your using it while yours is being fixed."

After leaving his car with a mechanic, Kenny gets a lift to our house from a friend. Soon they are involved in the Super Bowl game. His buddy leaves at half-time and Kenny falls asleep on the couch. At 2:00 a.m. he is awakened by a crackling noise. Instantly he is on his feet. He knows that sound for he is a trained firefighter.

Quickly he checks the walls and ceilings. Hot. Checks the phone. Dead. He runs upstairs to see if there are any flames. He sees none, but the floor is hot. Kenny happens to be in my office, his old bedroom, and notices two telephones. He grabs one — my business line. Live! He dials 911. Then he calls Doug, Laura's husband.

"Mom and Dad's house is on fire, get over here quick so you can flag down the fire trucks." Flames are now shooting out the side of the house. Kenny runs to the garage for the fire extinguisher, emptying it on the flames outside the office window.

Kenny's training as a firefighter tells him that the house should have been engulfed in flames within four minutes after he discovered the fire. It wasn't. The house is saved. The family is safe.

Accentuate the Positive 5

There are two ways you can live your life:
(1) to believe there are no miracles or
(2) that everything is a miracle.

Albert Einstein

Childhood pictures of hard times and rationing during World War II diminish when I recall our country's pride in pulling together as a team fighting for justice. Upbeat, encouraging songs sprang from strong determined spirits to disable the worries, fears and hardships of that time.

A favorite song from those war years was "Accentuate the Positive[1]." Whenever we children pouted or felt slighted, Mom would sing this song which reminded us to put the accent on the positive to eliminate any negatives. The catchy lyrics stuck in my mind like peanut butter to the roof of my mouth. As I savored the message, my mood grew brighter, my spirit stronger.

A positive mental attitude (PMA), serves as a "vitamin" and remedy for finding rainbows in life's stormy times. The basics for emotional well-being, of accentuating the positive and eliminating the negative, promote a joy-filled faith that stands firm no matter how bad the storm.

Stopping to look, listen and learn enables us to find the affirmative, productive side of life. Giving thanks and praise keeps us focused on the positives, rather than negatives, of a situation. The three remedies combined lead us to discover valuable possibilities for productive results.

While a positive perspective won't bring deceased loved ones back into our lives, a change in focus often helps heal the

---

1 Lyrics by Johnny Mercer. Music by Harold Arlen.

pain. When we put attention on what is good *in* the situation, the pain softens into moments of joyful memories. We function better and more easily. I call this my Power Prescription because:

- Stuff happens. We can't change what happens, but we can change our feelings and reactions to it.

- Changing our feelings and reactions into a positive perspective strengthens the "plus factor" in our lives; we value life more.

- The more focused we become on what is authentic, honorable, loving and kind, the more we are empowered to improve and maintain good relationships.

Stuff Happens

The movie *Forrest Gump* became an elixir for me. "Mama always said, 'Life is like a box of chocolates. You never know what you're gonna get,'" says Gump. The pure. The simple. The truth. A positive attitude includes the *acceptance* of life's basic facts. When our lives get dark and dreary, truisms and affirmations become battle cries, filling our wounded hearts with courage to stand firm and fend off negativity.

In the movie, Gump's true love walks out on him, so he goes running. He runs and runs, crossing America and gaining national recognition. Gump does what he needs to do. One day Gump steps into a pile of dog manure during his run. The man running alongside makes a face. "Yuk!" he says. Gump looks down, and says, "It happens," and keeps on running. Whenever I feel life is getting "yukky," I remind myself, "It happens."

As the year-end holidays approached, the second year after my husband's death, I thought about making new goals for my changing life. When my daughter Laura's first annual follow-up test for cancer came back negative, we celebrated. My daughter Debbie's improving health allowed her to work again. With an assist from holistic medicine, my foster son Henry and his partner Hector were in a holding pattern with AIDS. Although each of my other children had met major challenges since their father's death, life for our family appeared on the upswing. Then Dad received a call from his brother, Richard, a retired minister in Florida.

Uncle Richard was dying of cancer. For Dad it was a Catch-22. He wanted to see his beloved Richard, but couldn't leave his wife. Completely dependent on Dad, Mom was too debilitated to travel, even if I went along. If Dad got out of her sight, even in their own home, she panicked. Dad couldn't bear the thought of upsetting her, so he and Uncle Richard supported each other via telephone.

On Thanksgiving Day, Mom developed pneumonia. The doctor felt she would improve more rapidly at home, and the antibiotics worked quickly. A week later, Laura left a message on my answering machine.

"Grandpa called while you were out. I was feeding the horses and took the call. Mom, he sounded awful. You better go over there right away."

Although it was after 10 p.m., I called Dad. When he finally answered the telephone, my fears were confirmed. Dad had pneumonia. He tried to fluff it off as his asthma, but I knew he was in trouble.

"I'll be right out," I said. He didn't protest my coming, but when I arrived, he wouldn't go into the hospital.

"I talked to the doctor and he prescribed something," said Dad. "I'm taking it. I'll be better tomorrow. But I'm really glad you came because now I can get some sleep." Mom only catnapped, so Dad seldom had sufficient rest. He leaned back into his lounge chair and closed his eyes, but his sleep was far from peaceful. All night I prayed as Dad wheezed and gurgled.

The next morning, I washed, dressed and fed Mom. Dad wasn't hungry. I called his doctor again. The nurse told me, "Doctor is busy. He'll phone in another prescription." Dad grew progressively worse. The doctor remained unavailable. The pharmacist received no prescription. When I could stand it no longer, I called Laura to take care of Mom while I drove Dad to the hospital.

In the emergency room, I learned that Dad's oxygen level was so low he was on death's doorstep. The doctor began treatment immediately. My sister Vicki and I mobilized our families to help care for Mom so we could stay with Dad. In the hospital, Dad realized he could no longer care for Mom and asked me to make arrangements for her nursing home care.

"I've looked into both places," said Dad, referring to the two facilities in the small town where they lived (a 45-minute drive from my home). He preferred one, but said they already had a waiting list. Sending up a fervent prayer, I called that one first. "Yes, we have room." We learned that it had been years since there had been no waiting list, and a room had now become available. The whole family sent up prayers of thanksgiving.

Four days before Christmas, we moved Mom into the nursing home. She didn't understand and was quite agitated. She kept asking, "Where's Ralph?" She did not comprehend our answers. The doctors released Dad from the hospital the next day, saying he shouldn't be alone. Since I was having our family's Christmas at my house, I asked if he minded coming home with me. He was reluctant, but when the family brought over his favorite chair, he decided it would be okay "for a little while."

Our Christmas Eve celebration was special with Dad there, and then he spent Christmas Day with Vicki and her family. That evening, Dad asked me to drive him to the nursing home to see Mom. Afterward we drove around the little town of New

Carlisle where he once served as Chief of Police. We sat on Main Street, and I listened while he reminisced about the people, the children he helped cross the street, the "good old days." He had only good memories to share about all the years of his life. But five years of caregiving took its toll two days later. Tired and brokenhearted, Dad died of a heart attack in my home. And the new year rolled in on a tidal wave of troubles.

Accentuate the Positive to Keep Going

The day before Dad died, my sister Vicki's husband, Julius, was admitted to the hospital intensive care unit with a heart attack. A chaplain accompanied Laura to get Vicki from her husband's bedside to tell her about Dad.

Two weeks after Dad's death, Mom's sister, Rebecca, called to say she was diagnosed with liver cancer. Unable to bear children of her own, Aunt Becky had taken a special interest in her nieces and nephews. I considered her my "other mom." She died on Palm Sunday, the year following Dad's death. Uncle Richard also died that spring, and my cousin, Tom. Soon after, Tom's father, Merrill, my mother's only brother, joined the heavenly crowd, leaving Mom as the last of her immediate family. In two-and-a-half years, seven family members were gone.

The pain of losses merged with rising pressures to supervise estates and assume guardianships, swirling around me in a dizzying pattern of frustration and, sometimes, panic. Like a victim caught in a raging river grabs for flotsam, I grasped for something to keep me afloat: books to read, affirmations to bolster my spirit and people to make me laugh.

As the eldest, I was named executor of Dad's and Aunt Becky's wills and guardian for Mom. I also helped Uncle Bob with his finances and with clearing out Aunt Becky's personal belongings. When Vicki lovingly agreed to share the duties of

Mother's guardianship and Dad's estate matters, relief surged through me. Vicki has always been a model of exuberant determination for me. She refuses to let anything get her down.

Mother hated the nursing home, begging Vicki and me to take her to her own home. To make matters worse, she fell twice that year, breaking a hip each time. Surgeries fixed Mom's hips, but the second break left her wheelchair bound. Apparently Mom's fear of falling again, rather than the injury, immobilized her. She refused to walk except for the physical therapists.

Another old song that helped me keep going that year was, "Is That All There Is?[2]" Peggy Lee made my favorite recording of it. You can hear the emotions — up and down — as she sings, about a burning house and other sad, unalterable situations in life. Peggy sings about the various problems, then decides if that is all there is to it, well, she'll just keep on dancing. At one time, this song seemed negative to me, an example of a selfish, uncaring attitude. My Locust Years gave me a different perspective.

While I can't change what happened, I can change my feelings — and my reactions. I can keep on running... walking... dancing... or *living*... and *loving*.

Keeping on, a generic form of the "Stop, Look, Listen and Learn" remedy, takes less energy, yet effectively allows us time to get over the worst ordeals, heal to some degree and think about what is left to be grateful for. To look for the heavenly on earth, especially in those hellish parts, builds hope and perfects love.

"Keeping on keeping on" comes in many forms. Walk dog. Wash dishes. Pay bills. Chop wood. Carry water. Everyday tasks serve as grounding wires when the negativity hits us full charge. Engaging in familiar activities lessens the destructive

---

2 Words and music by Jerry Lieber and Mike Stoller

shock. Although our world has drastically changed, daily routines for life maintenance and diversion give a measure of certainty, assurance that somehow we will get through this stormy
time.

We can face grim reality even as we enjoy life. We can be
aware that crime happens and people do get sick and die. That
doesn't mean we have to live in terror of walking down a street
or worry about every bite of food we eat. Nor do we have to
obsess about what we might lose or how we're going to die.
Living in negativity drains life from mind, body and soul. As
Jack Lemmon says in the movie *Dad*, "There's no sin in dying
— but not to live — now that's a sin."

I remember days, however, when each moment demanded
every ounce of positive thinking I could muster. That's when I
realized the significance of maintaining an optimistic outlook
simply by living one day at a time. Savoring each moment.
With the right attitude, the heaviest burdens can be carried one
moment at a time.

Before their deaths, Dad and my mother-in-law, excellent
models of a cheerful outlook on life, served as my mentors.
Mom Hill's indomitable spirit carried her through many rough-
weather years. In addition to the care of her seven children,
Mom Hill worked as a waitress, took in laundry, cleaned other
people's houses and baby-sat their children. In her ninth
decade, she still lived proudly alone in her own house, which
she cared for with deep pride.

One teatime, I braved a question that I had pondered for
years. "Mom, when big trouble came in your family, I noticed
you went down into the basement and scrubbed everything in
sight. I always wondered why you did that."

"That was the only way I could get away by myself to pray.
I sure did have a clean basement," she grinned.

Dad took care of his first wife until her early death of heart
disease, a result of rheumatic fever in childhood. Then he met

my mother and took on the responsibility of three children along with a new wife. Later, when Alzheimer's gobbled away Mom's mind, Dad made it his personal mission to be her care-giver for as long as he could.

When Mom began to balk at leaving the house, Dad focused on watching the stock market on television. Beside his chair he kept pad and pencil, recording the stocks as they went up and down, making some money in the process.

Time with my personal heroes, Dad and Mom Hill, turned into rich rewards of shared insights, wisdom and invincible optimism. And some ideas for keeping on track.

Sometimes, when the heartaches and troubles seemed at tidal wave proportion, I wavered. Then the memory of prior painful times, when I had let myself get sucked into the quick-sand of depression and negativity, spurred me to hang on, to get back into balance. A positive mind-set cannot be just a desire, it is a necessity.

Accentuate the Positive
for Enlightenment

PMA develops a clear-headed perspective that allows us to see possibilities for solutions rather than crumble under over-whelming problems. Looking for the constructive, the useful and the worthwhile brings enlightenment that produces mind-ful, rather than mindless, choices. During my Locust Years, par-ticularly that crushing third year of constant stormy times, I had a multitude of choices to make.

I had the responsibility for closing Mom's and Dad's house and the disbursement of all their possessions, Aunt Becky's affairs and belongings, disputes with hospitals, Medicare and the IRS. Some days my PMA came out as, "God, please bless the jerks who mess up records and thank you for keeping me from doing something rash."

These difficult years proved the Rainbow Remedy theory. By refusing to decide hastily (stop, look, listen and learn) and insisting on finding something in the situation to give thanks and praise for (Dad and Aunt Becky were meticulous record-keepers so all insurance and tax difficulties ended in beneficial solutions for those I represented), my health and sanity stayed strong. During that time, some people referred to me as "Pollyanna," a reference they associated with "unrealistic."

Pollyanna, an orphan girl in a children's classic[3] of the same name, lives with a wealthy, stern, sour old-maid aunt. Although Pollyanna experienced tragedy in her short life (her missionary parents were killed), she remained cheerful, too cheerful for her new family and neighbors who were caught in self-pity and old hurts.

Pollyanna gets a bum rap when her name becomes syn-onymous with an airhead living in a fantasy land. Because someone chooses to see the bright side of life doesn't mean she can't face reality. God's reality makes Pollyanna's viewpoint look like a dim light bulb. Life can be wonder-filled and mirac-ulous every day, even in the midst of violent storms, if we're willing to accept the *possibility*. In every storm there is a gift — like the rainbow — if we're willing to look for it and accept it.

The negative viewpoint of Pollyanna's cheeriness is an excellent example of the "half-full, half-empty" syndrome. In the story (as in real life), people who criticized Pollyanna's per-sonality cheated themselves. Pollyanna's attitude came from a discerning mind, honing in on a higher standard of living. Every time we choose to see life from the dark side, we shut out the light.

The townsfolk's misconception about Pollyanna was that she was a positive thinker only. In fact, she was a positive doer. She managed to rescue many of the townspeople from their troubles by her creative ideas and simple acts of kindness.

---

3 Author, Eleanor H. Porter

Thinking positively but without action is simply "metafiz-zling," says Maria Nemeth, Ph.D., in *The Energy of Money*.

"Our inner visions inspire us, but we can't be content mere-ly to 'metafizzle' our ideas without taking any action in the real world," Nemeth says.

When Pollyanna falls out of a tree, her aunt and the towns-people fear she will die, for the little girl has lost her sunny dis-position. She has caught the negativity of the town. Through the tragic accident, the family and neighbors finally come to understand Pollyanna's message and rally around her with affirmations that help her recover. Affirmations are the cheer-leaders of the spirit. Pollyanna's recovery demonstrates how a PMA focus helps free the body from undue stress to heal itself.

Accentuate the Positive for Good Health

Looking back, I realize that with each new baby in my life, my energy diminished. My body reacted with a variety of aches and pains. Medical bills mounted, yet my health grew worse. The doctors couldn't find anything wrong — which didn't stop them from giving me prescriptions. Pills to help me digest my food. Pills to relax muscle spasms. Pills for headaches. Pills to sleep.

One time when I complained, my husband left to call the doctor from a pay telephone. "What's wrong with her? Why isn't she getting better?" The doctor answered, "She won't take her medicine."

After that, I took prescribed medicine faithfully until I start-ed nodding off if I dropped my guard the least bit. Keeping awake was agony. "This is not living," I finally said to myself. "This is slow death." Flushing all the medicines down the toilet brought on the worst case of flu I ever had. Later, as a member of the Drug Abuse Action Council, I realized my "flu" had been drug-addiction withdrawal.

A few months after dumping the pills, I got out of bed and went sprawling to the floor, coiled in an agonizing muscle spasm in my back. Refusing to give into a propensity for sickness again, I refused to see a doctor. For eight days I walked in pain, bent over. A friend suggested chiropractic treatment. I walked out of the chiropractor's office, straight and tall, free of pain. Along with this safe, drugless treatment for most of my physical problems, I also found a remedy for my soul in Dr. Paul Pierce's office: *Guideposts*.[4]

Guideposts is a small-sized magazine (circulation 2.6 million) of inspiring stories about real people overcoming real problems through a positive attitude. Dr. Norman Vincent Peale started the magazine to give people enthusiastic messages of hope. *Guideposts* led me to Peale's book, *The Power of Positive Thinking*, which started me on an attitude adjustment that turned my life completely around.

Using techniques and affirmations from my reading, I grew stronger in spirit, mind and, yes, in body. Several years later, I needed a physical for a life insurance policy. The examining physician said, "You are in excellent health." Exciting news for a person who was told earlier that she would probably end up in a wheelchair, a mental health institution or an early grave.

The power of our minds is incredible. What you think *can* kill or cure you. Does that mean all I have to do is think positive thoughts to cure some horrible disease, such as cancer? No, that's not what I mean, although there are numerous stories of miraculous healings, including some among my family and friends. Many books written by survivors using their PMA to overcome tremendous odds, along with traditional medicines and without, are on library shelves and in bookstores. Studies now prove that such an attitude benefits medical treatments, giving patients greater odds of winning against their disease.

---

4 Find Guideposts @ www.dailyguideposts.com

Bob Stone, author of *Where The Buffaloes Roam,* says, "Depression and negative thinking (fear, doubt, worry and self-pity) are cancers of the *mind.* Just as deadly as the cancers of the body — worse, maybe, because they nibble away at the soul."

True healing occurs in the soul. We are eternal beings, created by a Creator who loves us, and some day we'll return to our heavenly home. This body is only temporary housing for our soul. When we work on our soul, the body usually takes care of itself and does a mighty fine job too.

I am convinced that my husband, Ken, would not have lived as long as he did, nor enjoyed a rich, rewarding life, if he had allowed pessimistic thinking to take over. All of our children have demonstrated the healthful effects of an optimistic spirit.

Laura's bout with cancer six months after her father's death is one example of using mind power to work with modern medicine. Laura's theme from her youngest days has been to focus on the sunny side of life.

Although Laura had two small children, a husband, a house and assorted animals to care for, whenever I needed help or a supportive hug during the months following her father's death, she was there for me. Laura also intuitively knew when to give me a boot instead of a hug. If she felt I was sleeping too much, she'd say, "Well, that's fine for today. Now what are you planning for tomorrow?"

Since Laura's horses lived on our twelve acres, she came twice a day to feed and care for them. During this difficult time, she made an extra effort to come back to my house daily to keep tabs on me in spite of her own growing health challenge. My other children also supported and helped during those difficult times with frequent phone calls, notes of encouragement and visits.

Laura's diagnosis of thyroid cancer came right before Christmas in that first year of the locusts. Her diagnosis came a few weeks after my mother's surgery for breast cancer. Mom's cancer was hard enough to face, but she was getting up in years. And, with Alzheimer's, she wasn't aware of what was happening. However, Laura's children, Heather, age five, and Michael, age one, needed their mother. And Doug needed his wife. I couldn't bear to think beyond the diagnosis.

Laura remained strong in her own positive beliefs, and comforting to family and friends, as she faced her own challenge. Although she didn't tell me, I think Laura's biggest hurdle was the required isolation during the radiation treatment and after she got home. Because she was still radioactive, Laura was not allowed to hug or touch her children. So from a distance, she hugged with smiles and her cheerful disposition. Laura is completely recovered.

> THERE IS NO DANGER OF DEVELOPING
> EYESTRAIN FROM LOOKING
> ON THE BRIGHT SIDE.
>
> CHEER

Accentuate the Positive for Strong Relationships

Capitalize the "i" and "m" in impossible and you have: "I M Possible." Almost everything we use or own or visualize today was once considered impossible: electricity, radios, airplanes, automobiles, walking on the moon. People focus on the possibility of favorable outcomes; they invent things, generate ideas and improve objects and systems, so why can't the same theory be used in human relationships?

Quality relationships begin with ourselves. I M Possible. I M Capable. I M Worthy of loving, kind, caring and respectful relationships.

When we get caught in the difficulties and blockages, we become so frustrated with what's not working that we kill off our chances for happiness. Our negative mental attitude (NMA) drives away the people we need the most: our encouraging supporters. Now we are like two weather fronts about to collide, the kind that develop into tornadoes. Allowing the negative to overpower the positive sucks us into a whirlpool of cynical-thinking relationships that will destroy us. We must always stand guard at the door of our minds.

Developing PMA eases tension and increases joy. An authentic, cheerful spirit attracts devoted, supportive friends and partners who help us through the stormy times and join us in celebration of our achievements. Accentuating the positive develops strong coping mechanisms for dealing with hurting, confused and difficult people in times of crisis.

When we look for the good in each person — *and focus on that good* — we'll find more good than we ever knew existed. Good is there because God put it there, and each person needs us to recognize and utilize that fruitful asset. Another side to that paradigm is trusting that the other guy really wants good in his life, the same as we. Because he sometimes behaves otherwise doesn't mean that we should retaliate in kind.

Do Unto Others: Children have a unique knack for clarifying these concepts.

A first grader and a second grader were playing. Suddenly the mother heard a cry and ran to see what the trouble was.

Missy was crying. Jodie was gleefully smiling.

"What happened?" said Mother.

"She hit me," sniffled Missy. "Hard!"

"Jodie," said Mother, "Did you hit your sister?"

"Yes."

"Why?"

"Well, you said, 'Do unto others as you want them to do to you.' She hit me first, so I figured that's what she wanted me to do to her."

When tempted to give a payback, think twice, unless you have a mother to bail you out before the other party decides to also "do unto others."

Some days I notice many sour faces, particularly on young people, making it difficult to maintain my own cheerful outlook. Although some people say our world probably is not as safe as it once was, I believe that a smile can still go further than a glare to chase away the fears and suspicions of others. Here's another example illustrated by a child.

A Child Shall Lead: Pregnant with our fourth child and accompanied by the others, ages five, four and three, I set out to run some errands. The day was hot and I was irritable. Hauling the kids and purchases in and out of each store didn't help my disposition much either.

At the last store, I needed to run in long enough to pick up a package. I prayed for (and received) a parking spot in front of the store's big window. I left my three children in the car with firm instructions to "stay put."

While waiting for my package, I looked out of the window to see three-year-old Kenny Jr. standing on the sidewalk greeting each passerby. Soon his two sisters joined him. As each person passed, Kenny, Debbie and Cindy beamed their smiles upward saying, "Hi!" Even the grumpiest faces broke into smiles. As the clerk arrived with my package, she said, "Oh, how sweet. They're getting everyone to smile."

The clerk was right, the children were cheering passersby, including a harried clerk and a tired mommy. All the way home the children talked about how happy they made everyone. While tucking Kenny into bed that night, I asked him why he got out of the car when told not to.

"Everyone looked so sad," he said. "I wanted to make them smile." Then he gave me one of his sweet, dimpled grins and said, "And I did!" All of his life, Kenny made a priority of cheering up other people.

"Smiling is the only physical sign that is understood the world over," says Robert Aztell in his book *Gestures.*

Maybe my smiling and thinking or speaking positively won't change the whole world, but it will make a difference in my corner. Change the atmosphere of your corner and maybe those who come to visit will take the sunlight home with them.

The Relationship Estate: Getting through the Locust Years, particularly those involving the handling of estates and co-guardianship for Mom, called for more than smiles. To preserve good relationships, a family must stay focused on love, while preparing for estate sales and division of personal properties. The one in charge sometimes needs the wisdom of Solomon. I certainly was not Solomon. Not even close.

In order to do my job as designated executor for the estates and guardian for my mother's affairs, I took two major preliminary steps. My first step was to stop, look, listen and learn. My second step was to ask for help. I also found quiet times to take a good look at my intentions. Were they simply to fulfill the job designated to me? Now that I was in a position to "call all the shots," would my bossy ego's intentions get in the way of wise, fair decisions? Would my personal biases cause problems? Just what outcome did I truly want to see as a result of my efforts?

The desire for happy, peaceful growth in family relationships through the estate settlements led me to ask for help from my sister, Vicki. This action gave the two of us many opportunities to work through our grief and strengthen our friendship as we solved problems and worked out an equitable distribution plan for personal properties.

The plan that came was three-fold. First, an appraisal of all the items. Secondly, a gathering of family members. Thirdly, a system of dispersal.

The dispersal system began with family members going through the house and noting what they would like to have as a memento, or what they would be willing to purchase. Each family member numbered items on the list, number one being a first choice. If several people wanted an item, such as a lamp, as first choice, their names were put into a hat for a lottery.

The first name drawn took first choice in that round, then the name moved to last in the next round, until everyone received a first-choice selection. Then the process started again. To keep it as fair as possible for value, a set total amount was "credited" to each person. The value of each item selected was deducted from that amount. After that, they had first option to purchase other items still available.

In every household, many useful items are accumulated over time (linens, tools, small appliances). They don't bring much in a sale, but are valuable to young people starting housekeeping. We changed the plan slightly for distribution of these items. Everyone thought it fair and fun.

The cousins got together at their grandparents' house for one last party. We displayed leftover items as in a garage sale and put all the cousins' names into a hat. First name out got to go first to choose an item, then the second, on down the line. Then the process reversed, with the person who went last now going first, and back up the line. Then we put the names into the hat again and continued the process until each cousin was "first" to choose an item.

Although it was not a perfect system, my loving and helpful family made it work. The event was blessed because everyone's intention was to preserve the family relationship, not hold out for their personal desires. PMA looks to possible outcomes, intentionally choosing ways in which the highest good can come to all involved.

Another family I know distributed play money, the same amount going to each immediate family member. After a professional appraisal, the family held a private "auction" conducted by an impartial friend. Family members said they had a great time, creating another happy family experience.

Another example of putting a constructive emphasis on creating family harmony came about from my half-brother John. When my parents, Glenn and Helen, divorced, Glenn moved to California where he met his wife-to-be, Jonnie, a peach of a person. They had a daughter, Mimi, and a son, John. Vicki, Richard and I, all from the first marriage, lived in Indiana with our mother, Helen, and stepfather, Ralph. The five of us children really didn't get to know each other until we were adults.

When John, the youngest, graduated from army boot camp, he decided to stop in South Bend to get acquainted with Vicki and me. That led to a meeting with Mimi and another that included Richard. (Richard had an Air Force career and moved around a lot.) By the time cancer attacked Richard's body, and my Locust Years began, we all had developed a blessed, loving, supportive relationship. Accenting what went right in the families, rather than what went wrong, expanded our gift of family beyond any of our imaginings. We now have a special support system that has helped us through many stormy times. I thank God daily for the blessing of family.

Accentuate the Positive for Powerful Faith

Children are born believing that nothing is impossible. As soon as they can reach, they stick everything they get their hands on into their mouths. When they start to crawl, they trust flimsy tables and moving rocking chairs to help them stand up. Even with "no-no" commands and bumps and bruises, toddlers continue venturing into new territory. When encouraged, a child will accomplish far beyond "normal" expectations.

Affirming one's beliefs is another benefit of accentuating the positive. By stepping out in faith toward our expectation, going for it, we reinforce our faith power. We develop a *knowing* — a *certainty* that we can.

My granddaughter, Heather, began searching for four-leaf clovers as a toddler. Many times during my locust years, she knocked on my door.

"Would you like some four-leaf clovers?"

"Yes, I would."

In a few minutes Heather was back with a green bouquet clutched tightly in hand. Sometimes the bouquet included five- and six-leafed clovers.

After Heather left for her own home, I looked through my yard, but never found any. Heather *knows* they are *always* there. I wonder if that's why my little miracles are now coming in bunches. What do you think? Before the locust years, they didn't appear nearly as plentiful. They were not visible, because I frequently doubted their existence. Now, I know.

Accentuate the Positive to Create Miracles

An optimistic outlook doesn't keep away the crises that wrack havoc on our lives. What it does, however, is show us that within each chaos of crisis there are miracles. In his book *Making Miracles*, Paul Pearsall, Ph.D., puts it this way:

Crises are evidence of our survivability and continued development. Miracles are maps through the chaos. Without chaos, life itself and the miracles of living would not be possible. Like the air we breathe, chaos keeps us alive.

As we grow older, we find that believing in miracles takes work. We tend to be hooked on what went wrong, rather than what went right in our lives. That's when we need to take a review. We can look back in our scrapbooks and photo albums to see where we've recorded the happy hours. We can ask family members and old friends to help us remember the good times. If we keep journals, we can explore the good times in writing as well.

Jogging the Memory: I journaled as a child, although we called the receptacle a diary. However, when someone found my teenage diary and teased me about it, I quit writing my thoughts and feelings. Eventually, years later, the pressure of many problems, ill health and a growing propensity for worry led me back to penning my thoughts into a notebook.

My early adult journals were mostly depressing. "Woe is me. Why? Why? Why?" Full of self-pity and discouragement, I floundered in my own pessimistic words. Unaware of the power of my words (I forgot that God created the world by "speaking The Word"), I unwittingly brought more calamity into my life through that journaling.

Not until meeting Dr. Peale (through his writing), did I understand. His messages showed me how important good, happy and abundant thoughts and words are to bringing blessings into life. Uneasily, fearfully, I began to change my words. God must have appreciated the effort and ignored my doubts, for my life changed in exciting ways.

Instead of asking God why, I asked *myself* why. More specifically, I asked the writer's questions: Who? What? When? Where? How? All came before "why." My answers were connected to what I did wrong and what I could do differently to improve various situations. In my previous pity-party mode, the journal focused primarily on what *others* did wrong and what *others* should do to make me happy. Through the journals, I explored what I was learning.

The more proficient I became in searching, the more I focused on the good in my life. I watched doors open, leading to significant opportunities, delightful insights, fascinating serendipitous God-incidences and my ever-deepening faith. Life became a miraculous adventure.

That's why I continue seeking new perspectives, trying new experiences and stretching myself. I look to books, movies, audio tapes, music, pictures, quotations and anything that can plant cheerful thinking seeds within. Experiential workshops, adventure excursions or just saying "yes" to some new idea help cultivate, feed and water a brighter outlook on life. Confident thinking is simply taking charge of one's mind, focused mindfulness, setting it on course for an exuberant life.

Want to put power into your mind control? Try walking on burning coals. Or climbing a telephone pole and jumping off with only one person holding your safety line. These are two of the exhilarating experiences now in my journals. Journaling is a great cultivation tool, often serving as pruning shears as well.

Sometimes we have to let go of old emotional baggage before we can fully appreciate new experiences.

Bountiful Baggage: Each Locust Year, I hoped my life would be less chaotic, but the black cloud of loss and troubles persisted. In between funerals, visits to attorneys and caregiving, I sorted other people's stuff. My house, now empty of people, became packed with memorabilia.

I poured over my books and tapes and continued to attend personal improvement lectures and seminars to renew my previously confident spirit. Yet when the third Thanksgiving rolled around, I felt overpowered and prayed for relief. I tried counting my blessings, but there were too many tombstones blocking my view.

Two weeks before Christmas, my neighbor Bobbie called with an opportunity I had always dreamed about — a trip to Hawaii. Not just any trip, but a cruise around the islands with stopovers on several. My family was delighted and encouraged me to accept the offer.

At the time of the phone call, the trip (planned for late February) seemed a long way off. But when the day before departure arrived, I was nowhere near ready. Only twenty-four hours remained to pull myself together and decide what to pack for a ten-day trip.

At 3 a.m. I crawled into bed for some sleep, still not completely packed. Instead of leaving a clean and orderly house, as I intended, I had added to the clutter and disarray.

Early the next morning, with only three hours of sleep, I finished packing. My extra-large suitcase bulged. I put last minute items into my expandable carry-on bag, both ends extended, making it look like a giant golf bag. My experienced traveling partner warned me not to overpack, but I feared leaving something important behind.

Waiting for my ride, I roamed through my house. Boxes were in between, on top of and underneath nearly every piece of furniture. Boxes and boxes filled with stuff. Once again I heard the requests, "Jo, this belongs in our family, we can't sell it. You have such a big house — would you mind storing this for a while?" My parent's belongings and Aunt Becky's treasures were added to my own thirty-eight years of marriage accumulations. I tried to focus on my trip, but around me the house was bulging like my baggage.

I picked up a family portrait. My children and some of the grandchildren had their own homes now. My home was just someplace nearby. They had their own lives. Mine was on hold while I took care of guardianships, estates and insurance matters. They were making new memories. I sorted through old ones.

Our... my home now... had become an after-funeral gathering place, a holding place for loved ones' belongings, while family members adjusted and decided what *stuff* they wanted. As I stumbled on leftover luggage piled in the living room, my pent-up emotions ignited. From deep within, anger and frustrations erupted like a volcano.

"My house doesn't feel like home anymore. It... it feels... STUFFED," I screamed to the walls. Sinking into a couch, I sobbed, knowing no one would hear. Fatigue, grief and doubt hung in cobwebbed corners. I felt like a small weak moth caught in a sticky spider's web. The harder I struggled, the more stuck I became. Was Widow Spider sitting in a corner waiting to devour me?

The phone rang. "We're on our way to pick you up," Bobbie announced. I hurriedly washed my face, repaired my makeup and put on a cheerful smile. "Thanks for this trip, God," I whispered, as I struggled out the door with my massive luggage.

"I hope there's room," said our driver, eying my huge suitcases. Somehow we managed to squeeze the luggage into her van. At O'Hare Airport, my seven traveling companions were sure my carry-on would not pass. Surprisingly, it did. I ignored irritated stares from other waiting passengers.

In boarding, to my embarrassment, the monstrous carry-on bag became a major obstacle. The bag blocked the aisle, was too big to push under a seat and too heavy for me to lift overhead. Finally, an attendant, with help from a man built like a Chicago Bears linebacker, squashed it into an overhead bin. My bag filled the entire space and was pried out when we land-ed. After we deplaned, cruise ship personnel took charge of our luggage. I was so relieved, I nearly turned cartwheels.

As we walked up a gangplank to board the USS *Independence* in Honolulu, I felt as if I was *returning*, rather than visiting for the first time. Thousands of miles from my house I felt "at home" — at peace.

For the first time in months, I didn't need to work at being cheerful. Sunshine, the friendly Aloha spirit and my friends brought easy smiles to my face and joy to my heart. My problems were thousands of miles away. Or so I thought. Sometimes, when least expected, however, unbidden thoughts drifted across my sunny disposition like a black cloud. My traveling suitcases weren't the only baggage I brought with me.

One day I opted to enjoy a sandy beach while the others shopped. *The deserted beach will give me solitude to find my spirit,* I told myself. *No baggage, physical or mental. Time to start reaping benefits of my PMA garden, all those seeds planted from books, tapes and seminars.* Nothing happened. My spirit was as flat as the beach.

"Don't worry about anything, Mom," my family had told me. "Everything will be fine." I tried to believe them, but thoughts of Mom in a nursing home, Henry and Hector fighting AIDS in California, Debbie struggling in Florida, the various troubles of Cindy, Kenny Jr., Brenda, Laura and their families in Indiana, all our pain blocked the sunshine. Pesty fears attacked like flies before a rain. Stacked boxes of memorabilia and a mess of stuff left strewn about the house from packing cluttered my thoughts.

I thought being in Hawaii would fill me with happiness. Why can't I think of the good stuff? Why do worries torment my mind? What am I going to do now? God, you know I can't take much more.

There was so much trouble around me, it was hard to find room for anything else, even something fun and exciting, like a long-awaited cruise. I walked and pondered. Wandered and prayed. Although still apparent, my confidence wasn't as strong as it had been in times past. What was this sinking feeling? Was there a danger I'd slip back into the old depressions and negativity?

As I pondered my life with my Creator — past, present and future — I realized I was overdosing on jaded thinking. Those nasty grasshoppers (fear, doubt and worry) had swarmed again.

When I asked God how to stop the deluge, another thought came, "You have a choice." When I lamented the injustice of it all, the regrets, the anger and frustration, I heard a message from deep within: "Have you tried forgiveness lately?" The medicines prescribed, choice and forgiveness, brought more festering thoughts to the surface.

If I choose happiness most of the time, am I neglecting my "job" in caring for everyone else? Since they are suffering, shouldn't I suffer also? What about memories? If I don't think a lot about people who are no longer with me, might I forget them?

What am I to do with the guilt I feel at spending my dead husband's insurance money and enjoying inherited family treasures?

Forgiveness... what can that do? I'm the one who needs to be forgiven. I don't do enough, care enough. I need forgiveness for resenting all the extra responsibility, for resenting being left alone to take care of everything.

The ruinous thoughts blocked out Dad's directive to "Remember the happy hours." Thoughts of unhappy times menacingly seeped into mind, blocking warm happy memories and prevented me from seeing that they, too, were filled with self-pity.

I tried to push away thoughts of my deceased loved ones' "imperfections." Every contact with living loved ones challenged me to make a "meaningful" memory. Self-chastisement nibbled at my senses for compliments not offered, assistance not given and for using insurance death benefits to take a cruise. Negativity became a giant octopus entangling everything I did, including my dream-come-true holiday.

As I walked the beach, wrestling with the moods rising and crashing like the waves washing upon the shore, a message flowed into my mind. *Life keeps moving along as it always has with sunny times and gloomy times, like the weather. You are simply riding out the stormy times, looking for the rainbows.*

That night it stormed as we ate our dinner. Our ship rocked and rolled. Our server became seasick and I didn't. Was this a sign that I was adjusting after all?

The remainder of our cruise was lighthearted and fun, until packing time came around. Because of tight cabin quarters, we decided to take turns. I asked to go last. While everyone was top side enjoying the evening farewell party, I frantically packed and repacked my stuff. Because I bought gifts for everyone at home, plus a few souvenirs for myself, there were more items than luggage space. I finished barely in time for my three roommates' return for the last night's sleep.

At 2 a.m., I awoke in my lower berth to a gentle rocking of the ship. Quietly I eased out of bed for a walk up on deck. The night was clear with a full moon. Zillions of stars twinkled in a velvet indigo sky. Soft island breezes gently massaged my body. I walked around the ship, breathing deeply of clean fresh air, salt mist cleansing remnants of pain and grief from my soul. Coming to the ship's stern a second time, I paused. From the disco below, soft bits of music wafted up to me. My heart took a musical ride to another place — another time.

> *Feeling like a heroine in a romance novel, I gazed across the ink-blue water of Sister's Lake toward a dance hall. Sweet love songs flowed back on rays of moonbeams reflected in the water. We held hands and listened to the music. Ken put his arms around me.*
>
> *"I love you," he whispered.*

"I love you, too." I smiled.

Ken stepped back, reached into his pocket and pulled out a small white box. He opened it. A moonbeam spotlight transformed a tiny solitaire diamond into a beacon of love that bounced straight into my heart. I looked up to meet those sparkling blue eyes I loved so much.

They were not there.

"Gone," roared the ship's wake.

"Gone," cried my heart.

Tears rolled down my cheeks. Finally, the message sank in. It's over, Joanne. He's gone. They are all gone.

"Oh, God, what do I do?"

"Let them go," came the answer. And I did.

Into the ship's wake I dropped all the memories, good and bad. In went the memories of Ken, followed by those of my brother, Richard, our stepfather, Ralph — my very special dad. They were followed overboard by memories of Aunt Becky and all the others who had recently passed beyond my earthly eyes.

Then I virtually threw the emotional baggage into the waters — fears for my children, the heartache of Mom's Alzheimer's and nursing home visits plopped into churning waters. Swirling whirlpools hungrily gulped Hopelessness and Helplessness which quickly followed.

Finally, I threw in STUFF. ALL of it. Tears dripped into my neck. I searched for more tissue. One left.

"Well," I said aloud. "This is it. No more tissues, no more tears." After drying my face and neck, I turned and walked to the bow.

Warm breezes once again greeted me like soft kisses. Stars twinkled their joy. The moon beamed a welcome. My heart calmed like the quiet shimmering ocean surrounding the ship. *Everyone is sleeping, maybe I should too,* I thought.

"Before you go, please do something for me," whispered Someone.

"What?"

"Look out there — that's your future. What do you see?"

I looked. Fear tugged at my chest.

"You're okay, Joanne. Walk through it... you can do it. You'll be fine, I promise."

Taking a deep breath, I looked again. My thoughts took form: a little apartment, clean and neat, a motorhome and a long adventurous road ahead — free of excess baggage.

"Thank you, God."

Next morning, as we stood on deck, watching our ship move into the harbor for final docking, a rainbow formed. Its arc came from somewhere on the island, landing on the water at the very edge of our ship.

I knew then that, deep inside each of us, there is always a flicker of light, a tiny remnant of God's perfect love. The Love that casts out fear. That's what negativity is: fear in all its ugly disguises. When we connect to that spark within, we rekindle hope. Hope to survive the offenses of this world — of life. Hope is like the sun shining through the clouds, reflecting off the raindrops to create rainbows, a promise that good is in all things.

From my visit to Hawaii, our Rainbow State, I came home refreshed and determined to continue in my quest for seeing the good in everything. As I tackled my house organizing project and various problems in settling estates and managing Mom's affairs, the messages from Hawaii grew stronger. Finally, I was ready to embrace the two other remedies for Rainbow Living: Power of Choice and Forgiveness.

Rainbow Ingredients
for
Accentuating the Positive

- Keep on keeping on.

- See the glass half full.

- Expect to find good in each storm.

- Prospect for possibilities.

- Be cheerful.

- Smile.

- Use affirmations.

- Let go and let God.

- Keep a Rainbow Journal.

- Know it can be done and you can do it.

A God-incident

Mom rarely spoke, due to Alzheimer's, so Dad and I spent most Saturdays visiting with each other that year following the deaths of Ken Sr. and Richard.

One warm August Saturday, as Mom slept on a couch inside, Dad and I sat outside on a deck overlooking the pond behind my house. I was chatting away when Dad's eyes grew big. "Don't move," he whispered. "There's a hummingbird hovering at the corner of the deck."

"It's okay, Dad," I said, laughing. "That's my friend." Dad sat in amazement as the iridescent little bird flew close beside me. A minute or two passed as Mr. Hummingbird hovered nearby, watching Dad watch him. Then it zoomed off into a dogwood tree.

"I've never seen anything like that. He wasn't the least bit afraid," said Dad.

"I think Ken sent him," I said, then told him the story of Mr. Hummingbird's first visit shortly after Ken's death. With my little friend's visit, a door opened to share other coincidental happenings in each of our lives. As we shared, I learned more about my special stepfather and about myself. Until his death, Dad and I spent many hours reminiscing about past happy times, as we created new ones.

Power of Choice 6

The difficulty in life is the choice.

George Moore
The Bending of the Bough

Have you ever felt that in certain situations you had no choices? That whatever you were facing was absolutely, totally impossible to handle? You are not alone.

There are times in life when we feel so out of control that helplessness and hopelessness become constant companions. But choice, like breath, is something that is a part of us. *We always have a choice.* Even when we think we are not, we are still choosing. What is our choice? To give up, to let despondency take control, to perpetuate a difficult time and defeat ourselves. Or, we can choose differently.

In every circumstance, we have a selection process between options and preferences. Sometimes options are limited, or we are unaware of them. Sometimes our preferences are in conflict with our options. Sometimes options are better for us than our preferences. At other times, although the preferences outweigh the options, effects of outside influences limit our choices to the less preferable options.

For example, our preference is to buy a new house, but our income is insufficient to support that decision. At first we see no options and feel defeated. But as we stop, look, listen and learn, we see a number of options. I may opt to take a second job and save to buy the new house, then gripe about having to work so much. I may opt to redecorate what I have and start a savings account for the new house. I might decide to do nothing at all, blaming society or the economy for my "misfortune." We each decide how we feel. We each are in charge of our actions.

Michael's Choice: Four-year-old Michael stomped through the doorway, yanked off his shoes and plunked down on my couch. With a big sigh he crossed his legs and arms and stuck out his bottom lip. *Boy, it's going to be one of those days,* I thought and decided to ignore Michael for a while, hoping he'd relax a bit.

My son-in-law Doug brought Michael to me every morning before he went to work, so I could care for my grandson until his mother, Laura, came home from her job three hours later.

My glimpse of Doug's face as he brought Michael in told me their morning hadn't gone well. They arrived late, and I suspected their tardiness had something to do with Michael's hating to be rushed.

"I'm unhappy," Michael announced, after his father left.

"You are? How come?"

Michael's lip poked out further. "He yelled at me."

Doug is not the yelling type. I walked over and sat down beside Michael. "Looked like your dad was a little upset. Were you being pokey?"

Michael hung his head. "Yes, but he didn't have to yell at me."

"I'm sure he didn't want to, but sometimes, Michael, that's the way things happen. People get frustrated and they yell. But it's over now. You don't have to be unhappy all day about it."

"Yes, I do! It makes me very unhappy. I can't help it!"

"Well, I think you can. I believe we can *choose* how we feel."

"We can? How?"

"We just do, that's all."

Michael looked puzzled. "But... but how can I be happy when I'm unhappy?"

"If you are unhappy about something, you choose to think about something else. Instead of thinking about this morning and how everything got off to a bad start, you might play with the blocks or read a book or listen to some happy music on the records. Then you'll be happy again. Or you might think about something that makes you happy. What makes you happy?"

Michael thought a minute. "I got to ride my dirt bike last night."

"That's right," I said with a grin, remembering how seriously he handled the mini-dirt bike he had received for his birthday.

"What else?"

Michael grinned. "I ate my breakfast all gone." He looked wistfully at my cookie jar.

I grinned, too. "Go get one," I said.

Throughout that morning and for several mornings following, whenever Michael's mood sagged (and with preschoolers that can happen every other minute), I reminded him he could choose to be happy. After a couple of days, Michael didn't need reminding. He changed his attitude with an announcement, "I choose to be happy."

Then one day he stomped into my house again, lip sticking out, a scowl wrinkling his brow.

"Hey, Michael, remember? You have a choice."

"Yup," he snapped. "And today I *choose* to be *unhappy.*"

That day I told Michael he could choose to be unhappy if he wanted to, but I didn't choose to participate, so I was going into another room for a while. It only took a couple of minutes before I heard a little voice calling, "Grandma, you can come out now. I choose to be happy."

As Abraham Lincoln said, "We can choose to be happy or we can choose to be sad."

Choice, Not Chance

Sometimes we believe that chance takes away our freedom to choose. Chance may take away some of the options, but it can never take away our choice of what we will do about a situation.

You're So Lucky: One evening, a few months after Ken Jr.'s death, an old friend I'll call Maggie told me her doctor said she was going blind. I felt deep sadness for Maggie's impotency and her desperation. Praying silently, I tried to guide her to that core of peace within herself, to help her see she still had options even if her sight should go.

Nothing I said worked. My words gave her little comfort. Maggie's spirit seemed as blind as her sight was becoming. Her parting words rang in my mind for days, "You're so lucky. You have so many people who care about you. No one cares about me." I cared, yet I was unable to convince her. I felt certain others cared also, but they couldn't reach her either.

Shortly after Maggie's call, I slipped into a depression, the kind I had known too well from younger years. I remember believing that no one cared about me — not even God.

One memory of that earlier time still hurts. I was screaming at my mother, "Don't talk to me about God. I'm not sure He even exists, and if He does, He sure as hell doesn't care about me!" Mom looked as stunned as if I slapped her face. I'm sure in that moment she, too, felt inadequate and deserted.

Even when we don't believe God exists *He still cares about us.* That is what I feel in the inner calm during turbulent times. How I experience that feeling is not through luck but from constant and focused self-determination.

Wake Up Call: When Kenny Jr. died unexpectedly, emotions rushed through me. I felt vulnerable. Powerless. The moment I learned of his death, I knew my life, and the lives of those dearest to him, would never be the same. At first I refused to accept that he was gone. My preference was to block out the awful news. My body obliged by fainting. When that didn't last, I raged. I might be raging still had I not chosen to listen to my friend Naomi's concerned words.

Naomi chose to be with me, although she could well have delegated that task to someone else. She chose to care, voicing her concern and sense of helplessness as well. Her comment, "I don't know what to do," mirrored my feelings. When the words penetrated the raging storm within me, touching that part deep inside where truth and wisdom live, the answer came. *I don't have to do this. I can choose a different reaction.*

Suddenly, I saw other options. I could change my thinking, change my focus and perhaps, in the process, find peace. Which is exactly what I did. When I stopped to look, listen and learn, I found something to give praise and thanksgiving for, even in that awful moment. I became free to put the accent on the positive and exercise my power of choice constructively.

I began to feel acceptance, a calmness like the depths of the ocean during a storm. At the time of my son's funeral and many months following, I felt a core of peace in the midst of deep sorrow and pain.

This peace amazed me. Where did it come from? How did I get to that comforting place? How was it possible, after all I'd been through — losing loved one after loved one — to believe I still had a choice? That I could choose to be happy, to find peace? It was not luck.

PREPARATION + OPPORTUNITY = LUCK

"The Universe cannot help you in the same way that it can if you are trusting of it, because it cannot overshadow nor penetrate your choice," says Gary Zukav, author of *The Seat of the Soul.*

"Luck is when preparation meets opportunity" insist many motivational writers and speakers for success. Life is not simply a game of chance; it is the evolution of our choices. True success is simply choosing to live each day joyfully, with thanksgiving, no matter what happens. That doesn't mean that a funeral is filled with joy. But when we come prepared to "stop, look, listen and learn," we find joy in the worst of times. We have the choice to bless or damn our circumstances.

In my family we create some joy at each loved one's wake. We put up poster boards filled with pictures of the happy times. We tell stories. "Remember the time when… ?" We look for things to laugh about. When Dad died, we put five playing cards in his hands: the ace, king, queen and jack of spades, and the jack of clubs. A winning euchre hand. Ken Sr.'s casket was nearly full of crayoned pictures from his grandchildren. We laugh… we cry.

I feel sorry for people who choose not to cry, who stand staunchly by like "brave little soldiers." When we put a lid on our emotions, they can fester into diseases that eat away our bodies. Some medical reports claim that severe trauma in a person's life can cause life-threatening illnesses, even death, within a year. I think the inability or refusal to release emotional suffering leads to illness.

That happened to me. As a young woman, I had so many ailments that it was difficult for me to buy life insurance. The only policy offered for me to purchase came at a premium price, but not because of any family history. I had internalized my anger, frustration, fear, doubt and worry into intestinal problems so severe that an insurance medical examiner rated me "high risk." I was told, "You are a good candidate for colon cancer."

Today, in spite of one trauma after another for several years, I am healthy in body and whole in mind. Not because of Lady Luck, but because I decided to make different choices.

Good fortune comes from preparation, developing strong skills to assist and support us through anxious times. We do it by controlling consciousness, perpetuating preparedness, perusing the past, recycling relationships and propelling prayer power.

Controlling Consciousness: We train ourselves to be alert. Aware. We don't go through life as sleepwalkers. We teach ourselves to see options, lots of options. We keep ourselves in top mental and physical condition to avoid vulnerability. We avoid laziness. We take charge of our choices, perceptively prepare and learn from the past.

We allow ourselves time enough to determine what our intentions are, to be aware of the other person's intentions. We ask ourselves: How does that affect me? What can I do about it? Clarifying intentions, particularly our own, is the foundation for making sound decisions; ones that will stand up through every storm.

Perpetuating Preparedness: We can take the Boy and Girl Scout's motto: Be Prepared. Read, ask questions, observe other people and how they make choices. We master researching options through self-help books, support groups, the library, workshops, church. Novels provide insights into what works, what doesn't. The Bible gives us stories about how people's choices affected their lives. Fairy tales and children's books are splendid resources. Playing "What if… ?" with friends and family creates laughter and reveals intriguing options.

Like most children, my youngsters became restless on car trips, so we often played the "What if… ?" game. What if someone asked you to get in their car and go for a ride? What if your best friend wanted you to help her cheat on an exam? What if Martians came to our house? Some questions were serious, others funny. The idea was to get the children to think about their options, get them to dig deeply and come up with many ideas, no matter how weird. The important thing was to get them to THINK. Thinking helped them gain experience in searching for options, become creative in problem-solving and develop confidence and ability to find alternatives. They could then act, rather than react, to new and troubling situations.

Perusing the Past: For some people, journaling is a tool for growth. When we realize, "Whoa! I've been here before," we can go back in our journals to see how we previously handled the situation. If we are new to journaling, we may discover that we have a behavior pattern that is actually perpetuating a problem, rather than alleviating it.

According to personal growth expert Anthony Robbins, "Insanity is doing the same thing over and over again, expecting different results." With a journal we quickly learn where we are "insane" and where we are using our heads as God intended.

As we grow and journal, we'll find we are adjusting. On the other hand, although our choices improve, we may slip back into old habits, forgetting what works. That's when looking into our journal gives us a real boost. "Oh, right! I remember now."

Journaling brings our consciousness into greater clarity of how we deal with life's stormy times. The more cognizant of our choices, the better our decisions become. "There is no better school than adversity. Every defeat, every heartbreak, every loss, contains its own seed, its own lesson on how to improve my performance the next time," writes Og Mandino in *The Greatest Salesman in the World, the End of the Story.*

Recycling Relationships: We choose good trainers to teach us how to exercise power of choice for maximum benefit and minimum damage. Every person we meet and have a relationship with, even briefly, can teach us something. A discerning review of our various relationships gives us clues to how we make choices. Sometimes, however, we don't immediately recognize the "friends" God sends us.

Gregg Levoy, in his book *Callings,* warns us not to "confuse obstacles with enemies." In reality, our obstacles are friends who truly are trying to help us grow stronger, to triumph over adversity and to grow in wisdom and spirit.

When we surround the sand of an irritating relationship with fresh understanding, we create a lifeline made of precious pearls of wisdom. Wisdom to hang onto when we get that sinking feeling.

Propelling Prayer Power: Like journaling, prayer is a sounding board, a comforter and an anchor. We can't always find a friend to talk to, but we can always talk to God.

There was a time when I got upset because God didn't talk back in a human voice. I often railed, "I want an answer. Now! One I can hear... do you understand me?" When I didn't hear what I wanted to hear, I quit praying. Perhaps God took that to mean I was finally listening, for that's when spirit-filled authors opened my mind to the Power of Choice.

Reading powerful writings expands consciousness. We begin to see God's hand in everything. We hear God's Love through others who are caring, kind and helpful. We feel God's Spirit through our loved ones, in the kindness of strangers and the beauty of nature. We find God's Comfort in the midst of an inferno.

Mitchell's Choice: Several years ago, while riding his motorcycle, W Mitchell was hit by a laundry truck and severely burned. He was a former marine, twenty-eight years old and had everything a young man could want: a satisfying job on the San Francisco trolley line, a new Honda 750 motorcycle and a successful solo flight piloting a small airplane. Mitchell was handsome. Women loved him.

In one day his dream life became a nightmare. The accident left his face badly scarred, his fingers burned to stubs and his dreams for the future shattered. But, over time, instead of bitterly regretting the accident, Mitchell chose to use the recuperation time as an "R & R" for his spirit. He decided not to just survive, but to thrive.

As his burns healed, Mitchell planned a new life. In spite of facial scars so severe that children ran in fright while others called him "monster," Mitchell did not hide. His Marine Corps training taught him to face problems and deal with them.

After his recuperation from the accident, Mitchell became a successful businessman in Colorado. Eventually he went back to flying and purchased his own plane. One cold day, while taking off in his airplane, Mitchell experienced another tragedy. The plane stalled and crashed. Mitchell's four passengers got out with only scratches, but he was paralyzed from his waist down.

Mitchell still refused to let discouragement get to him. He reviewed his past for what he could still do. "Before the plane accident, I could do ten thousand things. Now I can only do nine thousand," says Mitchell today. Included in those nine thousand was eventually serving as mayor of Crested Butte, Colorado.

Mayor Mitchell's agenda was to take on the largest mining company in the world, AMAX, Inc. His mission was to stop a planned mining operation that would forever ruin the pristine beauty of the land. The David-versus-Goliath battle to protect Mount Emmons, "The Red Lady," lasted four years and thrust Mitchell into the limelight. Appearances on national TV programs, such as the *Today* show, and quotes in major publications, such as *Time* magazine and the *New York Times,* brought national attention to Crested Butte. The publicity also established Mitchell as an outstanding spokesperson.

Although Mitchell and his constituents were unable to defeat the mining company, they slowed it down enough for the 1981 recession to give AMAX an excuse not to proceed with their plans to mine the area. However, Mitchell and his band celebrated their accomplishments. During the battle they created legal precedents that helped other small communities fight similar battles against huge corporations loaded with

money. They forced AMAX to clean up pollution left by a previous company that had owned the old lead and zinc mine
AMAX had purchased in anticipation of their own mining
operation.

During the fight, Mitchell refused to sit back and feel sorry
for himself. He put himself on the front lines, spending
$160,000 of his own money to help make this world a better,
cleaner, safer place in which to live. Through that choice,
Mitchell's destiny came into view — to help others make positive choices.

"That destiny is a matter of choice is not something I
learned early in life," he says. Today, as an inspirational speaker, Mitchell is in demand worldwide.

Responsible Power of Choice

Free will is a gift. How we use that gift is our choice — and
our responsibility. If you ever asked to do something "because
all the other kids were doing it," no matter what "it" was, your
mother may have replied, "If everyone jumped off a bridge,
would you?" I have a political cartoon that says it well. The picture is a big, shapely apple with a worm crawling out of it. The
caption on the apple is "Freedom." The worm is labeled
"Responsibility."

> *God lets some things happen to us through "permis-*
> *sive will." By giving us free choice, He permits us to have*
> *the free will to do whatever we choose to do. If we choose*
> *to jump off the Sears Tower, He might just allow that to*
> *happen. Then again, being God, He might choose to*
> *find a better way for us to learn our lessons.*
> Catherine Marshall
> *Something More*

Responsibility is heaviest when our choices are limited by
outside forces. Sometimes our job is to buck the system, fight

back, ignore the experts and go in search of our own truths. In practicing the art of wise decision-making, we gain power over our environment. That's when we find rainbows.

Maggie's Choice: Two years after receiving the telephone call from my friend who was going blind, I was Christmas shopping at a local mall. Dodging around crowds of people, I heard my name. Looking toward the familiar voice, I saw Maggie's beaming smile as she waved from about twenty feet away. We hurried toward each other and hugged in greeting.

"You look wonderful," I said in amazement, remembering our last contact two years prior.

"I feel wonderful," she responded. "My last eye exam showed no further deterioration in one eye, and the other one is improving! I drink carrot juice and eat spinach every day. I decided to take charge and research alternative treatments." She shared other blessings she'd received since last we spoke, among them a renewal of a former broken relationship.

Maggie told me that when she looked for other options, she gained her sight — literally. "Our choices determine how high we fly," says Thelma Wells, author of *What's Going On Lord?* Maggie's flying as high as the rainbow these days.

Reliable Choices

The privilege of free will comes with the responsibility to choose carefully, mindfully — to know our intent. Reliable decisions, those that bring true happiness and peace to ourselves and others, come from honorable value systems.

"Core values can help guide your choices. They are both your anchor in the rough sea and the lighthouse that helps illumine a positive and principled course," says Terry L. Paulson, Ph.D. "They are your foundation for what you do or say. They are what you stand for and what you hold yourself accountable to — no matter what the cost."

To find our core values and determine our intent for making choices, we need to ask ourselves probing questions. For some questions, see pages 147 and 148.

Maintaining Our Power of Choice

When we refuse to accept responsibility to take care of ourselves, we risk losing our options. We must stay alert to what influences us to maintain our power of choice. Giving away our power by allowing others to think for us leads to apathy, then resentment and finally, rebellion. Next comes hatred and war. I can think of few things worse than war and the horrors that go with war.

Wars do not pop up like mushrooms. Seeds of war are planted and cultivated through years of dissension. Disagreements and misunderstandings accumulate to a point that everyone's right to choose becomes obscured. By the time we feel obliged to take up guns to insure our freedom of choice, we've already given away much of what we believe we are fighting for. We don't see clearly anymore, because the situation has become a power struggle, rather than a negotiation for a peaceful win-win agreement.

Wars do not bring peace. They merely overpower the enemy. What a wonderful world this would be if we would all choose to love, rather than fear; forgive, rather than hate; give, rather than take.

In spite of wars, in the midst of wars, people still have freedom to choose. Limited, but never eliminated. Dictators, terrorists, abusive parents and prejudiced people limit our options, but they cannot stop us from choosing our thoughts, our reactions. This is where our love and faith is tested. This is where our love and faith can grow deeper and stronger than ever before. This is the time we go within to strengthen mind and spirit.

Concentration camps, particularly those in which Jewish people were put into fiery furnaces, are among the most horrific examples of human atrocities. Yet, even there, we find examples of victims choosing love, peace, forgiveness and truth. Sometimes, when I feel myself slipping into self-pity, I look for encouragement from survivors of these camps who chose to forgive, to love and to move on: People like Corrie ten Boom, Viktor Frankl, Gerald Coffee and George R. Hall, whose inner work during their internments has enriched other lives as well as their own. I pray that humankind will choose to subscribe to their messages, rather than to those of hate mongers.

P.O.W. Choices: In *The Hiding Place,* Corrie ten Boom tells about a strange decision to give thanks and praise. Caught helping Jews escape, Corrie and her sister were confined in a Nazi concentration camp. With many other women, the two were herded into a small building, a building already occupied. Fleas abounded!

Taking the Bible's counsel to "give thanks in all things," the sisters' prayers of gratitude included the original occupants: the fleas! Nazi guards refused to step foot into the infested building, so the women were free to worship together. The fleas became their blessing.

In *Man's Search for Meaning,* Viktor E. Frankl, M.D., Ph.D., shares observations of man's free will demonstrated during his three years in Auschwitz and other Nazi concentration camps.

> *Even though conditions, such as lack of sleep, insufficient food and various mental stresses, may suggest that the inmates were bound to react in certain ways, in the final analysis it becomes clear that the sort of person the prisoner became was the result of an inner decision, and not the result of camp influences alone.*

Fundamentally, therefore, any man can, even under
such circumstances, decide what shall become of him
— mentally and spiritually.

Dr. Frankl chose to use his time in the concentration camps to continue studying how human beings react, so he could share the findings with all who would listen when the awful experience was over.

During the Viet Nam conflict, Gerald L. Coffee was taken prisoner and confined for six years in the infamous "Hanoi Hilton." There Coffee learned to communicate through a tap-code system created by the prisoners of war held in solitary confinement. The tap code allowed the POWs to "talk" to one another and they became quite creative with other sounds that lent themselves to the tap code. Some prisoners assigned to clean-up duties would work their brooms into rhythmic swishing messages. Through these messages, the POWs kept their spirits up. Today, Coffee shares his experiences in speeches that inspire and motivate thousands.

Another Viet Nam POW, George R. Hall, was confined for $7^1/_2$ years. His first year was spent in solitary confinement. To help him get through this oppressive and lonely year, he visualized playing golf.

"I played nine imaginary holes every morning and nine more every afternoon. This got me out of the cell mentally for a few hours each day. I pictured every course I had ever played and every person I had ever played with.

"Upon returning home, I was invited to play in the New Orleans Open Pro Am with my old friend, Orville Moody. He helped me with my swing on the practice tee and I was pleasantly surprised to shoot an 81. It's not that close to par, but a respectable score for someone who had not played in several years."

Al Siebert, Ph.D., says that life's best survivors use their inborn abilities better than other people. "They are resilient and durable in distressing situations. They regain emotional balance quickly, adapt and cope well. They thrive by gaining strength from adversity and often convert misfortune into a gift." Siebert is the author of *The Survivor Personality.*

Fine Tuning Power of Choice

Life is a constant process of making choices, usually unconsciously. Normally, we don't think about how we drive a car, walk or eat our food. We do those things from habit. We might call some people "accident prone," but in truth, they are sleepwalking through life. They have chosen not to see hazards, not to correct their dangerous habits such as daydreaming while driving.

Does this describe your life? When did you last sit down to list all the options you can think of for a frustrating situation or important decision? When you do this, you will often find you have more options than you originally thought, and that your decision turns out better than you expected.

As we become more conscious, we automatically move from panic possibilities to positive probabilities. We recognize that everything that happens hinges on choice.

Will we take a chance and go past the railroad-crossing gates? Or will we be smart and wait a few minutes, even if we're running late? Will we look for good in our situation? Or will we be sucked into pits of despair? Will we embrace anger? Lust after retaliation? Or decide to forgive? Will we react without thinking, or will we think, then act? Or will we choose taking no action, letting others make the choice for us? If we do, we give away our power.

Students Teach the Teacher: There are many reasons we give away our power to choose. Following are a few accumu-

lated from college students, who attended my "Power of Choice"
classes:

- to make others happy
- fear of reprisal
- denial [of responsibility]
- laziness
- to avoid conflict
- really doesn't matter [trivial matter]
- to get another opinion
- undecided
- to gain information
- don't know the options
- [effects of] previous choices
- mental state
- physical state

There are times when it makes sense to wait because better
decisions come when we are rested and alert. The wise delay
important decisions until they have enough information and
do not waste energy on trivia. While we are influenced by society, adversities, religion, family, peers, role models, government, advertising, media and other factors, we can still be discerning. Bottom line: *we pay the consequences for our choices* no
matter whom we blame. We might as well take responsibility
at the start and at least have the satisfaction of knowing we are
doing it "our way" like Frank Sinatra.

A Husband and Father's Choice: We are all on a pathway
back to the heaven we came from... a place many, including
my husband, Ken, call Home. Although we don't have a choice
about leaving this planet when our allotted days are spent, we
do have a choice about how we will make our journey.

Will we choose a dark, dingy road of regret and sorrow? Or will we make our trip along a golden road filled with missions accomplished, happy hours and rainbows? Some people find optimism easy and some find it hard.

My husband, Ken, had little difficulty making choices. He never understood why some of us agonized over our decisions. He was only thirty-eight when his first heart attack severely damaged his heart. Since his veins were too small for open-heart surgery, he was told he had no choices. Basically, Ken's doctors pronounced a death sentence. One prediction was "about a year."

Ken didn't accept that and went in search of other options. He found a doctor who encouraged him to live, rather than die. Live he did, for another seventeen years, the last seven of them with less than twenty percent of his heart functioning. The worst damage came as a result of a severe heart attack on his forty-ninth birthday. We celebrated his fiftieth birthday with a surprise party where family and friends "roasted" him. He loved every minute of it, laughing until tears streamed down his face.

Although Ken's options shrank, he lived life fully, cutting firewood, lifting his grandchildren for hugs and helping rebuild portions of our house after they were burned. Fortunately for his family and friends, he chose to make other people happy.

"When I die," he asserted, "if just one person says, 'My life was brighter because of Ken Hill,' I will know it's all been worthwhile." Ken succeeded. The visitors' line at the funeral home went outside the door and down the street. Strangers shook my hand and said, "You don't know me, but Ken came into the restaurant where I work. He always made me laugh."

One man told me, "We've never met, but Ken helped me get through some tough times after my wife died. He could always cheer me up."

Doctors predicted Ken's death would be instant, come without warning. "He won't suffer," they said. They were half right. He had little suffering and plenty of time to see everyone he loved before leaving. When the time came, Ken chose to walk through it all the way. He "held court" in the intensive care unit for twelve hours as family and friends came to say goodbye.

10 Questions to Ask Yourself *Before* Making a Decision

1. *What are the motives (and emotions) that can (or are) affecting my choices? (Love, anger, frustration, peace, greed, survival, lust, commitment, etc.)*

2. *What is really going on here? Look for all the perceptions... from every viewpoint.*

3. *What will I have to give up if I make this decision? What will I get? What price will I have to pay?*

4. *Will this choice affect my life, short term? Long term? How will it affect me personally: health, time, energy, mental and emotional balance?*

5. *How will this decision affect my current relationships? Future relationships? Other people in general? My community? The world? Finances? Work?*

6. *Is my intent to overpower someone else or only to assume responsibility for myself? Does my decision carry with it the possibility of causing irreparable harm to myself or to someone else?*

7. *Will it be beneficial to others? Help make this a better world in which to live?*

8. *In my old age when I look back at this decision, how will I perceive it?*

9. *How will this choice affect the eternal part of me — my soul, my spirit?*

10. *What other questions should I ask myself before making this decision?*

8 Questions to Ask *After* a Decision is Made and Results are In

1. *Why did I choose (or not choose) this? What was my intention when I made this decision? What did I hope to accomplish with this decision?*

2. *Did it truly benefit me? Did it benefit or hurt others?*

3. *What did I give up? What did I get? What price did I pay? Was it worth it?*

4. *How will this decision affect my future? Do I need to make some adjustments? What? How will I implement them?*

5. *How do I feel about my choice now that I see the results? Was it a wise one or could I have done something differently that might have worked out better for me? For others?*

6. *Have I set anything in motion that caused or could cause difficulty or harm? Are there decisions I can make now to change, heal or mend the situation? To stop the situation from getting worse?*

7. *What have I learned? How will this affect future decisions?*

8. *How can I put power into my choices? Where do I give my power away? To whom? Why?*

Rainbow Ingredients
for
Choosing

• Remember: You **always** have a choice.

• Stop and think: Choose to act, rather than react.

• Stay alert: Be conscious every minute of every day.

• Be prepared: Learn problem-solving techniques.

• Use: Past experiences, your own and others.

• Plan ahead: Continually improve your choices.

• Choose to see life sunny side up.

A God-incident

In July of 1994, I was attending a National Speakers Association convention in Washington, DC. On the platform was Captain Gerald L. Coffee, U.S. Navy (Ret.). I had heard him speak before and was excited about hearing him again, especially since I had a new friend, Barbara, to share the experience with.

Barbara and I lay awake quite a while going over the events of the day. She was as impressed with Coffee's speech as I had been when first hearing it. Coffee always ends his talks by tapping out "God Bless," just as the Viet Nam POWs did each night just before going to sleep. When Barbara and I finally settled to go to sleep we told each other "God Bless."

In a dream during the night, my son Kenny came to me and said, "Mom, I am just fine." He repeated this several times. Early in the morning, as I was waking up, I heard the tap code for "God Bless." My roommate was in the bathroom and I thought she had tapped the message to gently wake me up. I grinned to myself, thinking, I'll have to thank her.

Just then she came out of the bathroom.

"Well, God bless you too," she said.

"I didn't do that. I thought you did."

"No, I didn't do it either."

We giggled.

"Well, maybe the person next door did it."

A few hours later I learned that my son was dead. Although I was in shock and quite distraught, the dream and tap code message hovered in my mind waiting to anchor me in the truth that God does bless us, even during our darkest storms.

A Golden Nugget

It's my choice!

© Janice D. Cowen

Forgiveness   7

*We must make our homes
centers of compassion
and forgive endlessly.*

Mother Teresa

Getting through a crisis is only half the battle. There is always debris left from the storms. Grief. Fear. Anger. If we don't deal with them, they become obstructions to a joyful, healthy life.

Anger is a common part of grieving, whatever the loss. "Anger is a normal emotion if it is expressed when it is felt. If it isn't, it develops into resentment or even hatred, which can be very destructive," says Bernie S. Siegel, M.D., author of *Love, Medicine and Miracles.*

Siegel, a surgeon and holistic health advocate, says that resentment leads to life-threatening diseases, such as cancer. Forgiveness is a potent potion that heals, empowers and frees us from tormenting resentment. Did you know that a synonym for resentment is malignancy?

Like most others, my life has been full of occasions to forgive — opportunities not always taken. The Forgiveness prescription is a bitter pill to swallow, particularly if what or who we need to forgive is still hurting us. Yet when we choose to use this remedy, miraculous results evolve like breathtaking rainbows.

The first sign is the lifting of a dark bitter fog blocking our happiness, imprisoning us in anger, hurt and frustration. When we forgive, awareness heightens, love and joy spring up and peace flows from within. If forgiveness is so great, what holds us back? Judgment. Fear. Doubt. False hope. Pride.

If we forgive someone, are we saying that what they did was all right? By our forgiveness, are we condoning atrocities, such as slavery, killing or rape? What if we forgive someone and they do it again?

What if our forgiveness seems to tell the offender, "I'm a pushover. Keep on hitting me. I'll just turn the other cheek. Then when everyone sees how bad you are, they'll take care of me." What good will forgiveness do then? Will it make our enemies treat us better?

How do we forgive the past? What will forgiveness do? If the one who hurt us is dead, it's too late, even if we wanted to. Isn't it?

Forgive? I've got my pride.

"You may not be able to change your oppressor or save your life by your love, but you can keep hatred from destroying *your* heart, mind and life, as it has destroyed his," said Martin Luther King, Jr. Our resentments do not hurt the other person, but they are killing us. Literally.

"Resentments trap us from the inside," says psychologist Phil McGraw. "It's a myth that the other person has to be sorry or he doesn't deserve to be forgiven." We forgive because we must. Our lives and the quality of our lives depend upon it.

There are two ways to forgive, direct and indirect. Some take the direct approach, face-to-face. Others send letters, make telephone calls, send e-mails or a card. In some cases, an indirect approach works better, particularly if the person pardoned isn't interested in a pardon. Indirect approaches use methods that only the person forgiving is involved in, such as writing a letter, then destroying it rather than sending it.

While there are some cases in which forgiving someone helps transform the forgiven as well as the forgiver, that is not the purpose in forgiveness. *We forgive for ourselves.* We forgive to set our spirit free. We let God take care of the other guy or gal.

Cleansing, Healing and Freedom

Forgiveness cleanses, heals and frees our festering spirits. "Forgiveness is giving up the hope that the past would be different," shared a guest on *The Oprah Winfrey Show*. Somewhere inside us, at least inside those who are still grieving over the past, is a little voice that tells us to hit that rerun button and see a different picture. But it won't happen. We can't change the past, but *we can change our feelings* about it.

Wayne Dyer, philosopher, writer and speaker, tells the story of forgiving his father. Dyer's father was an alcoholic and wife abuser, eventually deserting his family. He died at age thirty-nine. Dyer went to his father's grave and poured out his heart, first with his anger and pain, then with forgiveness.

At his father's grave, Dyer found release and forgiveness for the man he had hated and resented most of his life. Hearing that story for the first time, I pondered on waiting until someone died to feel relief from the misery I felt he/she caused me. Through that pondering came an awareness that I was hanging onto resentment to have enemies to blame for my difficulties.

Growing awareness taught me I could choose not to be hurt by others' behavior and *my* need to forgive them. Obviously some people are so certain their ways are right and others' ways are wrong, they do not want nor feel a need for our forgiveness.

Realizing that my forgiveness was unimportant *for them* made it easier for me to forgive and let go of the outcome. Sometimes their behaviors did change. But even if they didn't, I was less affected by them. When their behavior irritated me again, it was time for another dose of Forgiveness. Eventually the offending people left my life or toned down their behavior when around me.

Sometimes I wrote letters about particular situations, then burned them. Other times, talking with the offender in my head or face to face helped release my anger and frustration. Although these methods helped, I needed something more, something to dig out those deep-rooted resentments that lingered long after the person or event had gone from my life. Something that would truly set *me* free. I found it in Catherine Marshall's book *Something More,* in the chapter called "Forgiveness: The Aughts and the Anys."

"Aughts and Anys" Adventures: In this chapter, Marshall shared her frustrations with unanswered prayers. The first time I read the book, I had a lot of unanswered prayers, particularly for my marriage. Although Marshall didn't have marital problems, she did have other difficulties that discouraged and frustrated her. As I was diligently praying for God to change Ken and noticing few results, I plunged eagerly into the chapter.

Marshall's friend, Rev. David du Plessis, told her about an insight he received about the problem of not getting answers.

> *It isn't your faith… No, it's something else… When you stand praying — forgive if ye have aught against any. That's your trouble. That's why your prayers aren't answered. You go about with a lot of aughts against a lot of anys.*

Thinking about all that distressed her, Marshall decided to give the "aughts and anys" a try. Her plan was simple. Each morning Marshall and her husband Len spent about thirty minutes in separate rooms, putting irritating aughts [things] and anys [people] on paper. Afterward, they met together for verbal prayer release of each burden on their lists. Then they tore the lists into small bits and put them in a large manila envelope. Eventually they burned them.

Strengthening, Energizing and Blessing

My first experience with Marshall's Forgiveness treatment restored my strength and energy and brought many blessings. Since I didn't have a prayer partner, my aughts "against the anys" worked a bit differently.

Taking a writing tablet, I began with my husband's deficiencies (as I saw them). Marshall said to include everything that plagued us. The list grew long, covering several pages, taking much longer than the allotted thirty minutes. I even included his leaving the toilet seat up. If my aughts were green stamps, I would have been driving a Cadillac. Instead, pain and sorrow oozed out of my stockpile of grievances.

After listing everything that I held against Ken (he wasn't that bad; I was that picky), I took a brief recess to brew a cup of tea to fortify me for the hard part. Forgiving.

Beside each item I wrote, "I forgive." On some, "I want to forgive. Please help me." Although I prayed for help in the releasing, part of me held back, clinging to the hurt and heartache that I believed Ken caused me. Now I think differently. No one causes us to feel emotional pain. We do that to ourselves.

Letting go can be as frightening as flying through the air. Two months before his sixty-second birthday, founder of Upward Bound[1] Sam Keen took up the flying trapeze. "To learn the art of flying on a trapeze, you first must learn the art of falling," says Keen. "To date, I have been better at holding on than letting go." Keen is not alone. I, also, am better at holding on.

Letting go was harder than making the list. Desperately wanting to be free of the destructive thoughts cluttering up my head and squeezing my heart, I said a prayer of relinquishment, tore up the paper, piled the pieces in the fireplace and lit

---

1 Upward Bound is a trapeze workshop for anyone facing deeply rooted fears.

a match. As hot flames leapt up the chimney, warm tears of release rained down my cheeks. All my grievances against my husband became only smoke and ashes.

Ironically, *I* changed. Somehow most annoyances on my list were no longer vexations. In fact, some of them turned into endearing qualities over the years. Like Ken's snoring. After his heart attacks, my husband's snores became sweet music, telling me he was alive and by my side.

"When we learn to pardon, we rise above those who have insulted or aggrieved us, and this act of forgiveness puts an end to the quarrel," says Wayne Dyer in *Wisdom of the Ages.* Forgiveness changed our marriage for the better.

For several months following my "aughts and anys" effort with Ken, I followed Marshall's example, diligently forgiving someone or something every day. Then I put the book on the library shelf. Guess I thought once it was done, the process wouldn't have to be repeated. Oh, how I deceived myself! There was much to be forgiven in the years to come.

The Big Test: After ten years of working in crisis intervention, I decided it was time to pursue my writing career. Shortly after I completed my first writing assignment and received a paycheck, my husband suffered his first heart attack.

Fear gripped me, then anger. Anger with Ken because he was a smoker and loved foods high in cholesterol. Anger with God because the attack seemed so unfair. (I hadn't realized yet that it's not God who punishes us, but that we punish ourselves by our own choices.)

After many years of financial and personal struggles, our marriage was finally in a "settled" state, giving me a secure feeling for the first time since our wedding day. Ken's business was going well. We had built our dream house. I was breaking ground on a long-cherished writing career. Then Ken's heart attack tore our life apart and nearly paralyzed me with fear.

My new mantra became, "Life is a roller coaster ride, and I hate roller coasters!" To me, a roller-coaster ride is nothing more than a laborious ride up and a painful jerking down. With lots of screaming! Give me the ferris wheel any day: a nice and easy go-around with time to enjoy the view. That, however, was not my life at the time.

Since Ken was the sole employee in his own business, major adjustments were in order. He sold and delivered automotive parts to car dealerships and auto repair shops. I kept the account books and occasionally made deliveries, but knew nothing about automotive parts. Kenny Jr. did know about automobiles and parts, and he was a good salesman, just like his dad. He was also looking for a short-term job to earn college money. That took care of the business, but didn't supply enough income, especially since Kenny Jr. needed payment for his work — payment that normally went to his father.

The doctor said that Ken Sr. shouldn't go back to work for at least six months, possibly a year. Yet I knew that my taking a full-time job (which would be necessary to even come close to meeting expenses, particularly with medical bills) would leave little energy or time to write. My resentment grew. Ashamed of my feelings, I kept them to myself. As my anger and resentment piled up, so did old fears of a punishing God. But instead of punishment, help came.

For the first time in my life, a job came to me: administrator for a women's service program at a salary I'd only dreamed of before. In addition, Ken qualified for disability benefits. (I was very grateful we had taken our accountant's advice and purchased insurance.) For nine months I felt secure again, blessedly unaware a storm was brewing. Like a tornado, the trouble stirred up quickly and destroyed almost everything and everyone in its path.

In nine months' time, I was writing grants and secured enough money to considerably expand the program. But somewhere along the way, enemies plotted against me. During my vacation, those enemies laid their plans. When I returned from my holiday, the board president asked me to resign.

I asked for a hearing. The officers agreed to meet with me. No actual charges were brought against me, although two points of contention came to light. Both pertained to personnel decisions I had made as administrator of the program. The decisions had been approved by the board, but now there seemed to be a change of minds.

When I asked for a full board meeting to discuss the issues, the meeting was granted. However, only a few members spoke, expressing only vague grievances. The bottom line seemed to be that I would not officially say that I was a feminist. (I believe labels limit us.) Since I did nothing wrong and no formal charges of wrong doing were filed, I refused to resign.

There is a law in our state that not-for-profit board meetings must be open to the public except for personal matters such as the final vote on personnel. At the hearing before the board, I brought an attorney and my husband. The president opened with a statement that she was sorry to have guests attending, for they might think "we're just a bunch of catty women."

I told the board that a major grant which received favorable verbal consideration for the following year's funding was based upon my being the administrator. The attorney advised the board that if I were terminated, it would be without just cause. Still, the board voted unanimously to terminate me.

A few weeks later, someone gave me a copy of a woman's magazine with a feature story on "trashing," a term used in those days for women tearing down other women. Now I faced the biggest test of my life (to that time). Not only was I fired, but the board of directors' decision was unanimous. The magazine article described my feelings exactly: Trashed! Here was a huge aught against a lot of anys.

Storm Aftermath: I received unemployment compensation, and Ken was still receiving disability benefits. However, our combined incomes barely covered the basics, and our house taxes were due. Somehow our local Lions Club heard of our dilemma and paid the taxes, even though Ken was not a member. Just when I thought the whole world had turned against us, God brought along a few of his "human angels."

Fortunately Ken's health was improving enough for him to begin looking for a job, so our financial difficulties were soon taken care of. (Due to the stress of self-employment, he discontinued his business.) But my emotional wounds were beginning to fester.

Many of my depressions of the past had descended out of the blue. This time I had a reason. A big one! I spent the first six weeks of unemployment wallowing in self-pity. Feeling like Jonah, I wanted a whale to crawl inside, so I could savor my "justified" hurt and anger. I earned it. I deserved it. I did it. Yuk! But even depression gets boring after a while.

At the library, I looked for something to help me out of the tar pit of anger and despair. Once again, Catherine Marshall's book, *Something More,* called to me. I didn't recall reading the book until the third chapter: "Forgiveness: The Aughts and the Anys."

Marshall's writings are hard to put aside, especially when Someone puts the book into your hands — *again.* Instead of throwing myself into the sea, Jonah-like, I explored my own library shelves. Yes, there it was. My very own copy, marked with my comments in the margins.

There is an old Native American saying, "If you understand, there is nothing to forgive." At first I didn't know what happened. It took many reading and pondering sessions — and much prayer — to understand the hurt and anger so that forgiving became a reality rather than a formality. Thankfully, as my list of grievances against the center's board of directors grew smaller, so did my feelings of resentment and pain. Finally, I was free to move on.

Freeing Others

Forgiveness is a mighty remedy that can free others as well as ourselves. As with my first experience with the "aughts and anys," my renewed strength and energy opened new vistas. I took a part-time job at *The South Bend Tribune,* which led to writing articles for the newspaper's *Michiana* magazine and a short series on ethanol for the daily paper.

With my confidence growing, I left *The Tribune* to start my own business, a bookstore and self-help center called "Horizons Unlimited." In classes, I stressed the importance of forgiveness. One day a student shared the story of her family, broken apart by a disagreement, every family gathering tainted by the aftermath. One family member wouldn't let the conflict die. Every time she brought up the volatile subject, the family took sides and dissension broke out.

One day Edie[2] came to me with a letter she wrote to her family. The letter began, "Dear Ones." Edie avoided the conflict details, focusing on her love for everyone, her desire for them to be a whole, loving family again. She ended with, "I, for one, will no longer participate in this behavior anymore." Edie asked if I thought she should mail the letter. I suggested she wait a few days and let her heart decide.

Edie came back a few weeks later to say she decided *not* to send the letter, to just leave it as a prayer and "let go and let God." Edie found peace, and a surprise "response." Without any knowledge of the letter, the primary agitator wrote Edie a letter stating she was thinking about the situation. She wanted peace in the family and asked if Edie would help her bridge the gap.

2 Name Changed

Edie's letter was void of criticism of any person, yet it clearly stated her awareness of a deep, festering problem that needed forgiveness and release. She had truly released the family through her forgiving "prayer" letter.

"Forgiveness means accepting the core of every human being as the same as yours and giving them the gift of not judging them," says Joan Borysenko, Ph.D., in *Minding the Body, Mending the Mind.* "You can be clear about whether or not a person's behavior is acceptable without judging the person."

Deep Wounds: Sometimes, we hang onto our hurts tightly, feeding and nourishing them through the years until their roots bind us in mind, body and soul.

"The freedom in a simple act of forgiveness saves the expense of anger and the high cost of hatred," says Dyer.

God's rainbows occur when the sun's rays shine on falling rain. The rainbow is a result of internal reflections of the sun's rays by the individual drops of water. A rainbow is a full circle, but only the arc can be seen from the ground. Our forgiveness becomes like the sun reflected through pain and sorrow. Through prayer intercession, we do the forgiving for those who are stuck and create a rainbow of love encircling them. Most of the time, we only see the results of our forgiveness from our side of the spectrum.

My Trusted Friend: During my childhood years, as I moved from home to home, Grandma Gladys became my refuge. Most families I stayed with didn't want to care for a sick child, so they shuttled me off to Grandma. Sometimes I think I got sick just to be with her, for she filled the deep emptiness inside.

After my mother remarried, I visited Grandma often. When I became a young wife and mother, Grandma was my confidant. I could always count on her, so when the time came for her to need someone to count on, I wanted to be that person.

As the years in the nursing home grew in number, my resolve weakened. My trips grew fewer and far between. One day I realized that a year had passed since my last visit.

Grandma was in a nursing home about forty-five minutes away and she had pneumonia. A nurse called Mom to tell her to call the family. When Mom called me, I opted not to go. Exactly a year before, we had received a similar call. That time I went with the intention of helping Grandma to "pass over" into heaven. I thought my love strong enough to let her go. I was mistaken.

The day was hot, the kind that no amount of air conditioning relieves. Grandma lay in bed, curled up like a newborn baby. Her snow-white hair blended into sterile-white sheets — her eyes were closed, her breathing labored.

Nurses attempted to make her comfortable, but she obviously was not. She was tense, her face drawn into a frown.

"Grandma, Grandma, it's Joanne, remember me?" I leaned down to kiss the sunken cheeks and gently stroke her shriveled body. In Grandma's era, a woman "with some flesh on her bones" was considered healthy and strong. Grandma had been such a woman. Healthy and strong in body and in spirit: always the caregiver, never the needy one.

Grandma took in the parents on both sides, a daughter with a heart condition and her two grandsons after her daughter died. She was a midwife and nursed other women's babies when they could not. Grandma had no formal nursing training, but I'm certain she could have passed any board exam. She read every medical article and book she could find. Friends, neighbors and sometimes even strangers came to her for homemade remedies and "tender loving care."

When Grandpa died, Grandma's mental and physical
health deteriorated. Two years later, a police officer
found her at 2 a.m. wandering the streets in her night-
gown. Grandma's three remaining children couldn't
bring themselves to put her into a nursing home, yet no
one could care for her in their own home.

I brought her to our house for a few days, but even
with two teenage daughters still at home and alert,
Grandma managed to leave the house and try to start
my car. So I found a high-quality nursing home. When
I visited Grandma in her new home, she recognized me
only as "the one who took me away, drove me in circles
to confuse me, then left me here."

The good visits occurred when my granddaughter was
with me. Seeing Melanie, Grandma cheered up and
talked to her at length about the good times when
Joanne and her other grandchildren were small.

Now, years later and grown up, I was at Grandma's
bedside, feeling helpless. Only this time there was no
soft lap to climb into, no bosom to lay my head on. The
arms that so often held me were black and blue from
thrashing around to escape a worn-out body.

A nurse pulled a chair next to the bed and I sat down.
She left and I took Grandma's hands in mine.
"Grandma, it's Joanne. I'm here. Don't be afraid. I love
you." Grandma Gladys didn't open her eyes, but I
thought she relaxed a little. Please Lord, don't let her
suffer anymore. Help her go in peace, I prayed silently.

"Grandma, it's okay. You can go now if you want. I
love you," I said aloud.

I closed my eyes and prayed the phrase over and over.
Peace filled me. Grandma's hands slackened. I opened
my eyes. She lay perfectly still, stretched out in a relaxed
position. Her breathing grew more shallow. Panic seized

me. I dropped her hand and fled, crying all the way home.

Grandma recovered to spend another year tied into a wheelchair, fed, dressed and changed like a baby. Ashamed about not being able to stay with her when she needed me most, I didn't go back. I felt responsible that she had to endure another year in the prison of her body. Now here we were at the crossroad once again.

One day passed. Then two. Grandma lingered. *I will not go,* I told myself. *I cannot do this.*

On the third day, I set out on some errands to take my mind off Grandma. Suddenly, I realized my car was heading in the direction of the nursing home.

My heart pounded. I slowed, then speeded up. Slowed again. Hesitating. Knowing I had to go. Fearing I was too late, or worse.

"Lord, help me stay this time," I prayed aloud. As if in answer to my prayer, my mind tuned into the words coming from the radio. "Goodbye to you, my trusted friend....[3]"

Trusted friend. Oh yes, Grandma, you truly were and are my trusted friend.

Grandma was extremely upset, thrashing back and forth. Bars were up on the sides of the bed, a nurse posted nearby. I took Grandma's hand in mine. No words came out, but in my heart I spoke to her.

Grandma, it's me, Joanne. I'm going to stay. It's okay. You can go now.

Grandma thrashed back and forth. Her hands gripped mine tighter. I sensed anger. Fear.

"May I put down this side so I can get closer to her?" I asked the nurse.

---

3 "Seasons in the Sun," English lyrics by Rod McKuen. Music and French lyrics by Jacques Brel.
   Used by permission. All rights reserved.

The nurse came around the bed to put down the safety rail. Then she pulled up a chair for me. Before I sat down, I leaned over and gently hugged and kissed Grandma, my trusted friend. I rubbed her back like she did for me when I was a child.

"Remember how you used to rub my back?" I whispered in her ear. "Remember how we slept spoon fashion in the winter time to keep warm?" Grandma's grip relaxed a bit. Her thrashing slowed. The nurse left us alone.

"Remember how I used to come over to wash your collection of salt and pepper shakers? How you helped the other kids and me put on circuses and plays in your backyard?" As Grandma grew calmer, my panic of the previous year returned. Shutting my eyes tightly, I prayed silently. *Help me.*

Strength swept over me. I felt transported back in time with a clarity of vision I didn't know existed. I saw good times and sad times. In the memories, I saw a major hurt in Grandma's life. She and one of her sisters had a falling out that was never fully reconciled. I began heart talking again.

It's okay. You are forgiven for whatever you may have done. I know you are forgiving Mazie. Then I went through a list of people and events that I believed were problems for Grandma. *Grandma forgives X and X forgives Grandma.*

From the knowns I went into the unknowns. *Grandma, you are forgiven by everyone and everything. Everyone and everything forgives you.* I felt as though I were living the words, not praying them.

I felt the release. The peace that I felt briefly the year before came back stronger. It was as though Grandma and I were suspended in time with no regrets, no fears, just a deep loving incredible peace.

When her hand relaxed completely and her breathing quieted, I did not move away. *It's okay, Grandma, it truly is okay.* We held hands in the silence... in the peace.

Some time passed before I noticed sound in the room — piped-in music from the same radio station I listened to on the way to the nursing home. The same singer's words floated to my ears, "Good bye to you, my trusted friend...."

Tears spilled down my cheeks. I felt a gentle hand on my shoulder and opened my eyes. Nurses in white encircled Grandma's bed. They, too, were weeping.

Grandma looked so beautiful. A glowing smile adorned her face, and her body radiated the whiteness of the sheets. The room seemed lighter, brighter. The nurses standing around her bed seemed surrounded by an angelic glow. Grandma's breathing was no longer labored, just slow and easy. I knew it was time for me to leave.

"Say 'hello' to Grandpa for me," I whispered and kissed her goodbye. I was almost home when I heard the song again. Same radio station. Same singer.

"Goodbye to you, my trusted friend...."

Grandma died two hours after I arrived home, the peaceful smile still on her face. My trusted friend and I had walked together through the valley of the shadow of death and found no fear.

Something is Missing

In the recovery years since Kenny Jr.'s death, I spent much time exploring the strengths that made it possible to get through the mayhem years of constant stormy times and loss. My search covered new authors' slants on old ideas, as well as those philosophers who served me so well in the past. My journals held many revelations, as did conversations with family and friends who share my journey through life.

As each memory came under the scrutiny of current events, doubts dimmed, fears faded. Still, something ate away inside, keeping me from experiencing the total peace I knew was possible.

Like Grandma, I was holding onto some unfinished business. Regrets for things not done or done in anger or malice churned up like lava from a volcano. Although my head told me that some of my actions and omissions stemmed from ignorance and inexperience, I still had trouble letting go the remorse. To forgive another for actions stemming from their ignorance or inexperience is far easier than to forgive oneself.

For me, the regrets of not living up to what I perceived to be a "good and responsible" mother went the deepest. I apologized to those who were living so many times they finally said, "Enough! You did that already. Get over it!" I am working on "getting over it," and every day the load seems lighter.

My heaviest burdens were regrets that I didn't do enough for Kenny Jr. and Henry. Now it was too late to rectify. Ironically, Henry (my foster son) was born almost six weeks before Kenny (1955) and died almost six weeks earlier as well (1994). Although born to different mothers, they both called me "Mom."

After Ken Sr.'s death, Kenny Jr. came to visit me more often. In the last couple of years before his death, he set a regular appointment into his busy calendar for our visits. During those times we shared much. He obviously was concerned about me and wanted me to write the book I kept talking about. He gave me pep talks, books to read and much love.

We last met two weeks before his death. Kenny overslept that morning and was late for our visit. He seemed tense, fatigued. I searched my training, my intuition for questions that might help him find the answer to what troubled him.

Kenny's boss was both demanding and demeaning. I urged him to get his work experiences information together so I could write a resume. "Later, Mom," he said. "I have to prove he can't beat me down."

Kenny had worked three years to build a sales territory, then the company divided it in two. They gave the two parts to inexperienced sales representatives and assigned Kenny a badly neglected territory. Since most of Kenny's income came from commissions, he lost money on the reassignment.

Kenny's obvious stress concerned me, particularly since he was thirty-eight, the age at which his father first had a heart attack. I didn't want to plant seeds, but felt the fear so strongly that I asked the question. "Are you concerned about a heart attack?" Kenny's eyes filled with tears.

"Kenny, the Hill side is only one leg of your heredity," I said, trying to reassure him. "On my side of the family, people live long lives. You are not a smoker, never have been. You have a lot in your favor."

He smiled slightly, reached across the table and took my hand. "Mom, I'll be fine. You worry too much."

A week later he and his wife Lynn came to tell me the good news — they were finally expecting their first child. Kenny also told me that a few days after our visit he made a parachute jump. Kenny appeared happy, vibrant and free of stress.

Just before leaving for Washington, D.C., the following week, I called to ask him to retrieve my car from the airport. I learned he was upset because his boss was trying to delay delivery of a huge sale Ken had closed. If he succeeded, Kenny's commissions would also be delayed and cause him to miss a bonus and "Salesman of the Year" award. Yet he seemed confident it would all work out, telling me once again "not to worry."

Later I chastised myself for not pushing him to see a doctor, get a check up, write his resume or meet me someplace where we could talk more. Something that might have saved him.

These regrets piled on top of the self-blame I already harbored about Henry. Although I had often visited Henry in California during the years he struggled with AIDS and talked with him frequently on the telephone, I was not present when he died.

I had been, however, with Henry and Hector when Hector died. After that, I made several trips to see Henry, the final trip through severe winter weather, to be at his bedside in a hospital. Henry died and was revived (in spite of a Living Will), while I was en route. I remained with him for two weeks while he recovered from his brush with death. We talked a lot about death. We talked about my next visit.

"Don't come back," Henry said. "We've said our goodbyes. You've been through enough."

I returned home and was not with Henry when he died. At first, I consoled myself with the fact that I was with Hector when he died, and Hector's mother was with Henry at his death. In some ways, I felt she and I shared the burden and pain, making it somewhat lighter to bear. As time passed, I wasn't as sure.

Then remembering Grandma's story brought the question, "Have you done the 'aughts and anys' for yourself?" When I did, old guilts, real and perceived, surfaced as well. Amazing what comes up when we dig deeply. No wonder I needed forgiveness!

I agree with of a comment made by Saint Teresa of Avila: "It is a great grace of God to practice self-examination; but too much is as bad as too little."

Perhaps some will say that in my grief I did too much self-examination. Maybe. Maybe not. I once subscribed to a newsletter called "Scrupulous Anonymous," published by a Catholic order of monks. I referred to it as my AA group for people addicted to sainthood.

Sometimes we find it hard to separate regret for something we have no control over with true guilt for something we do have control over. That's where self-forgiveness can save us. Through the self-forgiveness exercise, the perceived separated from the truth, enabling me to accept what could not be changed and change what obviously needed changing.

As I worked on forgiving myself, I came to realize that there was anger with my loved ones because they were no longer here. "Forgiving others for their separations from us involves also forgiving ourselves for willingly being drawn to the mirage that we are separate," says my friend Doug Germann[3]. Doug's reminder that we are all one in the spirit helped me to remember that my loved ones are always with me in my heart.

Released, I could now read through my journal from the year of Henry and Kenny Jr.'s deaths. I discovered I had written about dreams forewarning me. In one dream, Kenny Jr. brought Henry to see me on Mother's Day. Both were still alive at the time of the dream. And, as mentioned earlier, I found the dream I had shortly after Kenny Jr.'s death when he appeared to tell me he was "fine."

I believe this was God's way of preparing me, but I didn't want to accept it. Forgiving myself has freed me to accept what is. According to Dr. Norman Vincent Peale, forgiveness may be no more than "the opportunity to try again, to do better, to be freed from the penalties and shackles of past mistakes." I would add: and freed from unfulfilled intentions and desires.

When we forgive, we release the need to blame or judge ourselves as well as others. We become compassionate, loving unconditionally. "When you begin to realize your own precious, unique self-worth, the need to defend yourself will diminish, and your body will naturally relax," counsels psychologist Joan Borysenko. "The more accepting you become of yourself, the more you can see others in the same light."

---

3 Quoted from Simplifying our lives, by Douglas D. Germann, Sr.

Sweet Surprises

Forgiveness opens doors of opportunity for life-changing experiences and sweet surprises. These mysterious workings obviously come from a Source greater than ourselves.

Besides fewer quarrels, other interesting and surprising changes occurred between my husband Ken and me after my first focused forgiveness adventure. The biggest surprise concerned the toilet seat. Like many other husbands and wives, we often squabbled over that one. I could not understand how he could be so inconsiderate. He could not understand how I could be so stupid as not to check.

One day as I got out of the car, an inner voice said, "Move back the seat." Sometimes Ken would joke about the "midget" who drove the car last and left the seat wedged under the steering wheel. Other times, especially if it was raining or snowing, Ken would get angry as he tried to wedge his body far enough into the car to push the seat back. As I entered the house, an idea came.

"Honey," I said in my most casual voice. "Got a proposition for you."

Ken looked up from his newspaper suspiciously. Seeing the smile on my face, he relaxed. "What do you have in mind?" He grinned back.

"Well, I was just thinking. Maybe we could make a deal. I'll work at remembering to put the car seat further back and maybe you could try to remember to put the toilet seat down."

"Okay," he said, and went back to his paper. I don't recall finding the toilet seat up after that. However, I have to admit, the car seat was left under the steering wheel a few times. Yet there were never any more arguments about either one.

Rounding a corner in a large greeting card shop one day, I saw a familiar face. Although I couldn't place the name, a happy feeling came over me, so I smiled broadly. "Hi! How are you?" I said.

The woman looked startled. *Perhaps, I don't know her after all.* Slowly she smiled back. "I'm fine, Joanne. How are you?"

We chatted a bit, giving each other a brief update about family and work, then moved on. Twenty minutes later as I drove down the street, her name finally came to me. Twelve months before, she was on my "hit list" — a key player in the women's service program firing. I laughed all the way home. The joy in seeing her was real, and the happiness in knowing that I was truly free at last was awesome.

Forgiving is much like gardening — a continuous process. No matter what method of forgiveness we use, sooner or later some pesky person or situation comes along and sows a nasty weed in our tranquil garden. Like the bugs and weeds in our flower beds, hurts and slights need immediate attention if we are to remain healthy and happy.

Forgiveness... the richest gift you can give or receive.

Rainbow Steps
to
Forgiveness

- Say it in person.

- Write a letter.

- Make a telephone call.

- Do the "aughts and the anys."

- Pray for help.

- Include yourself.

A God-incident

When my children were little and people hurt them, especially the kind of pain that affects the heart area, I'd tell them, "Go ahead and cry. That's what God gave us tears for... to wash away the hurt."

However, we can cry too much. During many of my younger days the PLUM disease got the better of me. Remember that "Poor Little Unfortunate Me" curse that erupts into pity parties which can last for days? During my pity parties, I cried. Boy, did I cry! I cried so much my eyes puffed shut and my nose stopped up. When I got going, so did my family. They got as far away from me as possible.

I'll never forget my last "good" pity party. I don't remember what I was "celebrating," but I do recall it was a bang-up job. I wailed. I howled. I sobbed. (Everyone cleared out of the house, including the dogs.) I could barely breathe. Still I cried. I couldn't stop. I cried because I couldn't stop crying!

Scared, I began to pray. Rather, I **changed** my prayer request. Usually, I demanded that God change everyone and everything in my life. Why do I always have to suffer? Why do I have to do all the changing? Life's not fair! Finally, the realization came that God seldom answers why questions. He lets us find our own answers to help us remember them better.

That day, the day of my final crying jag, suffering came because **I chose to suffer.** The reality of that truth didn't set in on that fateful day. However, I became keenly afraid that if the crying didn't stop, I might drown in my tears.

"Oh, God, please help me to stop crying. I truly don't want to do this anymore." With that realization, the wailing started to wind down. When I get up to full steam, it takes a while before the brakes catch hold.

As the last sobs shuddered through my body, something weird happened. Warmth flowed over me, as though Someone had laid a soft blanket across my face and shoulders. I peeked through the slits that had once been eyes. An afternoon sunbeam was streaming in the bedroom window, caressing me.

One last tear drop caught in the corner of my eye. A tip of the sunbeam touched the tear, and in that tiny droplet I saw a rainbow. I believe the tiny rainbow was God's promise that I'd never cry like that again — and I haven't.

Oh, I've shed plenty of tears over each loss and tears of joy during my happy hours. But my eyes don't swell shut, nor does my nose get plugged. When I'm tempted to punish myself through pity parties, God reminds me of the teardrop rainbow.

Soul would have no rainbow
had the eyes no tears.

A. Philip Parham

When I forgive,

I walk lighter ...
breathe easier ...
smile broader ...
live longer ...

Yes
I do!

© Janice D. Cowen

Helping Others Help Themselves

8

*Cheered by the presence of God,
I will do each moment, without anxiety,
according to the strength which He shall
give me, the work his Providence assigns me.
I will leave the rest; it is not my affair.*

François Fenelon

A t first, in the Hotline program, I felt confined by the limitation to serve only as a guide, leading and encouraging callers to find their own answers and make their own choices, and in complicated issues, to seek professional assistance. In the beginning, all our volunteers and the one paid staff (I) were college degreeless, and community mental health professionals feared we would overstep boundaries and cause harm. This sounded harsh, but as I look back, I see God's hand in it.

As a crisis specialist, I loved to meddle. (This is the first time I've admitted this, so please don't tell anyone.) Since I had many personal problems and seemed to be dealing with them okay, people called me to help solve their problems. I tried to do just that. Although I encouraged those most troubled to get counseling, the major drawback to my "consultations" was that I told others what to do, rather than help them find their own answers. Oh, what messes we make when we meddle in others' lives to solve their problems for them! My personal soap opera covered a wide range of protegees, not all appreciative of the results.

Being a crisis-*intervention* specialist confined me to helping callers *help themselves.* The rules forced helpers (called Listeners) to become adept at interviewing and *listening fully* to the caller. Attentive listening enabled us to determine the questions we asked to lead callers to their own solutions. These questions helped them explore options and discover answers for themselves. We did not tell them what to do.

Those of us who prayed used this as a quiet tool to guide us as we guided those on the telephones. Then we let go and let God take it from there. A favorite prayer was the Serenity Prayer:[1]

> *Lord, help me to change the things I can,*
> *Accept the things I cannot change,*
> *And please give me the wisdom*
> *To know the difference.*

We are all part of the Oneness that is God, and we have a responsibility to do something constructive with our lives. Some call this a mission assignment. Some think only special people are called into a mission, that the calling usually applies to religious work. I believe that everyone is born with a mission tucked inside of them. Some of us haven't discovered it. Don't worry. We will... or we may already have and don't realize it yet.

A personal mission is an inner calling to undertake an activity or perform a service. That service can be caring for children as in parenthood, teaching or babysitting. It can be building bridges or sweeping the streets. A mission is what fits our talents, brings harmony to our spirits and puts passion into our lives. We may have what seems like several missions, but when examined closely, we'll see they all have a common thread.

Through the Hotline experience, I discovered my mission was helping others help themselves. Even as a child, I knew that helping others gave me a thrill. Starting the Hotline program did that. The Hotline also brought restrictions; that part

---

1 Reinhold Neibuhr ©1926

about "helping themselves" was new to me. I believe it was the first time I truly let go to let God direct the way.

I had no college degree or special training that qualified me for the job. Yet, when I said "yes" to the calling within, doors opened in exciting and novel ways. In the beginning, there were so many God-incidences in my life, I felt rushed. In one day I had several offers of help, the best coming through the Administrator of St. Joseph's Hospital. Sister Margo promised a room for our telephones. Free of charge!

I nearly skipped out of her office. Praise and thanksgiving flooded my mind, along with questions of what to do next. In the midst of this barrage of joy mixed with worry, I stumbled. My conversation with God was so intense at that point, that without thinking, I looked skyward. "You don't have to push," I said. "I'm working as fast as I can!" A couple coming into the hospital viewed me with concern. (The hospital also housed a psychiatric unit.)

To help others become empowered, we do *not* do for them what they should do for themselves. When we do, we teach dependence. Dependency drains us and diminishes the dependent. We know we've been truly helpful when the person we are assisting becomes independent, capable of solving his or her own problems.

Most of you probably don't deal with the down-and-out person — home-less, jobless, hungry, iso-lated — on a daily basis. Yet every day someone needs help. Some situations are simple: carry a grocery sack, hold a door, watch a child or parent to relieve a caregiver, drop some money in the kettle. That's when we just lend a hand, step in, do the job and leave.

Other circumstances challenge us. A family member, a friend, a co-worker or perhaps a stranger is in crisis. They are bright individuals who can actually empower themselves, but for the time being, they've forgotten how. That's where we come in, not to do it for them, but to help light the way out of the tunnel.

The best helpers possess the following attributes:

- Heart-centered intentions
- Respectful listening skills
- Trusting spirits
- Exploring attitudes
- Loving unattachment

Heart-Centered Intentions

Our intentions determine the kind of help we give. They need to be honest and clear, truly kind and caring about the other person (no hidden agendas) and accepting of the person's *feelings* without judgment. We want to be open and receptive to working toward understanding and unconditional love.

"From the perception of the multisensory human, the intention behind an action determines its effects, every intention affects both us and others, and the effects of intentions extend far beyond the physical world," says Gary Zukav in *The Seat of the Soul.*

Zukav's wisdom makes sense, particularly in the hindsight view of various experiential outcomes from events in my life. When I compare the experiences of the crisis intervention service, the Hotline, and my work at the women's service center, I see a vast difference of intention going into each employment experience.

With the Hotline, my original intention was to provide a service to the community, to bring awareness of a growing drug abuse problem. The women's program, however, was just a happy opportunity for me to earn some money. Once I became familiar with the project, my true intention came into focus. I admit it was not an altruistic one. While I did want to help women improve their lives, my major goal was to show what a great fundraiser and administrator I could be. I was still smarting from being "demoted" at the Hotline. (I was also looking for an increase in pay when the grants came through.)

Looking back, from the viewpoint of intention, I also see a point in the Hotline adventure when I became disenchanted with the bureaucracy. Anger and resentment pushed aside benevolent intentions. I got off course and helped set in motion events that led to my leaving the program, hurt and spent. What a lesson!

Without those experiences, I would not have learned how to deal with the years that followed. Nor would I have had the satisfaction that comes from rising out of the rubble and building anew. That is the feeling we want to see in those we help to help themselves.

To accomplish that, we must be willing to accept each person as God's child with the potential to decide on his or her own solution. We must be unattached to the outcome.

As we begin to help someone in distress, we drop into the silence. We look and listen to our hearts. We ask the questions that will focus our intentions on that which will benefit the one we serve.

> *What is my intention?* Answer honestly, clearly.
> *Is my intention kind and caring?* No hidden agendas.
> *Is my intention accepting of the other person's feelings?*
> *Is my intention free of judgment?*

*Is my intention open and receptive to working toward
   understanding?*
Is my intention built on unconditional love?
*Am I willing to allow the other person to decide for him-
   or her-self?*
Am I willing to be unattached to the outcome?

Respectful Listening

Successful helping begins with respectful listening. We make contact at a feeling level. The Hotline was a telephone service only. So we had to tune in our ears. Many listeners had difficulty at first, but I watched with amazement as one volunteer, Donna, breezed into the task with fervor. Blind since childhood, she taught us a lot about the power of intentional listening.

Knowledge sometimes stands in the way of listening, particularly if that knowledge comes from years of experience. Our inclination is to jump in, quickly solve the problem for the person in crisis and leave. That is like giving a man a burger and fries so he can eat today, but he won't know how to find food for tomorrow unless he goes begging again.

Sometimes we are afraid of the silence. We're afraid our silence will scare away the person we want to help. "When we let natural silences fall, we'll still stay connected," says Lee Glickstein in *Be Heard Now.*

When our intentions come from unconditional love, our silence says, "I trust you. I'm here for you. Feel free to speak for I am listening. I will wait until you are ready."

Respectful listening is compelling, it draws from the deep well of truth inside. Every Hotline training session began with a reading of Marjorie Holmes prayer, "Lord, Make Me Aware of People."[2] My favorite part is:

---

2 From *Who Am I, God?* by Marjorie Holmes. Used with permission. All rights reserved.

Remind me to listen, really listen when people open their mouths, like small doors to that [their] world, and try to share what's inside. Remind me to look, really look, into the hopeful windows of their eyes. I can never really enter, no, but how much I can learn from these brief glimpses. How much my own world can be expanded. (And how much I can give just by listening.)

Our most effective listening comes in silence... ours. We keep our focus on the person speaking and listen not only with our ears, but with our hearts, tuning into their emotions as an *observer*. We put our emotions aside. Connecting at a heart level means we listen intently to what is said, and what is *not* said. Heart listening means acceptance and caring, not judgment and advice.

If the troubled person becomes stuck, we can help them reconnect to their own thoughts by mirroring back what we heard through questions or associative statements, such as:

"How does that make you feel?" If they don't respond, or say it doesn't bother them, we can say something like, "Hum. I think if I were in your place, I'd be very hurt... angry... lonely... " or whatever emotion we sense coming from the person in crisis. When we listen with our heart, we intuitively pick up the feelings.

Sometimes we won't be quite on target and the person will correct us. This is great, for we cannot always know what it is they feel, and our sensory perception may be off. They may also be testing us, to see if we really do care. When we accept their right to feel as they do, even when those feelings fluctuate, we show trust.

If we come across as condemning or judging, the speaker will feel rejected. Given the same circumstances, we might feel the same way. Accepting another's feelings can become a good lesson in self-help. When we judge others, we also judge ourselves.

"When people are talking, there's no need to do anything but receive them. Just take them in," advises Rachel Naomi Remen, M.D. "Listen to what they're saying. Care about it. Most times caring about it is even more important than understanding it.

"Listening is the oldest and perhaps the most powerful tool of healing. It is often through the quality of our listening and not the wisdom of our words that we are able to effect the most profound changes in the people around us."

Intuitive listening is a basic element in practicing medicine, maintains Dr. Remen in her book, *Kitchen Table Wisdom*. Physicians who attend Remen's workshops and open themselves to their own intuitive powers find interesting results.

Sometimes our intuition tells us what to do at the time. Perhaps it's reaching out and taking hold of a hand, or offering to say a prayer. Other times, intuition may surprise us with a common-sense response to a strange situation.

I remember a story related to me by a psychiatrist friend from his intern days. In the state hospital where Hal interned lived a man who could climb the library shelves and squeeze himself into the tiny space between the top shelf and the ceiling. One day, as Hal stood pondering what he might say or do to get the man down, a cleaning lady came into the room. She looked up, called the man by name and ordered him down immediately. The man obeyed. Instinct triumphed over scholarly learning.

Dr. Remen gives four questions we can use to test our intuition: "Is there some reason not to do this? Would following my intuitive insight cause anyone harm? Would it delay or negate some needed treatment? Would it embarrass or humiliate anyone?"

Trusting Spirit

We must trust the ability of the other person, ourselves and God's Spirit within each of us to solve problems. Every individual has an inner creativity that pushes to find solutions. So why do people get so down? Why are they homeless? Drug addicts? Alcoholics? They've forgotten how to use their creativity in a *positive* way, or they weren't taught how to use it or were discouraged from trying. How else would a homeless person manage to survive for years on the street? A druggie support his or her habit?

What about those who don't survive? They give up. They push themselves to the point of no return and let go of that creative power within. The power doesn't fail them, they fail to use it wisely, constructively.

Effective helping is trusting the other person, ourselves and God's Spirit within each of us to come together for healing and empowering resolution. There is a danger, however. As we trust enough to open ourselves to the other person's emotions, we sometimes fall into their pit of despair and therefore become ineffective.

"A helper does not do for the other person what he can or should do for himself," Melba Laird, MSW, advised each new group of Hotline volunteers. "You can't help someone out of a ditch if you crawl in with him." True. If we crawl in and push him out, we're stuck. But we can put down a ladder and encourage him to climb out.

The Ladder of Encouragement: We've all seen miracles happen when the underdog is cheered to victory by an impassioned crowd. People accomplish amazing feats through brief encounters with enthusiastic encouragement.

At a seminar for professional women, the speaker asks for a volunteer to break a board in half. She wants someone who has never done this before and has no experience in a martial art. The speaker chooses a middle-aged kindergarten teacher, a cuddly grandmother type, sweet and shy.

The speaker asks for two volunteers to serve as cheerleaders. She stations one in front on the audience's right side, the other on the left. Then she helps them get the two sides competing in cheering: "Yes. Yes! YES!" Once she feels the cheerleaders and their groups are strongly competing, she combines the two sides for even more energetic confidence building: "YES! YES! YES!"

Next, the speaker shows the teacher how she wants her to stand, hold her arm and thrust it forward when the audience shouts, "GO!" The two go through a few practice runs. The speaker tells the cheerleaders to get the audience fired up. "YES! YES! **YES!**" At the peak, the seminar leader nods her head. The audience shouts, "GO!"

No one is more amazed than the teacher when the board splits in half with one swift movement forward. Her face goes from amazement to joy. Her body stands taller and straighter at the realization of her own empowerment. Such success demonstrates that our ladders are tools that teach, guide, encourage and empower others to help themselves.

The Ladder of Guidance: Ladders come in all sizes and shapes, especially when used as a tool for guiding. Art therapist Lemuel Joyner uses music and art to help people climb out of their ditches of despair.

Back in the 1970s, when our government mandated the closing of mental institutions, our local Mental Health Center opened a Day Care Center. Many patients, institutionalized for years and now released, had low self-esteem, a history of helplessness and few skills for living in the world. They were terrified. Lem was in charge of the local program.

The Hotline office was in the same building, so there were many occasions when I had the privilege of watching Lem at work. One day vividly stands out.

The program was new and untried: the building was an old house with many small rooms. Lem was showing the clients how to work with clay. Since clay modeling is a messy project, the group squeezed together in the tiny kitchen.

On the floor, Lem placed a large square of wood. On it, he piled several lumps of wet, gray clay. To show his clients how to work air bubbles out of the clay, Lem demonstrated each process. Slowly, he kneaded the clay, gently explaining each step. At times he punched and pounded on it, pointing out the subtle changes in the clay as he worked to make it pliable, ready for sculpting. Most of the clients watched in fascination. One sat cross-legged in a corner, a blank stare on his face.

Picking up the mound of clay, Lem raised it high overhead and slammed it down. Whop! Some startled, laughing nervously. Splat! The clay splattered into pieces. The man in the corner began to sob.

"What's wrong?" Lem asked empathically.

"That's me," he sobbed. "That's me."

Lem smiled his gentle smile, knelt down and calmly pulled the pieces into a smooth ball. "Ah, but look," he said. "We can put ourselves back together." The man blinked, smiled and moved in closer. Later Lem showed me a shapely bread loaf sculpted from the clay. The man in the corner formed the piece as a symbol of his rising from the clay into a nourishing substance.

Lem also used music in his programs, particularly a recording of the *Desiderata*[3], to help his clients find self-worth. One time, after listening for several hours to a distraught friend, I played the recording. Since it worked well with Lem, I thought it might help my friend Jean[4].

Jean's problems were numerous and complicated. Even if she had been receptive, I found no questions to ask her. Jean's

---

3 ©1927 by Max Ehrmann. All rights reserved. Reprinted by permission
   Robert L. Bell, Melrose, Mass. 02176
4 Name changed

need was simply to vent and vent she did. When she was finished, I asked her to relax in a lounge chair and listen to the
words and music of this magnificent poem. It includes the message, "You are a child of the Universe, no less than the trees
and the stars; you have a right to be here."

My intuitive spirit led me to this action. The words of the
song touched Jean's spirit. The next day she acknowledged a
drinking problem and joined Alcoholics Anonymous.

The Ladder of Assurance: One day my daughter Laura told
me about the prenuptial classes she and her husband Doug
had attended years before.

"I don't think we got much out of the classes except for one
night," she confided. "That night Father Murphy came in, put
on a record and left. We've both said that listening to that song
made the most sense of all the instructions."

"What song was that?"

"'Do You Love Me?'⁵ from *Fiddler On The Roof.*⁶"

I grinned, remembering a time when the same song served
as a ladder to help Ken and me climb out of the trouble in our
marriage. I shared the story with her.

"Remember when your dad and I went to a Marriage
Encounter weekend? We were separated at the time." Laura
nodded.

"Had the leaders known our situation, I'm sure we would
have been asked to withdraw, as the program was not designed
for marriages in trouble. I went with a bag of books to read,
and your dad took his portable bar. Since we each felt the other
was to blame for our problems, I think our hidden agenda was
simply to be able to say, 'See, I tried, but I knew this wouldn't
work either.' At least, I know that was mine.

"The Marriage Encounter leaders did as the priest did for
you and Doug. They put on the same record and left the

5 Music by Jerry Bock and Lyrics by Sheldon Harnick
6 Stage and screenplay by Joseph Stein

room." Laura and I fell silent, remembering the song and our experiences with it.

According to tradition, matchmakers, not the individuals involved, arranged marriages. In *Fiddler On The Roof,* three daughters, Tzetel, Hodel and Chava, are rebelling against the tradition, wanting to make their own choices. "Because I love him," they beseech their father. Tevye doesn't understand this. He is the "Papa." His children do as he says. Besides, "What is love?" he asks himself.

Pondering the question, Tevye goes to his wife, Golde. He wants to know if she loves him. This begins a musical discussion about love. Golde thinks it might be Tevye's indigestion. But Tevye is serious; he needs to know. Golde sings to her husband.

Now Golde ponders the question, recalling all the things she's done through the years: tending the children, washing the clothes, cooking the meals, even milking their cow.

The couple then reminisces about how they met on their wedding night. Tevye admits to being afraid and Golde acknowledges she was shy. Both were nervous. Because they were obedient to their faith and family tradition, they accepted the arrangement. But now their children are questioning, defying tradition. They want to make their own choices based on love.

As Tevye and Golde reflect on their life together in song, they come to realize that the greatest demonstration of love is tending each other's needs and doing their best to help a family grow.

As Ken and I listened to the song, our marriage and our love, took on a different hue. We went home and for the first time in our married lives, we both worked on our marriage *at the same time.* The Marriage Encounter put us in touch with each other's spirits by helping us understand how we were wounding each other's spirits. It worked. Our thirty-eighth wedding anniversary came seven weeks after Ken's death.

In both instances, the music was turned on and the leaders left the rooms, trusting the listeners to find their own answers. Trusting ourselves and the other person is working from a point of reverence for the God-given wisdom within each person to bring revelation and renewal.

Today there are similar programs for troubled marriages. One is called Retrouvaille. (For more information on these programs, see Resource Section.)

An Exploring Attitude

My most memorable episodes of helping others to find their own answers come with little input on my part. However, there are times when a person needs something more than a non-judgmental ear. That's when a kind, careful, loving exploring attitude is useful.

When we remain observers and stay unattached to the outcome, we become expert explorers, getting better results and having fun in the process. Exploring is asking open-ended questions to lead the crisis-affected person into a calm, thinking mode for possible solutions. Good questions also act as guides for testing various possibilities.

Anthony Robbins, a leader in self-mastery workshops, stresses the importance of questions. "Questions themselves have the power to make the most changes in your life... or to bring you the most pain," he says.

Empowering questions that help us help ourselves or someone else are those that begin with words and phrases that will bring positive answers. For example, don't look for answers to, "Why does this always happen to me?" Instead, ask another question: "What can I do that would prevent this from happening again?" When the person we are helping asks the disempowering "why" question, change it into an empowering "what" question.

Asking questions that help to find solutions is a good mentoring technique. "A mentor is a kind of soul mate and carrier of souls, a kindred spirit who sees something special in us, not just as we already are but as we could become," says Greg Levoy. According to Levoy, author of *Callings*, there is another side to mentoring — being a "tor-mentor."

"A tor-mentor is supportive but won't mechanically slather on reassurance at every turn when what we may need is an honest acknowledgement that the path is slippery when wet, and it's often wet. The outcome is iffy, as it is with all risks, and every dream has its small print," maintains Levoy.

I like Levoy's definition and his coined spelling of the word "tormentor," for it signifies a proceeding with caution. There are times when confrontation is the answer. Pursued in anger, with an intention to control another, it will surely backfire. Pursued with careful consideration and love, our chances are pretty good it will succeed.

Remind yourself and the person you are helping that most things take time. The real world isn't like a fast-food restaurant, and we wouldn't want it to be. One flavor. Fried. Yuk!

This chapter covers only a brief summary of the most important elements behind our questions, not the myriad of possibilities for questions. We can keep in mind the steps covered in the crisis dynamics chapter: trust our intuition, pray and expect our questions to bring positive results.

Crisis dynamics for helping others help themselves:

- Make contact at a feeling level.
- Identify feelings.
- Accept the right to feel that way.
- Reflect what you hear and see.
- Explore the problem *now.*
- Explore resources for options and resolution.

Remember also to:

- Hand down a rope or ladder. Stay out of the ditch.
- Trust the person to make his or her own right decision.
- Praise the effort made. Cheer them on.
- Learning comes from failure.
- Let go and let God work out the details.

Loving Unattachment

When I love enough to remain unattached to my own agenda for another, to let go and let God guide me in the relationship, I feel a spiritual bonding. When that happens, the experiences we share bring about the best for both of us.

"Again I say to you, if two of you agree on earth about anything they ask, it will be done for them by my Father in heaven."[7] The key word here is "agree." When our only intention is to be of service — to help someone find his own answers, and to trust him to decide *for himself* — then we can easily let go and let God take care of the outcome. We have fulfilled the "agreement" between all parties to share in this marvelous life experience called "growth." Here are some ways to help us let go:

Pray Affirmative Prayers: Silent prayer, prayer partners and written prayers all help to make this world a better place in which to live. One potent prayer method came during a time when I felt totally helpless to help someone who seemed incapable (at the time) of helping herself. Since Debbie is my daughter, it was hard to stay unemotional. In fact, I was frantic.

---

7 Matthew 18:19 Revised Standard

Shortly after Debbie's diagnosis of bipolar depression, I received a midnight telephone call from a Florida hospital emergency room. Debbie was brought in for treatment, refused it and left. No one knew where she went. I was in Indiana. There was no way I could get to her in a short time. Trained in crisis intervention, I knew that by the time I did get there, her crisis would be past. In the meantime all I could do was pray.

I lay back in bed, tears streaming into my ears, frustrated and afraid. *All I can do is pray. What good is that?*

"What good is prayer? That's all you can do? All!" The words rang in my head so distinctly I sat up to see if anyone else was in the room. Seeing the room empty, I pondered the words. "All," is that "all" you can do? Feeling ashamed that my doubts had brought the message so strongly to mind, I mumbled aloud.

"Sorry, God. No offense. It's just that I need to feel like I'm doing something."

God's a good listener. He shuts up most of the time and just lets me talk. I rambled about wanting to let go, how hard it was, how I needed something tangible to hang onto... yackety-yak. He must have grown tired of my whining about "something I could see... do," for an idea of a power prayer page came to mind.

Like a treasure map, a prayer page is a collage of words and pictures to help us visualize what we want. I got out of bed, found a clean piece of white paper, a picture of a happy, smiling, healthy Debbie, scissors, glue and a pen. As I continued to pray for her safety and Divine guidance, I pasted her picture in the center of the page, surrounding it with optimistic statements: "Joy!" "Inner Peace." "Whole Healthy Body." I put in prayers for myself: "I am guided to help my child attract and express only good."

Each time I got nervous about her well-being, I looked at the power prayer page and read every affirmation aloud, ending with a thank you and affirmation: "Debbie is surrounded by guardian angels, and all is well."

Two days later, Debbie called to say she was getting the help she needed. She now enjoys good health, a happy marriage, a rewarding job and a beautiful home. I now have a notebook filled with power prayer pages. They are part of my "help" while God and his other children do their work.

Plant Seeds: We can also give support by planting "seeds" of helpful information. For years I left my self-help books and tapes around the house, hoping the family would read or listen to them. Now they discover exciting new concepts and buy me tapes and books. When Oprah Winfrey started her "Finding Your Spirit" segment, daughter Brenda called to tell me to tune in. "I know you don't like talk shows, Mom," she said, "but Oprah sounds just like you. You've got to hear this." I tuned in and was hooked.

Encouragement through the sharing of books, tapes and other little treasures serves as pick-me-ups, touchstones and optimism boosters. We can also put positive nourishment around the house with fun posters. Kids get turned off by preaching, but they love posters. For Christmas gifts one year, daughter Cindy made parchment scrolls. On them she carefully calligraphed various truisms. My favorite was, "The best way to get even is to forget."

We can send greeting cards, funny and motivational enclosure cards. Small pins or figurines make good ladders to help friends or co-workers out of a slump. When my husband died, my friend Marilyn sent me cheerful notes and cards. She continued this on a weekly basis for two years. Each arrival filled me with joy and gratitude.

For nearly forty years, my friend Marie Leddy has given tiny ladybug pins. "This is a symbol of good luck, good fellowship and love," she says as she pins the bugs on people. Most recipients are in awe of this loving gift from a stranger. Watching Marie spread the ladybug message is as wondrous to me as watching a rainbow form. Frequently the recipient will relate how timely this little gift is, as they have just received disturbing news and need a sign to give them strength to face what lies ahead. Other times they say they will share the pin with someone else who "really needs this." When they do that, Marie gives them a second pin.

Cheer Lead: Friends and family supply me with mugs, magnets and plaques with rainbows, hummingbirds and angels. Some carry messages, such as "Don't Quit" or "Hang In There." In every room of my house, in my car and in the "Hummingbird" (RV), I see touchstones that cheer me on, reminding me of those who help me. Their gifts remind me that someone believes in me.

No matter what the problem, how difficult the situation or how minor, there is always a ladder to help us help others help themselves. Know what we get when we do? Awesome rainbow feelings.

Good Scouts are Prepared

The Boy and Girl Scouts' motto is "Be Prepared." This advice must be heeded if we are to be at our best in helping others. Here are seven tips for keeping prepared and for gaining new techniques for helping others.

1. Read books, listen to tapes, attend self-help workshops.
2. Watch how other people listen; give support.
3. Listen to how others ask questions. What kinds of responses do they get? Are they helpful? If you can stand it, tune into an occasional talk show that incites. See how it should not be done!
4. Make changes in yourself. People, particularly children, learn by observation. Monkey see, monkey do — an old

saying more true today than ever before. As parents, teachers, ministers, mentors, leaders, we have a big job: offsetting advertisers' and media gurus' erroneous messages of self-indulgence and self-pity.

5. Take care of your body as well as your mind and spirit. This helps you stay alert and prevents burnout.

6. Be open and receptive and share the responsibility for saving the world. We all have a stake in this planet.

7. Remember, it is the silence between the notes that makes the music. Take time out to be in the silence, to listen to your intuition.

Together we sing a chorus of love and understanding as we help each other help ourselves.

Rainbow Ingredients
for
Helping Others

- Heart-centered intentions

- Respectful listening

- Trusting spirit

- Exploring attitude

- Loving unattachment

- Preparation

- Prayers

Remember: God is in charge and all is well.

A God-incident

Carrabelle, FL
(Journal entry eight months after Kenny Jr.'s death)

It was an overcast day today, but still quite nice, as it wasn't cold or rainy. As I walked the beach this morning, I was lost in gloomy thoughts... to match the sky... and not looking at anything in particular, when I felt there just might be a dolphin. I began to watch the ocean then, and sure enough there was one, not too far out. He swam along with me for quite some distance; then I turned and headed back as he kept on going.

For a few minutes, while walking along with the dolphin, I stopped feeling sorry for myself and actually began to think in a joyful manner. The feeling, like the dolphin, came and went... but at least it came!!! Tonight, just before sunset, I walked again. Once again lost in thought... only this time I was having a little discussion with God about why I had to wake up depressed in such a beautiful setting. The feeling [about the dolphin being there] returned and as I looked, there he was. This time he stayed with me. If he got too far ahead, he would disappear for a bit, then suddenly be swimming in a circle right in front of me. So close I was afraid he'd get beached.

In my mind I talked to him. Thanked him for coming. As it happened a couple of more times, I became concerned that maybe he was in trouble. I prayed he was okay and told him to go further out, that he had the whole ocean.

Then the thought came that maybe he, too, was staying close to shore all alone to get his thoughts together. I began to think about our similarities. He was alone, but he belonged in a pod. Isn't that their usual way? He seemed lost and confused. I feel that so much. I came out here to be "alone" and I've done a pretty good job of keeping my distance from people. They are friendly, but not pushy to *get me to join in. I'm glad… and sad. For I feel anti-social, yet I know if I get involved in the little nonsensical conversations, I won't get done what I came here to do.*

What did I come here to do? Forget? I can't forget because I don't want to. I long to be able to enjoy just one more day with them [those who died]. Yet, I'm not enjoying days with the ones who are still living. I feel guilty for that. I feel guilty for not writing, for sleeping so much, for not staying in touch with all the people who want me to stay in touch, for not wanting to take care of anyone else's stuff anymore.… Those ugly thoughts race around in my head like the little crabs on the sandy beach.

I feel guilty every time I leave… like I'm betraying my family and friends and guilty whenever I stay at home… like I'm betraying myself and my spirit. I think I know my mission, but I don't do it. I feel beaten even though I'm not running a race… have no competition.

I'm running away but there is no place to run to and nothing to do when I get there. Oh, there is something to do… only I don't do it. Every little thing I do is an extreme effort… whether it is fixing myself something to eat, taking the dogs for a walk, writing a postcard or taking a shower. I put off taking showers for days now. I'm beginning to get scared that I'm losing ground… sinking. I don't think I can tread water anymore, and I don't know if I remember how to swim.

My dolphin seemed to say to me that we all need to get away by ourselves to get ourselves in balance. I feared that the dolphin would come in too close and get beached. I kept saying, "Go out… you need to leave the shore or you'll die." (He was so close I could have walked in and petted him.)

I thought about myself on the way back to the Hummingbird… I had to leave the safety of my family and go into the deep water of traveling down that lonesome road. Yes, I do have to take precau-

tions, for I can get myself into trouble... get beached if I go too far away... in mind and thought. But the dolphin's odd behavior, it's obvious focus upon me, seemed to be a special message from God. "I'm here. Don't worry. Be happy. You'll be safe."

I was so energized coming back from my walk thinking about writing in my journal that I was really clipping along. No pain.

The sun is out again... outside, and in my heart. Praise God.

The dolphin stayed with me the entire walk, about two miles, turning around when I did to come back to my starting place.

Support Systems 9

A faithful friend is the medicine of life.

Ecclesiastes 6:16

A good support system provides protection, comfort and assurance during good times, bolsters and sustains us through the difficult times. To thrive, not just survive, our support system must nourish spirit, bolster courage, comfort, console and confirm, assist in maintaining or regaining equilibrium and sustain us during difficult times. To build and maintain a good system, we must know our needs and inner strengths, be in touch with our authentic selves. We must remember that support systems work two ways: giving and receiving. They support us and we support them.

This rainbow remedy begins with a strong foundation of faith, framed with family and friends, filled with books, tapes and other tools to comfort, teach and insure us that we will make it through the challenging times. Helping networks are expanded through church, work and social groups, augmented with special interest clubs and associations. The goal is for a structure where we feel safe and free to ask for the blessing of assistance, an arrangement that can include prayer partners. Asking for help is opening the door for God's special people to lend a hand, bringing angels knocking on our doors.

Richard Ackenhusen, a Methodist minister and my stepfather's brother, gave a Thanksgiving service one year that I never forgot. His theme was so foreign to me that, at first, I felt shock. Uncle Richard began by sharing his gratitude for being needy. Did I hear him correctly? Gratitude because one needed help? Support? Weren't ministers supposed to preach about how we were to give? How other people's needs came before ours? As Uncle Richard spoke, the concept took shape, and for the first time in my life, I realized the selfishness that comes through the pride of total self-sufficiency. We are here to receive as well as to give. A support system is also the other half of helping — the receiving half.

Foundation of Faith

What we learn as children forms the bulk of our faith, begins to shape who we are and what we need. We are exposed to a variety of beliefs as children, and what we choose to learn from that exposure builds our basic belief system. Mine was a combination of Bible stories and fairy tales portraying the good conquering the bad. In that early gathering of knowledge, my faith in something good coming out of trouble took root. Finding positive role models to emulate developed my strong survival skills — skills that included helping others as well as myself.

No matter what we are taught, we still have a choice in what we believe. We take the messages inward, examine them in our spirit self to find our true authenticity and our life purpose. When we do this, our systems provide true benefit and empowerment. When we resist the messages and claim we have no faith, we choose to believe we are victims of circumstances with no purpose.

In doing this, our systems are no longer supportive, but dependent. Dependence on another to decide what is best for our lives, traps us in situations that leave us powerless, even though we may feel "cared for." This is what is known as "codependence," an unhealthy and non-supportive relationship. True support helps us achieve independence.

We must take an active role in preparing and using the system we help to create. Remember the Power of Choice remedy: even when we feel the most vulnerable, we still have a choice.

For some, life and death situations bring a sense of powerlessness. We feel that we have no choice in who controls our situation, that we must accept the experts' opinions. If you ever felt that way, take heart in Della Reese's story.

When the talented singer and actor was stricken with an aneurysm, she was rushed to a hospital and examined by a prominent neurosurgeon. However, the doctor was pessimistic, lacking in faith. Della Reese's inner wisdom told her this was not the person to strengthen her in the positive faith-filled way she needed, and she ordered him out. The next physician had the deep faith and positive outlook she was looking for, plus a new medical intervention clip he had designed that saved her life.

What do our beliefs have to do with getting help? What we believe in will determine what kind of aid we get. The backing we want to receive is freeing, spiritually uplifting and strengthening. Unfortunately, not all beliefs uphold freedom. In Della Reese's case, the first physician believed only in the surgery process, and although he was a skilled surgeon and willing to do the surgery, his prognosis was negative. For the actress that was not enough. She wanted someone who believed as she did — in a Higher Power working with the doctor and her for complete recovery.

When we look to others to do for us what we can and should do for ourselves, we become dependent. That is not support; it is control. We must become fully aware of what we believe if we are intent on building a nurturing foundation that frees us.

For many, the first awareness of faith comes through the family's religion. My childhood religious training was confusing, as the messages received in Sunday School seemed in conflict with what was preached in church services. In Sunday School I learned about a Jesus who was loving and caring. He forgave the sinner, found the lost and healed the sick. "Gentle, meek and mild." In the church service that followed, the message came across differently. The pastor might begin slowly, on a light note, but when he sucked in a deep breath, I knew the next message came with pointed finger (straight at me, it seemed) in a voice strong enough to shake the windows. "Gawd's going to get you if you don't change your ways. NOW!" The pulpit shuddered as the minister's fist pounded his point across it.

When it came to who God really was, my heart told me one thing, my head another. Although Jesus was the son of God, somehow they were also one, and I didn't know which one carried the most weight. Jesus loved me; God punished me. I thought if I could just be "good enough," Jesus could go to bat for me and persuade God to heap rewards upon me. But no matter what I did, or how good I thought I was, bad things still happened.

After Mom married my stepfather, we went to a church that emphasized God's love. Still, my early training was to see God as judging and punishing, rather than loving, helping and forgiving. Harder still was accepting God as already within me,[1] and all I needed to do was be still and know.[2] Until I recognized that foundation, none of the other systems God had put into place could reach me. Faith's core is to *know* that no matter what happens, you already possess whatever you need to get you through every difficulty you encounter. First comes desire to know, then comes trust that you know and then comes the knowing.

We also build our faith through watching and learning. Some of the watching and learning comes firsthand with real

1 Luke 17:21
2 Psalms 46:10

individuals, some through reading, watching movies or hearing stories. We've all heard stories or seen movies of heroes who make daring rescues. When asked how they did it, they reply, "I don't know. It was just something inside me that happened." To discover more about your beliefs and strengths, look at whom you most admire.

"People live in direct relation to the heroes and sheroes they have," Maya Angelou told the Economic Club of Southwestern Michigan College.[3] Who were your earliest heroes and sheroes? Who are they now? What did you learn from them that bolsters you in time of need?

One of my earliest heroes was *The Little Engine That Could.* The Little Engine watched big engines steam their way up steep hills, then puff with pride at how "easy" it was for them. But every time the Little Engine tried to climb the hill, he got bogged down by fearful thoughts. "I hope I can. I hope I can," he puffed unsuccessfully. Trying to get up the hill was frustrating, but the Little Engine refused to quit trying.

One day The Little Engine took a different approach, chanting, "I think I can. I think I can. I think I can," as he chugged slowly up the hill. As the top came into view, he joyously puffed harder. "I know I can. *I know I can.* **I know I can.**" Whenever faced with the "can't-ers" of life, something inside me still kicks in with, "Yes, I can. Yes, I can."

As I grew older, "Wonder Woman" sprang from the comic book pages to give me courage to stand tall, take on the mighty challenges of the teen years and do all in my power to be my best. She taught me to fight for the underdog, look for the good and resist evil.

Angel stories were also a favorite, particularly the ones in which angels served as protectors or guides. With angels around you, how can you not feel protected? Accepting guidance isn't as easy.

3 May 18, 1995

Through those early years, when my faith was a tiny seedling, I often imitated my heroes and sheroes. When life was good, I thought my way was working, but my way soon came disillusionment, discouragement and dejection. Then I tried begging prayers. Demanding prayers. Those didn't get me far either. Not until I figured out the praise and thank you formula, did my life begin to take on a happy glow.

> ## NOTHING HAS CHANGED BUT MY ATTITUDE. EVERYTHING HAS CHANGED.
> ANTHONY DE MELLO

Some people feel they do not need faith. Yet they use faith every day in driving the freeways, flying in airplanes or eating in restaurants. To participate in these activities, they trust that a drunk driver won't cross the center line, the airplane motor keeps running and the food is not poisoned with bacteria. We all put our faith in something every day. Why not put it into our Higher Power? That power does more than get us through the traffic; it transforms the wait into enlightening experiences.

Inner Wisdom

Faith also comes from inner strengths discovered through those quiet times when we stop, look, listen and learn. When we dig past the problem to see how we handled it, we are often surprised to learn that we did much better than we thought. With each realization, our victories come more quickly and easily through gained insight, wisdom and strength. Others may point out a strength we've not been aware of before or something that may seem to us as a weakness.

Some years back, my oldest daughter, Deborah, became ill and lost her job. By the time she recuperated and found another, she had accumulated many debts. I visited her home the day she received her first paycheck from a new employer. On the table was a beautiful Pocketbook plant, named for the puffy purse-shaped blooms. I stared at the plant.

"I know it was foolish," she said. "I have so many bills... but it was only $3.00 at the market and I needed something pretty."

For a few moments I struggled to respond without crying. Foolishness? No. Strength. Courage. Wisdom. That's what I saw. Debbie's inner wisdom knew her body was on the mend, and her soul needed to celebrate the survival. I shared my observations with Debbie and made a promise to give myself flowers. When was the last time you gave yourself a bouquet in celebration of making it through the storm?

Books, Tapes and Other Stuff

I once read that Margaret Mitchell used her original manuscript of *Gone With the Wind* to prop up a legless couch. In our family, large books often served as booster chairs for the smallest children so they could reach the table. "A book may look inanimate, but like a home, it lives, breathes, and expresses your being," writes Sarah Ban Breathnach in *Simple Abundance*. When opened and read, a book becomes teacher, friend, therapist and lover — as real as another human being. Each book, each story, each quote, whether in the Bible or from an inspirational author, is molded into firm foundation blocks to hold us up in times of distress.

Whether it's stories of real-life survivors or fantasy heroes and sheroes, it makes little difference. Each brings words of wisdom, sparks ideas and plants seeds for personal growth. My love of books has given me the tools to build confidence, courage and strength to face life's storms. Authors and characters became my friends, my mentors. Magazines served equally, particularly the women's magazines: *Woman's Day, Family*

Circle, McCall's, and *Good Housekeeping.* The self-help articles always held some nugget of advice or inspiration to use in my life. "Can This Marriage Be Saved?" in *Ladies Home Journal,* was a priceless resource for me during my marital strife.

Music is another great supporter. Melodies and lyrics reinforce determination or soothe the soul. Old-time gospel songs such as "In The Garden" and "In His Hands" wash away fears. Current uplifting songs like those sung by Barbra Streisand in her "Higher Ground" CD buoy the spirit and renew energy. Motivational and storytelling tapes bring the authors and heroes alive, filling the ears with wondrous sounds, the mind with fresh ideas and renewed joy.

Support for Life Changes

When I sold my house to my daughter Laura and her husband, Doug, mixed emotions flooded my days and disturbed my nights. I needed to move on. With the house still in the family, a connection remained, yielding a sense of security and peace. Yet I was a beginner starting over. That was scary, mind-boggling. Then once the decision was made, inertia set in.

To counteract that inertia, I played motivational and storytelling tapes as I painted and prepared my new apartment for temporary housing until I decided on permanent quarters. One story on a tape given to me by my daughter Cindy carried me through my first steps into a new life. The tape is by the Celestial Navigators.

The story is about a man who comes to "The Wall"[4] that no one gets through. The Celestial Navigator storyteller becomes the man; he vividly recounts finding the wall, climbing through the debris of those the wall defeated and finding his way out.

---

4 Story by Geoffrey Lewis. All rights reserved. www.celestialnavigators.com

My Wall: I am painting the walls in my new apartment when I hear the story for the first time. My hands tighten on the roller, my ears strain to catch every word: "... which no man has survived." I dip slowly into the paint, ease off the excess and reach toward my wall. *Will I be stuck now? Will I just grow old, shrivel and die?*

"I find a hole ... " comes the raspy, exhausted voice. Sweat pours off my face down my neck. My heart pounds. *Will he make it? Will I?* Paint dries on the roller as I hold my breath... waiting... waiting... as he struggles with the wall. I exhale in a burst of air as the storyteller breaks through the wall and into an incredible, surreal adventure — a downhill ski race through the northern skies.

Smiling broadly, I redip the roller and race along with my hero. He shoots off into space, then drops into a canyon. As my roller races to the mop board, the skier races to the finish line. "I did it! I did it!" he shouts. "I broke through the wall of inertia!" I rewind the tape to listen again. And again. Finally, I shout aloud, "I did it!" I, too, break through the wall of inertia, my freshly painted walls symbolic of the fresh start I am making.

Jesus said we should become as little children. Children love repetition. Why? Repetition helps them to remember. Repetition cultivates the seeds that grow into wisdom. My favorite tapes are dubbed, the master stored for future copying when the duplicate wears out (which is often).

I highlight my books, often writing dates and comments in margins; they become dog-eared and full of Post It® notes. Favored books and tapes that bring comfort during stormy times are close by, on nightstands, end tables, library shelves and in a bathroom basket. I keep booklets and affirmation cards in purse and pocket. Inspiration is always at my finger tips.

My "support staff" (the authors and speakers) expands as I scour bookstores for more self-help guidelines to help me keep on keeping on. Through the books, tapes and life-enrichment seminars and workshops, I continue to grow and find new strength.

A variety of items serve as reminders of friends and family who fortify my spirit. Two favorites are in the Hummingbird (my RV). One is a poster of a man running down a road that leads far into the horizon, with the caption, "The race is not always to the swift but to those who keep on running." Another is a small plaque created by Jan Cowen. The "Little Tramp" on the plaque is swinging in a swing. Jan's caption says, "What is a swing without the ups and downs? Life is like that too!"

With each challenge conquered, each bit of information that settles into our personal resource databases, our inner wisdom grows and our confidence expands. So what happens to that confidence when disaster strikes? Will our inner wisdom still guide us? Oh, yes. That's when it reaches out and chooses those who will be most helpful in our hour of need. Inner wisdom knows that we are not alone upon this earth; we are part of a whole, and it's time for us to be the receiver.

Family and Friends

We inherit our families, choose our friends. Both can serve as strong reassuring units *if we are willing to accept their help.* We may just be stubborn, unwilling to accept help because we want to believe we are self-sufficient. In Pat Conroy's *The Prince of Tides,* a father says, "I don't like to ask people for anything." His son, Tom Wingo, replies, "That makes it very difficult to give you anything, Dad." We need to find a balance between our self-sufficiency and asking for and accepting help that benefits us and our helpers.

Some years back I read of a single woman with no living family members, who learned she had a terminal disease. She had several close friends, but they didn't know each other. Knowing she would need a strong support system to get through her ordeal, she called all the friends together and asked if they would be willing to form a team of helpmates. They willingly agreed. The friends formed a friendship like that of a close-knit family. When the woman who brought them together died, they comforted each other.

We may be unwilling to accept help because it comes with strings attached, is not useful to us and, sometimes, may even be harmful. In that case, we teach others how to help us. When seeking help, we must beware of those who pity, overprotect and overpower us. It is better to refuse the help if strings are attached. Co-dependency is not what we want. Neither do we want someone who will do for us what we can, or should, do for ourselves. Yes, they love us, but sometimes it takes tough love to make us strong. In some cases we may need to be the ones who insist on getting tough love.

When I began the *Crafters' Link* newsletter, I asked my husband to read my writing and critique it.

"No," he said. "I don't know anything about writing or crafts."

"True, but you know a lot about sales and marketing, and that's what I'm writing about. Marketing and sales principles are the same whether it's auto parts or crafts."

"No."

"Why?"

"It won't work. You'll get mad and cry. We'll argue. It won't work."

I'd already given this a lot of consideration and was prepared. Although it was scary, I asked for tough love.

"I know. I do cry when I'm angry or frustrated. But it won't be anger or frustration with you. I would rather you criticize me, here, where I can correct it, than print it and hear it from some reader."

When I promised not to argue or be hurt, Ken agreed to give it a try. Actually, there were a few tears but he rarely saw them. He was right, he didn't know anything about writing or crafts, but he was expert at picking out confusion, repetition and vagueness. He also gave me many good sales and marketing tips. Together, we made a terrific team.

My favorite memories come from the times when he read something and said, "I don't have a clue as to what's wrong here, but it lacks something." That's when we held a "discussion," which we both came to realize was nothing personal, but needed to be done to help me get to whatever "it" was that the article needed. Ken had a knack for asking questions that dug deep into my inner wisdom to unearth something special. Sometimes I think that's what I miss most since he is gone. I am so grateful we persevered in developing a relationship that brought us pleasure and fresh perceptions. Thanks, Ken.

Fostering Family Fidelity: Sometimes, in the early days, I felt that my family and friends didn't understand me. (They probably didn't. How could they? I didn't understand myself.) Even in the midst of family gatherings, I felt isolated, the odd one out. Sometimes I was left out, but not because they didn't love me. I know now there were times when my attitude put a damper on the event. I didn't want to take part.

We can love and comfort someone we don't understand. Even if we disapprove of something someone does, we can still offer our love and be there for them. That's the way God does it. He doesn't approve all that we do, but He never deserts us. Sometimes it takes time for that wisdom to blossom.

As a parent, I came to understand what my parents went through. I'm grateful for my father and mother getting together long enough to serve as the channels for the uniqueness of me. I'm even more grateful they had the wisdom to separate so I could grow up in peace. I bless them for finding wonderful stepparents for me to love, as well as two brothers (Richard and John) and two sisters (Vicki and Mimi). Once I released my resentments of my parents, *they* became wiser and easier to understand.

Although my family didn't always embrace my way of thinking, it didn't mean they didn't love me or couldn't assist me, especially during emotional upheavals. Many times, they were my best resources for putting balance back into my life. This comes in hindsight, as I often fought their attempts to help me see how my thoughts and behaviors were actually creating the problems that tormented me.

Yet there are many happy memories also, as when Ken Sr., or one of our children or grandchildren, sat with me and talked about life, their own feelings and beliefs. These sharing conversations help us understand one another better, letting us know that someone cares. When the children were young, many of these conversations happened around the dinner table. Now that they own homes of their own, some in other parts of the country, we stay in touch through modern technology.

My oldest granddaughter, Melanie, reminds me of myself as a young mother. Grandma and I spent hours at the dining room table working jig-saw puzzles and talking. Melanie lives in Virginia, so we talk via e-mail, letters, the telephone and occasionally, faxes. When I visit, we play Scrabble or Yatzee and talk. Although busy young adults, my grandsons, Jeremiah, Matthew and Ryan frequently come to share a meal and conversation. Before Kenny Jr. died, he and I had a monthly breakfast date for sharing and supporting each other. Busy lives require creativity to keep in touch. Voice mail messages and "I love you" or "thinking of you" codes on pagers work wonders to reassure and gladden the spirit of someone you care about.

I learn much from my family by listening and watching. Two of my daughters are single moms. Watching Brenda and Cindy work full-time jobs, sometimes two jobs, to support their families, plus take care of their children, has often given me the courage to stretch my horizons. Lynn, my widowed daughter-in-law, now has the job of rearing her child alone. She, too, serves as one of my sheroes. We know we can lean on each other. We also know that we can stand by and let each other grow without interference. That's true validation, coming from a place of unconditional love.

Support by Teaching

Benefits often come from teaching and encouraging, rather than doing something for the person. Two years after the Locust Years ended, I bought a unit in a cooperative housing development. My new house needed some major remodeling and decorating. Since Brenda and Cindy had become quite efficient in all matters of house repairs, I asked them for help. They came with hammers, power saws and drills, which were used, in part, to teach me how to do much of the work myself. My girls, along with my son-in-law Doug and grandson Ryan, taught me how to care for my car, RV and lawn mower. They make me practice what I preach!

Although my sister Mimi and brother John live great distances from me, we are as near as the telephone. I know I can count on them along with my sister Vicki, and they know they can count on me. Before he died, my brother Richard delighted in calling from Texas during our northern snowstorms. Using his portable telephone from poolside, his first question was, "How many inches of snow do you have?" He made sure he was close enough to the pool so that I could hear the laughter and splashes of happy swimmers. Humor was the way Richard fortified me. He kept me laughing, even when it was hard to find something to laugh about. Uplifting humor has helped our family survive the worst situations.

After the flight from Washington, DC, into Chicago, the day of Kenny Jr.'s death, Barbara and I had a two-hour bus ride home. I dreaded arriving. As I stepped from the airport commuter bus, my daughters, Cindy and Laura, and my sister, Vicki, surrounded me like a cocoon. I let them hold me up with their collective embrace. Finally someone said, "Well, there must be one heck of a party going on in Heaven, with so many of them there now." We laughed through our tears as the agony of yet another loss lifted just for a bit.

Grandma Gladys often told me, "Honesty is the best policy." Honesty, I came to understand, is not just in telling the truth. Good supportive relationships need honesty of spirit as well. That is, to love each other as each is. That is rarely easy, particularly in diverse families, but diversity makes for a spicy, lively family.

Accepting our differences, as well as our similarities, is what has strengthened our family ties. We've grown stronger and closer in our crises, because we've put our love for each other first, because we forgive one another and we maintain a sense of humor. As H. G. Wells said, "The crisis of yesterday is the joke of tomorrow." Teach your family how to live life funny side up and see what a difference it makes.

Forming a Friendship Fraternity: Friendships form an essential part of our network. Some friendships happen spontaneously, others are cultivated. The best friendships help us grow in productive ways. These friendships are not based on needs or wants, but created through shared experiences filled with love, honesty and trust.

I have such a friendship with Shirley, whom I met in seventh grade. Her family moved to a suburban area of a neighboring city in September; my family moved to the same neighborhood

two months later. We were the new kids and immediately grav-
itated to each other, building a trusting friendship that still
exists, although she now lives in California. We keep in touch
via e-mail and telephone calls.

Shortly before Ken Sr. died, Shirley and I established a standing Saturday morning date for telephone calls, taking turns
calling. When I didn't call that Saturday morning of Ken's
death, she knew something was wrong and immediately
began praying for me. I always enjoy our conversations, but
during the Locust Years they became special blessings.

Through the years, Shirley and I have helped each other
through many stormy times and celebrated the harvests of
goals achieved, dreams realized. We've cried and laughed
together, shared our stories, our homes, our dreams and our
sorrows. What works for one doesn't always work for the other.
That's okay, because in the sharing we find something useful
that gets us where we need to be. Different lives, different
needs. One beautiful friendship.

Two weeks after the convention where I first met Mitchell, he
called me from his home in Hawaii and talked for an hour,
encouraging me to keep growing. Although we were just
becoming acquainted, he knew from experience how important it is to talk with someone who understands pain. (I told
him about the deaths of my husband and brother.)

"I came to see, more than ever before, how friendships are
'investments' that offer protection in a crisis that no insurance
policy can give," Mitchell says of the buttress of help he
received during his crises. Although my scars would not be as
visible as Mitchell's, the pain inside was as searing. Little did
either of us know, that day he called, that Mitchell would play
a role in my darkest hour by staying by my side and accompanying me to the airport.

Another new friend from NSA, Rosita Perez, invited me to
visit her when I was in Florida. We spent a whole day talking

about the speaking business and life in general. Rosita continues to be a great support to fledgling speakers even though she deals with her own challenges of multiple sclerosis.

I cherish the Girl Scout saying, "Make new friends, but keep the old. Some are silver, others gold." What a privilege to have friends and family in the good times and in the bad. Friends form the underpinnings of our maintenance program. Always there, always ready.

Several very special friends are self-appointed "humor buddies." They write, fax or e-mail me cartoons, jokes, quirky signs and newspaper articles that hit their funny bone. Jeff, a humorist, calls to share his latest version of what some people call a catastrophe. He and another friend, Marie, see life from the flip side. Marie calls to share a laugh — literally. All she says is, "Hee, hee, hee" until we both break out in giggles. During the difficult years, I feared losing my humor, but Marie and Jeff taught me how to find it in everyday living. The funnies are there, if we will laugh. Hanging onto grief is useless — and dangerous to our health.

Doug sends me interesting quotes. Marilyn sends self-help articles and rainbow stories. Barbara likes to use different accents and made-up stories when she leaves messages on my machine. Denny and Winona send friendship poems. Each contributes a bit of beauty, strength and fun to my life on a regular basis — truly a joy-filled support system.

Church, Work and Social Groups

My Unity minister friend, Amalie Frank, says we should choose the church where we "get spiritually fed." During the Locust Years, an informal group from St. Mary's of the Assumption Catholic Church near my home gave me spiritual nurturing. They call themselves "The Breakfast Club." Although I fell away from the church, and we saw each other infrequently, they welcomed me to join them the first Sunday after Ken Sr.'s funeral. They were friends from the young days of our families. Being with them on Sunday mornings gave me a sense of stability as my world fell apart. They helped refresh my faith.

When our children were very young, the First Methodist Church I attended, had a "Mother's Study Group." Mothers grouped according to the ages of their children. Our children were two, three and four at the time, so I went to the preschool group. The other mothers and I shared trials and triumphs and helped each other find solutions to problems.

One of our solutions was a shared "Mother's Day Off." We paired into teams to baby-sit all the little ones. As I recall, there were eight of us. For three weeks, we each had a free day, when we took our children to the home of one member of that week's team. The team planned a day for the children. My daughters still talk of the fun they had. We also shared tips we found in books, magazines or from our elders. Life as a young mother became easier when shared.

At various times, I left church-going because egos and politics pushed spirituality out the window. Negative events didn't sour me on church, only made me cautious. The Breakfast Club was a reminder that it's not the organization that provides the spirit of love and inspiration, it's the people.

The same is true of work places and social groups. We must look for places that respect us as persons, not simply as cogs in the wheel. Even though the board of directors didn't care for my management style at the women's center, most of my employees did. The memory of their validation still strengthens me in difficult times.

On the day of the board meeting, I saw my secretary, Polly, a single mother, standing by the window. A big tear moved slowly down her beautiful cheek. Like mine, this was the highest paying job she had ever had, giving her the opportunity to start saving toward a house of her own and now she was about to lose it. I put my arm around Polly. "I'm sorry," I said. "I'll help in any way I can."

She turned her tear-filled eyes toward me. "Oh, I'll be all right," she said. "It's just that I can't understand how anyone can do this to you, after all you've done for us." Her validation supported me that day.

Discovering loving, supportive experiences is like panning for gold at the end of the rainbow. If you look, you'll always find at least one beautiful nugget. Suggestion: rather than looking for a job, look for an *environment* in which to grow emotionally and spiritually, as well as financially. The right place will help you maintain good health, meaning more money in your pocket as well.

Social, Special Interest and Self-Help Groups

In my years of crisis intervention work, we made hundreds of referrals to a variety of mental health agencies, social services and self-help groups. Occasionally, when people's problems basically came from loneliness, we tried to find a special interest group for them.

Today there is a group or association for every problem or interest known to man or woman. A divorced friend has joined a bicycle club. Another is taking dancing lessons and joins a singles group for trips to dance contests. Several organizations helped to balance and confirm me, as well as inspire and motivate me throughout the many stormy times of the Locust Years. Remember, when considering support groups as well as personal interest groups, look for compatibility. Some friends in twelve-step programs tried several groups before finding the one that fit their needs and interests. Caution: be careful, not hasty, in assessing compatibility. What you want is loving support, that includes tough love.

For optimum benefit, choose groups where participants know how to listen, and where they respect both you as a person and your right to make your own decisions. They give empathy, not sympathy. Sympathy is getting into the ditch with a person. Empathy identifies with and understands another's situation, feelings and motives, but doesn't get caught in them.

Look at groups whose members are genuine, non-possessive, honest and respectful of privacy. They maintain confidentiality and are not dictatorial. You will know it's the right group when you feel the spiritual uplifting even as you walk together through the pain. Names and addresses of helping organizations are listed in public library reference sections, local referral information services, the telephone directory and the Resource Section at the end of this book.

Often one group leads to another, creating an interesting and enlightening adventure for living. For me, the National Speakers Association was a catalyst for finding a variety of new and dear friends and supporters. One support group began mid-way through the Locust Years, when I attended a storytelling workshop, where I met Lee Glickstein, creator of Speaking Circles®. After attending a couple of Lee's workshops, he gave me permission to start some Speaking Circles® in my own community.

The first one with friends, Doug Germann, Marie Leddy and Barbara Steele, lasted five years, evolving into a support group that I treasure dearly. We met every Saturday morning to share our thoughts, ideas and stories in the unique style of the circles. The focus on love and listening created transformation in our lives. So phenomenal is this process that Lee's groups are now called Transformational Circles.®

"A group that effectively gives us systematic listening with no expectation, even no demand to speak at all, is infinitely more powerful than any one person," says Lee Glickstein[1].

---

1 Author of *Be Heard Now!*

"With ideal listening you begin to trust your own voice; you begin to listen to yourself, hear yourself. ... *We need other people to listen us into existence."* [Emphasis mine.]

This is the primary ingredient of a true support system, whether one person or a group. This kind of listening allows us to reach deep within our own well of understanding, desire, creativity and personal mission to discover what it is that we must do to survive... and to thrive. No one else knows what we need most. They can give advice and tell their stories, but they cannot make our decisions. Advice and stories give us different perspectives and trigger ideas for answers, but *we must make our own decisions.*

Several other organizations helped me get through my grief: Hospice, Alzheimer's Association and Beginning Experience. Until Henry's and Kenny Jr.'s deaths, I didn't get involved in any formal grief programs. After all, I reasoned, family and friends provided tremendous support, and I was a trained "specialist" in crisis intervention. Still, something was missing.

The signs were there: I slept a lot, cried over nothing. When my thoughts turned to a desire to start drinking again or to ask the doctor for tranquilizing medications, I knew I was headed for trouble. The worried looks on loved ones' faces also told me it was time to get help before I succumbed to the damaging desires that would surely lead to addiction. I joined a Hospice grief group that took me past the deep hurt and into the awareness that it was time to move on. But how?

Shortly after the grief group work ended, God put another "angel" into my life, a new neighbor, Sue Ann Smith. Déjà vu. We were the new kids on the block and became fast friends. Sue was active in Beginning Experience (BE), an organization to help widowed, separated and divorced persons make a new beginning. Although I was keenly aware of being a widow, I hadn't had time or energy to think about what that meant for my future.

Beginning Experience is a weekend program designed to help widowed, separated and divorced persons make a new beginning in life. Although the international program was designed by members of the Catholic faith, it is open to persons of all faiths. The program consists of presentations by a specially trained team followed by personal private reflection time and dialogue in small groups. The BE weekend I attended opened my mind and heart to possibilities for the future, based upon the strengths they helped me discover from my past. I came away refreshed in spirit and renewed in physical energy. Throughout the process, I renewed my commitment to live joyfully.

I believe the modern group setting that focuses on individual growth with positive guidance parallels the experience Sam Keen, trapeze flyer and philosopher, describes in *Learning to Fly.*

> *Initially, I thought of the [safety] net as nothing more than a safety device that would protect me if I could manage to fall correctly on my back, seat, or stomach. As I gained skill in twisting, turning, and landing, however, I realized it was more than a concession to human fallibility; it was also a platform from which to launch new flight. A modern nylon net is essentially a large trampoline that invites a flyer to convert a fall into a rebound trick — a somersault, a suicide dive, a high balletic leap.*

Group experiences, such as BE, provide a safety net where we fall back into memory, examine our weaknesses and rediscover our strengths to bounce back into living fully once again. Group experiences help to strengthen individual relationships as well. As group leaders guide us through the maze of personal experiences, we learn to accept help from strangers; we learn how to ask for and respond to help from family and friends.

Ask for the Blessings: Why are so many of us reluctant to ask for help? Is it because we think we know it all? (Do we?) Is it because we fear — or mistrust — the advice or help? Help is a give and receive proposition and when it's our turn to receive, we must be prepared to ask.

"Instead of just searching for advice on what to do to respond to your callings, tell others what they can do *for* you. Guide the guides by telling them *exactly* what kind of help you need. If you don't specify, if you must tell people to help you, or that you feel stuck, they're likely to try to diagnose what sort of help you *seem* to need and administer it, however they see fit," writes Gregg Levoy in *Callings.*

Levoy shares an anecdote of how his brother, Ross, helped himself to get the help he needed. "Quit giving me your damn advice," Ross told his brother. "Just ask me questions and listen." If someone is unwilling to do that for us, then we should look for counsel elsewhere.

Sometimes our troubles serve as catalysts, a strong motivator to take some action, make a change or create something new. The Hotline program which I was drawn to set up, provided a listening ear to callers which was not always available to me when I needed it. In truth, sometimes the help is there, and we just need to ask. Hotline does not call troubled people. They must call the Hotline. There is no disgrace in asking for help when we are truly in need.

Were you taught that it is more blessed to give than to receive? Equal blessings come from receiving. How else can others give? How do we feel blessed by another's love unless we are willing to accept their gifts of caring? How else is God's purpose for each of us to be fulfilled?

Winona, another friend I met at a storytelling retreat, worked out a formula to help her husband's parents, who were both ill. Winona and her husband wanted to help, but they couldn't do everything, as they had obligations of their own. Neighbors, friends and church members wanted to help also. Winona listed tasks people could do and posted the list on the refrigerator. When friends came to visit, they could choose something from the list: do the grocery shopping, sign up for care so the caregivers could take an hour off, mow the lawn or do the laundry.

Everyone has a different approach to giving and receiving help. My beautiful mother-in-law taught us by example how to be considerate receivers. Mom Hill enjoyed her independence. She lived alone in a large house, which she kept in immaculate condition and good repair, although she had a very small income. As the years went by (she died shortly before her 96th birthday), she had to let go of some of her independence and ask for help. She did it in such a way as not to be a burden on any one person.

Fortunately, Mom Hill had a large family, so there were many to divide the work. She paired talents with jobs to be done. Since I liked solving difficult problems, I got the job of watchdogging medical insurance payments. Some shopped. Others cleaned. Mom Hill also included grandchildren and eventually great-grandchildren in the process. When her health was good, the worker went home with freshly baked bread or a container of cookies.

Sometimes Mom Hill insisted on paying the younger generations a little money for jobs such as cleaning the house or mowing the lawn. She met protests with stony determination. "I pay my way," she stated with pride. I think it was her way of setting an example, giving a lesson in responsibility to the next generation.

If one was willing to stay a bit, she enjoyed tea and stories. Sitting at Mom Hill's table, I learned much about coping with life. Her strength became my strength, her courage, my courage. Bless you, Mom, and thanks for the memories.

Don't Take "No" as Rejection

Back in the days when I was giving myself a lot of pity parties, I called a friend one night for some TLC (Tender Loving Care) conversation. He was a counselor and had said, "Call me anytime." Well, I called and he was not home. How dare he be gone when I needed him? After sulking a while, I stopped blaming him; after all, he was only human. He had a wife and children and other clients/friends besides me. Then I blamed God.

"Sure, I can be available for everyone else, but the one time I need help, it's not there." Now that's a deluxe pity party! I got into the dialogue so thoroughly that it became ludicrous, and I started laughing. "How ridiculous can you get, Joanne? You sound just like the chronic whiners that call in and tie up the Hotline phones. You don't want help. You want company for your misery."

I relaxed, leaned back and visualized connecting with my friend and immediately realized that had I connected, he would have put a quick end to the pity party. Now, I often find a quiet place for a heart-to-heart visit with my helpers (when it's not practical to call). No matter whom I choose to "visit," he or she is always there for me. Part of the program is using imagination and memory to "talk" with someone who has helped us before.

Prayer Power

Recent scientific studies prove the power of prayer. Shucks, I could have told them that! There are times when I know someone is praying for me... the message comes across as a warm feeling of peace.

One avenue of incredible benefit is prayer partners. Some people form prayer chains. This is a process whereby one person calls for prayer help, the person called then calls another, on down the chain until several people are praying for the person in need. Some chains are organized through Bible study groups and churches. Besides family members, I call on five friends regularly for prayer help. Some of them pass along the request to their personal prayer partners.

Another form of prayer partnering is through 24-hour organized prayer lines manned by dedicated volunteers. Through the years I frequently called Silent Unity, Unity Village, Missouri and World Ministry of Prayer in Los Angeles, California. When I call these lines, I hear prayers of certainty and affirmation that immediately bring me a sense of well being. Both have toll-free numbers for those on limited incomes.

A final reminder about prayer power. *It works.* Be careful how you pray. When Ken and I separated, a dear friend called to say she was praying for us to get back together. I asked her not to do that.

"Why? Don't you love him anymore?" she asked.

"Yes, I do. Very much. I'm just not sure that is what is best for him, or me, or the family. So please pray for what is best for *all* concerned."

She understood. The best was yet to be... for we did reunite with many good times ahead.

God's Special People

Then there are the surprises, those times when someone special appears serendipitously to bless our lives. As we develop awareness for what lifts and nurtures us, we open ourselves to the blessings of amazing experiences.

We are all God's special people, but some seem to have an aura similar to that of the angels. These people go out of their way to perform little acts of kindness. Meet a few who blessed me through the years:

- A man who crawled under my car in pouring-down rain on a cold March day to remove the rusted muffler that had caught on a pothole.
- The nurse who sat by my husband's side, tears rolling down her cheeks, as we waited and watched through that long night of his forty-ninth birthday.
- The neighbor who sneaked baskets of clothes from my house and brought them back freshly ironed.
- A gladiolus farmer who left fresh bouquets on my doorstep.

My friend, Marilyn, calls such people "God with skin on." God's special people ask for nothing and give their all. Whenever and wherever needed, they show up. These brief encounters of loving support bring much joy.

For effective and efficient Rainbow Support Systems, I use the *Stop, Look, Listen and Learn* remedy first. To strengthen my system, *I Accentuate the Positive* and give large doses of *Praise and Thanksgiving*. Should I find some difficulties, I pour on the *Forgiveness*. I choose carefully and ask for *Help to Help Myself*.

We're all in this world together, and there will always be stormy times. Let's share our rainbow blessings in love and peace.

Rainbow Ingredients
for
Support Systems

- Foundation of faith

- Inner wisdom

- Family and friends

- Prayer partners

- Heroes and sheroes

- Church groups

- Work associates

- Support and self-help groups

- Special interest clubs, associations

- God's special people

Remember: It's okay to ask for a blessing of help.

A God-incident

It rained in the wee hours of that February morning, then stopped. I went for my usual early walk on the beach, watching the sun and the clouds play hide and seek. Washed from the rain, the sand was smooth and clear of all but the most recent footprints. I counted four sets — three adult, one child.

Glancing up, I saw a mother and child walking ahead of me. The child stopped and held up his arms. The mother picked him up, then turned and headed back toward me. I smiled.

As they got closer, I could see that the child was about five or six, a pretty heavy load for his mother. He had his legs and arms wrapped tightly around her. I smiled. She smiled back, obviously unaware of any burden. As they passed, I turned to look at the child. His face was full of trust as he lovingly patted his mother on the back.

I smiled again, thinking of the times I'd carried my children, and how often I see my children carry their children. Lost in thought, I walked further than I usually do. Coming out of the reverie, I realized I was slowing down. I turned to look at the long walk back.

Looking back at the sand I saw, the child's footprints alongside those of his mother's. Then, I saw only one pair of footprints heading away from me — one set, deeper now. **I wish I had someone to carry me,** *I thought.*

The poem **"Footprints"** popped into my mind. But when I tried to envision being carried by The Creator, my adult mind refused to form a visual picture. I looked for the child and his mother. They were nearly out of sight. As I recalled his trusting face, his loving pat upon her back, pictures of my being carried came flooding in.

Before birth, I was carried in my mother's womb, The Creator's incubator. Next I was carried by strong, competent hands — those of the doctor called to the house to help my mother in giving birth. After my birth, I snuggled into the arms of my mother and father, and beloved maternal grandmother, who came to care for me as Mom recuperated. The line of arms outstretched the ocean spread before me: aunts and uncles, grandparents, teachers, husband, children, friends and even strangers.

When did they carry me? They came in my hour of need, even before I called. They sent loving notes, beautiful cards and bits of humor. The busiest ones put me in their "tickler file," so I wouldn't get lost or overlooked in their busy world. Their arms literally held me up as the blood drained from my broken heart in the dark hour of my son's unexpected death.

They carried me when they did for me what I no longer had the will to do for myself. I felt their loving arms when they forgave me, encouraged me and occasionally gave me a yank so I couldn't languish in the gutter of depression and self-pity.

Understanding arms lifted me when I could not understand. The wisdom of shared insights through other people's writing and speaking held me up even when they weren't physically there.

So to all my loved ones, family, friends and you who I've not yet met: I say thank you. Thank you for helping me make it through this life. I LOVE YOU!

The Pot of Gold

I believe in every experience, we can find gold. Mostly, it's tiny flakes, like those brief moments when a bit of humor breaks through the pain. Other times there are bits and pieces, varying sizes, coming in the form of a helper, new ideas and insights. Once in a while, we find a mother lode. Often, that is when we open ourselves to receiving. That is what happened to Steve Russell. Here is his story as written in the *Be Beacon*[4] newsletter.

> In mid-June, I was hospitalized and diagnosed with a very rare and fast-growing nasal cancer. On Saturday, June 24th, I quit breathing. It must not have been my time to cross over, for God spared my life. The heroic efforts of the nurses and doctors saved my life.
>
> I have never done well receiving gifts and compliments from others. It has been easier for me to give of myself than to allow others to minister to me. As I lay helpless in the hospital, and later convalescing at my dad's house, I started changing. Family members and friends started showing up, get well cards poured in, and a large amount of e-mail was sent to me. Prayer groups were seeking my recovery. Organizations I was a part of reached out to me with care and concern. Churches that did not even know me heard about my illness and started interceding. I had no idea that so many people cared about me. I was overwhelmed! I knew I could never repay or reply to so many people. Then I realized I did not have to.

---

4 Newsletter published by Beginning Experience of South Bend, Inc. September, 2000.
Used with permission of Steve Russell.

A dear, close friend handed me a CD to listen to as I lay in the hospital bed. She said especially listen to song number six, "I Will Carry You." If I remember correctly she said something like, "Steve, right now you are unable to carry yourself through this, let me carry you!" As I listened to the song, I broke in tears realizing this was God speaking to me to allow others the opportunity to help me. As I quit resisting and relaxed, I started to feel renewed by others' compassion and love. When I was unable to talk, a hand squeeze spoke of our mutual love and respect for each other. When I felt beaten down by the trauma my body had endured and anxiety towards my soul, their smile kindled hope within to go on living.

In just a few short years since my divorce, I had acquired a wealth of new friends who had become my extended family. The kindness in their spirit has allowed us the opportunity to bond to each other. As I lay near death's door, we cried in each other's arms. As my recovery took miraculous steps, we found that tears moistened our joyful faces. We are a part of each other. We in Beginning Experience are joined by common experiences. We have been united; our hearts are linked by turning the emotions of hopelessness, helplessness and unworthiness into hope, faith and love.

I can only say thank you to all my family and friends. Your help this summer has been deeply appreciated. The doctors say it is a miracle that I lived, and that I am cancer free. So to all my family past, present and future who have been, or who are in despair, I would simply say, "Can we carry you?" Welcome to our family.

With love, Steve Russell

When my spirit is worn,
or my soul is torn,
faith will see me to the morn.

When the day breaks,
my mind awakes
as the sun shines into my heart.

Melanie Stone

The Seasons 10

For everything there is a season;
and a time to every purpose under heaven:
A time to weep, and a time to laugh;
a time to mourn, and a time to dance.

Ecclesiastes 3:1,4

S eeing the triple rainbow with Ken was a turning point for me. I made my decision and continued with my newsletter, working odd jobs now and then for income. We managed quite well. In spite of the cut in income, we vacationed in Florida with each of our children and their families. Ken took several trips to see old friends, and we traveled to California to visit with Henry and Hector.

The four years following the awesome rainbow were blessed ones for us. Although we still encountered some stormy times (the natural elements and personal ones), we created many happy memories. Our relationship grew deeper, more loving, forgiving and individually freeing. Although the changes were gradual, developing over the years, we began to live our lives deliberately, more thoughtfully. We saw the miracles... the rainbows in everyday living.

Ken glowed with a beautiful tan from hours spent outdoors, walking in the woods, planting trees and golfing. He helped rebuild our house after a fire destroyed part of it, then enlisted the aid of our son-in-law, Doug, to build an addition to the barn for an office and small warehouse for me. Besides writing, printing and mailing my newsletter, I published and promoted a greeting card line and conducted craft marketing workshops. Occasionally I advised individual crafters how to market what they made. Although the business was slow in growth, life was good, rich and full of promise.

Going Home

My last day with Ken began at two o'clock on a Saturday morning in May, 1990. I awoke with a deep sense of peace and love. I saw tiny twinkling lights on the pink dogwood tree outside our bedroom windows. Ken had put them on the tree for Christmas. We enjoyed the lights so much that we decided to leave them year round. Hearing a slight noise behind me, I leisurely rolled to face the door. Ken stood silhouetted by the hallway light.

"I'm sick. Real sick," he whispered. He turned and staggered down the hall. I flew to the telephone and dialed 911. After giving the critical information, I left the phone receiver off the hook as instructed and ran to my husband slumped on the staircase.

I recalled his doctor's last words to me: "He won't know what hit him. He has so little heart left, he'll go quick." After the birthday heart attack, more than eighty percent of Ken's heart was dead. For seven years, he had lived with less than twenty percent of a heart. Ken's strong will, with a lot of prayer power, played a powerful role in extending his life.

"I love you," he whispered. "I'm going home." My tears mingled with Ken's and I hugged him close. He was cold and gray. Barely breathing.

"I'm not ready to let you go," I insisted.

"I know, but it's time. Tell the kids I love them."

As I sat holding Ken, terror and panic welled inside me. *Oh, God, please help me let him go.* The fear left — a strange sensation came over me. Was it a trick of the mind? The Spirit? As I sat on the stairstep holding Ken, waiting for the paramedics, a part of me separated off to one side and calmly watched us. There were two of me!

The part holding Ken was ready to jump up and down and scream, "Don't go! Not yet! I won't let you go!" But she didn't.

With the emergence of the observer (that part separated from me), I knew that no matter what happened, I would deal with it. At the same time, I also knew that I could feel whatever I needed to feel — rage, acceptance, loneliness, gratitude, whatever came, without going over the edge.

My observer stayed close throughout Ken's leaving, the funeral and on through the next year. She balanced me. I felt the pain, and through her, I also felt a joy and peace similar to what Ken revealed as he took leave of his earthly home.

The paramedics came quickly. I called my nearest daughter, Laura; then let a firefighter drive me to the hospital. Laura called the rest of the family. Our priest came, medical personnel came, family members came, friends came and Ken kept on breathing and talking.

Ken's words were the same to each special person. "Hi. Thanks for coming. I'm going home. I love you." There was an incredible sense of peace — almost joyfulness — in the room. Ken seemed to glow. He still looked the picture of health, except for the needles in his arms and tube in his nose.

"He'll make it, just like before," family and friends said in the waiting room. Hoping they were right. Knowing they weren't. About 10 a.m., Ken's vital signs declined, his breathing grew shallower and he closed his eyes. The nurse signaled for us to come closer.

Someone asked, "Where's Debbie?" Debbie, our oldest daughter, lives in Florida. "She's on her way," someone replied. "She'll be in at 11:20."

Ken's heartbeat inexplicably grew stronger. His eyes opened and he looked at the clock. Softly, he said to us again, "I'm going home." A smile lit up his face. "And it's *beautiful*," he added. Although Ken's voice was barely above a whisper, everyone heard his words, even his hearing-impaired mother who was sitting across the room.

When Debbie arrived, a nurse told her a miracle was occurring in Ken's room. Debbie assumed her dad was going to recover. "No," said the nurse, "but what's happening in there is a miracle."

Truly, it was. For Ken had waited for his daughter and continued to talk to us up to the moment his soul left for his eternal home. Clearly. Distinctly. Even though his lungs were filled with fluid, his heart barely pumping. People who were present that day still marvel at what happened. Some say, "Now I know there is a God."

Ken's sense of humor also remained intact. Once Debbie arrived, he motioned for all his children and me to move closer to the bed. "I'm proud of all of you," he said. Then, with a loving smile, he gave a slight nod to each of his divorced daughters and said, "Next time, pick a good one." With a twinkle in his eye and a nod toward me, he told his offspring, "And don't let her spend any money."

In the waiting room and for months following Ken's death, I pondered our life together and its end. With each memory, I relived the storm followed by a triple rainbow and a golden sunset... and its promise.

Welcome Home

After Ken's death, our family went back to Hill's Haven, our house in the woods that he loved so dearly. Coming down the lane toward the house, I surveyed each dogwood tree Ken had planted the year before. He was worried they weren't going to live. I encouraged him to be patient. Now I, too, wondered if they had survived the winter.

We were barely in the door that afternoon, when two of the younger grandchildren, Ryan, eight, and Heather, four, clamored to go mushroom hunting. "Paw Paw told us to go hunt mushrooms," they chorused. We all laughed. Although we'd found no mushrooms for two weeks, their mothers, Brenda and Laura, took out the bags and disappeared into the woods. Soon they were back, bags filled with huge fresh morels (the biggest ones found that year). The girls said that with every find, the children looked up and exclaimed, "Thank you, Paw Paw."

As their mothers cleaned the mushrooms and prepared us a meal, the children romped and played as though their grandpa were still with them. Rolling on the floor, they giggled as though someone were tickling them. The rest of the adults were making phone calls and putting together to-do lists for the funeral. The older grandchildren, Matthew, Jeremiah and Melanie, helped clean the house.

Cindy suggested I lie down for a while. I was relieved, but apprehensive. *What if I can't sleep? What if this peaceful feeling leaves me? I have to stay strong for the family.* I need not have worried, for when my head hit the pillow, I was out. My family remained strong for me.

The next day our children, Debbie, Cindy, Ken Jr., Brenda and Laura, went with me to the funeral home to make arrangements, something I always feared. As the funeral director explained various casket models, our offspring cried out in unison, "She can't spend any money!" We cracked up laughing. Their dad would have been proud.

Midway through Ken's funeral Mass, the parish school children were dismissed for recess. St. Mary's of the Assumption church is in the basement of the parish school building, so we heard thundering feet and joyful laughter as the children ran outside to play. I remembered stories Ken had told me about his experiences in parochial school with strict nuns. Ken boasted about testing their efforts to maintain obedience. At his funeral Mass, I could almost hear him gleefully shouting, "About time. Hurrah! I'm out of here. Going with the kids."

Our family looked at one another and burst into surprised grins and giggles. Stifled chuckles rippled through the church.

Even the priest smiled. I wonder, if heaven had a doorbell, would it sound like laughter?

The Bible teaches us to make a joyful noise unto the Lord. Isn't death supposed to be a glorious event — a journey home to our Heavenly Father for a joyous reunion? I wonder if I could have seen death this way when Ken suffered his birthday heart attack? I think not. I hadn't learned to trust. I wasn't ready to let go and let God, even though I had said a prayer of relinquishment at his bedside. Looking back, the thought comes that perhaps Ken wasn't ready to let go then, either. Perhaps it wasn't his season. Now it was.

As we drove into Hill's Haven after the funeral, another surprise awaited us. All the dogwood trees were in full bloom. Their time had come. For Ken and his loved ones, a new season also began. How would I adapt to widowhood? Would I bloom again? When? How?

During the months following Ken's death, I was acutely aware of lessons learned through the years to help me meet the challenges I now faced. With my "observer" self and the many God-incidents that first year, I felt confident I could handle anything that came along. I didn't know that Ken's death was the beginning of a long, stormy season in which I would be severely tested.

After Ken and my brother, Richard, died, I wrote a letter to all the *Crafters' Link* subscribers to tell them the newsletter would no longer be available. Meeting the deadlines, especially without my special "editor" (Ken), was more than I felt I could handle at the time. I needed the time to grieve my losses and adapt to a new life.

Many letters of support came back. One stood out — a letter from a woman who had faced the loss of seven people in her family in a short time. She shared her faith and strength with me, which touched my heart deeply... and calmed my fears. I couldn't imagine how anyone could survive and still have something left to give away. Now I know, and now I must pass on the gift she gave to me.

Like seeds, or cuttings from another's garden, we pass along our stories, our discoveries and our lessons learned. Some will take root and brighten our days with blooms and season our lives with sweet laughter or salty tears. Others will become medicinal, like the Rainbow Remedies, to serve in healing, restoring and protecting.

Our stories, our sorrows and joys must be shared, for this is our way of fulfilling God's promise: "I am with you always.[1]" We are the Holy Spirit's messengers of hope, of survival, of joy, of faith. Spirit is with us in each other's stories, each other's loves, each other's faith. We are all on this journey called life. In birth and in death, we share... we learn... we grow.

We dare not be afraid to share our stories. We dare not become so attached to them we get stuck or demand that everyone else see them the same as we do. We put them out there. We love enough to allow each listener to take just what they need. We know there is plenty more where that came from, especially when we get together in family reunions, friendship or strange encounters. Those can be wonderful "potluck" meetings of minds, hearts and souls. Bring a bit... take a bit. Put together, our stories provide a feast of faith, a banquet of love and a smorgasbord of hope.

Remember the promise... and look for rainbow blessings.

> ## DEATH, THAT GREAT PUZZLE, IS NO LONGER A MYSTERY... IT IS THE MOST WONDERFUL, JOYOUS, SENSITIVE, JOURNEY HOME.
> ROBERT CUBIN

1 Matthew 28.20 Living Bible

A Golden Nugget

We're given promises and if we don't claim them, it's like getting a letter and not opening it.

Jan Cowen, Artist

© Janice D. Cowen

Afterword

...and life goes on.

A s I write the final chapters, I'm sitting in the Hummingbird, my Jamboree motor home, parked in Carrabelle Palms RV Park, Florida. This is where I began the book, and here is where I am completing it. In the time following those years when "locusts" swarmed down upon my life, this beach became a safe harbor.

Here I come to renew my spirit. Here I come to dig deeper for the words that best express the Rainbow Promise that accompanies me from mountain top to ocean depth. When I leave this place of reflection and recovery, rest and restoration, I venture back into life's stream of wondrous encounters, adventures and discoveries.

In addition to my personal retreats, many new experiences helped to flesh out and refine the Rainbow Remedies:

- A storytelling retreat helped me remember my first healing rainbow.

- A cruise taught me how to get rid of excess baggage and gave me the strength and courage to decide to go forward rather than backward.

- Fresh insights were revealed about family and friends whose love and encouragement still fill my life with joy.

- A return to college culminated in a graduation ceremony and a first draft of this book.

- Life-enhancing workshops were attended where I walked on burning coals, climbed a twenty-five foot telephone pole, stood and leapt into space to signify "with faith all things are possible."

- Fascinating trips were taken to my ancestral homelands: England, Scotland, Wales and Ireland. On the Emerald Isle I did all the driving — left side of the road.

- I discovered that I can swim a half mile without stopping, lift weights, drive a 24-foot motor home, make a shelf, program a VCR and fix a water softener.

- I welcomed and cuddled Kenny Jr.'s daughter, Katelyn, and three great-grandchildren, Georgianna, Justice and Morgan.

There is much more I want to share with you, dear reader, but for now it's time to draw this book to an end. I'm sure we'll meet again. Soon, I hope. Perhaps it will be as we pass on the highway of life, share in a workshop or retreat, swap stories over a cup of coffee, sit beside a campfire or touch each other through the magic of e-mail.

Whether we travel together or apart, remember the promise in the rainbow. Like the porcelain figurine found after the tornado, you and I are protected and guided by a loving, unseen hand.

To see God's magnificence, *look for the rainbows.*

Blessings,

Joanne

Even if I could use all the languages of the universe, there would not be enough words to express my gratitude for all who have helped get this book written and published — and to those who have helped me in life. Grandparents, parents, step-parents, brothers, sisters, husband, children, grandchildren, great grandchildren, cousins, friends and enemies. To all who helped me get through life to this point, I humbly say "Thank you."

Putting this book together was another fascinating experience in God-incidences. I learned so much from my editors: Marie Stilkind and Sue Ann Smith, found in serendipitous ways.

At a storytelling workshop in St. Louis, I met Winona McLaughlin and mentioned I was looking for an editor. A few weeks later Winona met Ruth Fischel (*Time for Joy* author) from Massachusetts, who mentioned her editor, Marie, living in Florida. Winona excitedly related the news to me.

Marie Stilkind had edited the first *Chicken Soup for the Soul*, along with a number of other books and served as an editor for *New Woman* magazine.

Sue Smith moved into a house across the street one month after I moved into my present home. She left a newspaper career in mid-life to pursue a master's degree in communication and is now a college assistant professor.

These two women have been incredible teachers. Through their coaching I've gone far beyond my original dreams for this book.

Two other teachers greatly influenced my writing: Helen Amos and Kim Peterson. My fourth grade teacher, Helen Amos, was a master in bringing out the talents of her students. She encouraged me to write a historical play for our class which we presented to the entire school. (Helen is in heaven now with many other loved ones, and they are probably giving each other high-fives, saying, "She finally did it!")

Kim was my professor at Bethel College, where this book began to take shape. Kim is a great encourager and the sponsor of Bethel's Writer's Club — my oasis for refreshment and support.

I am deeply indebted to four editorial friends and mentors who opened the doors, encouraged and guided me in the earlier years of my writing career: Bill Sonneborn and Ray Gard, both former editors of *The South Bend Tribune,* Rita Winters, former *Muncie Star* "Lifestyle" Editor and Barbara Brabec, author of *Creative Cash* and *Home Made Money.*

I met artist Pilar de la Torre, from Australia, in Hawaii at an Anthony Robbins "Life Mastery" session. We were introduced by Anne Chen whom I met at an earlier Robbins' event. On a hot summer day, artist Jan Cowen rode her bicycle into my life, when she came by my bookstore/self-help center called Horizons Unlimited. And God brought my other artist, Heather Bare, into my life via daughter Laura and her husband, Doug.

Special thanks to Jody Brown for typesetting my manuscript into the first resemblance of a real book, and to Joya Helmuth for putting the final design touches to cover and text.

Many family members and friends bravely read and commented on my book at various stages. I am deeply grateful for their love, support and comments. They are my foundation.

In the seven years of preparation and writing *Rainbow Remedies for Life's Stormy Times*, my spirit grew stronger and my faith deepened. Whatever my need, it always comes just at the right time, always filled with love and support.

May God bless you all as you have so richly blessed me. Thanks.

ACKNOWLEDGEMENTS

I wish to thank all the writers I have quoted for their comfort, guidance and inspiration. An exhaustive search was done to determine whether previously published material included in this book required permission to reprint. If there has been an error, I apologize and a correction will be made in subsequent editions.

Real Magic & Wisdom of the Ages by Wayne W. Dyer. © Wayne W. Dyer. Reprinted by permission of Wayne W. Dyer. All rights reserved.

"Desiderata" prayer by Max Ehrmann. ©1927 Max Ehrmann. © renewed 1954 Bertha K. Ehrmann, © renewed 1976 Robert L. Bell. All rights reserved.

Who Am I, God? by Marjorie Holmes. ©1970, 1971 Marjorie Holmes. Published by Doubleday Books. Used by permission Doubleday Books. All rights reserved.

Quotes and stories from Dr. Norman V. Peale used by permission of Ruth Stafford Peale, 66 East Main St., Pawling, NY 12564.

Bible Quotes. King James Version (KJV) unless otherwise noted.

Resources

Suggested Reading

Like the trees in the forest, we have the best chance of surviving the storms of life if we have deep roots and a strong, healthy center. For me, much of this has come from reading. Following are some favorites which have helped (and continue to help) me get through the stormy times (or clean up and survive the aftermath). I pray they will bring strength, comfort and hope to you as well.

Allen, James. *As A Man Thinketh*. n.d. Mount Vernon, NY: The Peter Pauper Press. 1989 MindArt. A classic book on the mind-body relationship.

Bach, Marcus. *I, Monty*. Honolulu, HI: Island Heritage Limited, 1980. A delightful story of a caterpillar's metamorphosis and serendipity.

Bach, Richard. *Jonathan Livingston Seagull: A Story*. New York: The Macmillian Co., 1970. A small but mighty book of inspiration for all ages.

Barbara, Dominick A. *The Art of Listening*. Springfield, IL: Charles C. Thomas, 1958. Listening is ninety percent of good communication.

Berry, Carmen Renee. *When Helping You Is Hurting Me: Escaping the Messiah Trap*. San Francisco: Harper & Row, 1989. Here you will learn how to love others without sacrificing yourself; a must read for "pleasers."

Borysenko, Joan. *Guilt Is the Teacher, Love Is the Lesson: A Book to Heal You, Heart & Soul.* New York: Warner Books, 1990. 1991 New York: Little, Brown & Co. Borysenko's books are so full of inspiration and insights, I keep them for frequent reference.

_____. *Minding the Body, Mending the Mind.* New York: Addison Wesley Publishing Company, 1987. 1989 New York: Bantam.

Bosco, Antoinette. *Coincidences: Touched by a Miracle.* Mystic, CT: Twenty Third Publications, Second Printing, 1998. True stories of God's little miracles in everyday life.

Breathnach, Sarah Ban. *Simple Abundance: A Daybook of Comfort and Joy.* New York: Warner Books, 1995. A book you'll want to read again and again as it is so rich in insights you can't catch them all the first time around.

Browning, Norma Lee and Russell Og. *He Saw a Hummingbird.* Midland, MI: Northwood Institute Press, 1978. This book left an imprint on my soul that has literally opened my eyes to the wonders of miracles where least expected.

Buscaglia, Leo F. *Living, Loving & Learning.* SLACK, 1982. 1985 New York: Fawcett. Love makes life worth living. Buscaglia's books are about the real love — the love of Spirit.

_____. *The Fall of Freddie the Leaf.* SLACK, 1982. 1983 New York: Henry Holt & Co. For the young at heart, and those who want to find that place again.

Butterworth, Eric. *In The Flow of Life.* New York: Harper & Row, 1975. 1994 Unity Village, MO: Unity Books. This book will wake up your intuition and spark your spirit to living life fully.

_____. *Discover the Power Within You: A Guide to the Unexplored Depths Within.* San Francisco: HarperSanFrancisco, 1992.

Cameron, Julia. *The Artist's Way: A Spiritual Path to Higher Creativity.* New York: Jeremy P. Tarcher/Putnam/Perigee Books, 1992. Techniques that will open your heart, mind and spirit as well as your creativity.

Canfield, Jack and Mark Victor Hansen. *Chicken Soup for the Soul.* Deerfield Beach, FL: Health Communications, Inc., 1993. This was the first of many "Chicken Soup" books, every one a heartwarming experience. Great pick-me-ups.

_____. *Chicken Soup for the Surviving Soul.* Deerfield Beach, FL: Health Communications, Inc., 1996.

Carnegie, Dale. *How to Stop Worrying and Start Living.* New York: Pocket Books, 1948, 1966. 1984 Revised edition. S&S Trade. A classic that still speaks the truth in easy-to-understand language.

Charles, C. Leslie. *Why Is Everyone So Cranky? The Ten Trends That Are Making Us Angry and How We Can Find Peace of Mind Instead.* New York: Hyperion, 1999. Releasing anger frees the spirit, heals the body and expands the mind.

Chopra, Deepak. *Quantum Healing: Exploring the Frontiers of Mind/Body Medicine.* New York: Bantam, 1989. Chopra is a medical doctor who practices holistic medicine. His theories make sense.

Cole-Whittaker, Terry. *What You Think of Me is None of My Business.* LaJolla, CA: Oak Tree Publications, 1979. A freedom book — this one is focused on freeing yourself from dependency upon what others think.

Conwell, Russell H. *Acres of Diamonds.* New York and London: Harper & Brothers, 1915. A classic about the search for riches and finding them where you least expect them.

Dominguez, Joe and Vicki Robin. *Your Money or Your Life.* New York: Viking, 1992. A revealing book about how our attitude toward money can affect our well-being, physically, emotionally and spiritually.

Dossey, Larry. *Recovering the Soul.* New York: Bantam Books, 1989. Dossey's titles sum up his books. More than just a good read, Dossey's books help you find the healing you need in all areas of your life, not just your body.

_____. *Meaning and Medicine.* New York: Bantam Books, 1992. A great book with many true stories of how the body, mind and spirit interact to bring illness or health. A powerful message for anyone seeking wholeness.

_____. *Be Careful What You Pray for...You Might Just Get It: What We Can Do About the Unintentional Effects of Our Thoughts, Prayers & Wishes.* San Francisco: HarperSanFrancisco, 1998.

_____. *Healing Words: The Power of Prayer & the Practice of Medicine.* San Francisco: HarperSanFrancisco, 1995.

Dowling, Colette. *The Cinderella Complex: Woman's Hidden Fear of Independence.* New York: Pocket Books, 1981. I believe this book is just as timely, if not more so, than when first written.

Dyer, Wayne W. *Your Erroneous Zone: Step-by-Step Advice for Escaping the Trap of Negative Thinking & Taking Control of Your Life.* New York: Funk and Wagnalls, 1976. Reprint edition paperback, New York: Harper Perennial. One of my first discoveries in my quest for ridding myself of erroneous concepts. Fabulous.

_____. *Real Magic: Creating Miracles in Everyday Life.* New York: HarperCollins, 1993.

_____. *Your Sacred Self.* New York: HarperCollins, 1995.

_____. *Pulling Your Own Strings: Dynamic Techniques for Dealing with Other People & Living Life as You Choose.* New York: HarperCollins, 1994.

Estes, Clarissa Pinkola. *Women Who Run with the Wolves.* New York: Ballantine Books, 1992. Everyone's life is full of stories: those we live, those we think we live and those we want to live. Pinkola helps us see how each plays a role in helping us find our true selves.

Fields, Rick, with Peggy Taylor, Rex Weyler and Rich Ingrasci. *Chop Wood, Carry Water: A Guide to Finding Spiritual Fulfillment in Everyday Life.* New York: Jeremy P. Tarcher/Perigee/Putnam, 1984. This book is about balance, the key to maintaining sanity and good health.

Fillmore, Charles. *Christian Healing.* Unity Village, MO: Unity School of Christianity, 1992. This book shares true stories of the power of prayer in healing bodies as well as spirits.

Foster, Rich and Greg Hicks. *How We Choose to Be Happy: The 9 Choices of Extremely Happy People — Their Secrets, Their Stories.* New York: G. P. Putnam's Sons, 1999. Want to be happy? Here are nine ways to do it.

Frank, Amalie. *Amalie's Good Words: Signposts for the Journey.* Hays, Kansas: Joan Rainwater Publisher, 1998. A good word for starting each day; a book for all seasons and every year.

Frankl, Viktor E. *Man's Search for Meaning.* New York: Washington Square Press, 1963. 1997 New York: Pocket Books. Frankl's experiences in a Nazi concentration camp brought enlightenment. Thankfully, he lived to share his insights with the world.

Friends of Peace Pilgrim. *Peace Pilgrim: Her Life and Work in Her Own Words.* Santa Fe, NM: Ocean Tree Books, 1982. The story of a remarkable woman who walked over 25,000 miles as a self-proclaimed "wanderer for peace."

Fromm, Erich. *The Art of Loving.* New York: Bantam Book, 1970. 2000 Continuum. Learn how to achieve a life rich in the power of love, beginning with a healthy love and respect for yourself.

Fulghum, Robert. *All I Really Need To Know I Learned In Kindergarten.* New York: Villard Books, a division of Random House, Inc., 1986, 1988. Through humor, Fulghum reminds us of the basics for living a good life.

Fynn. *Mister God, This Is Anna.* New York: Ballantine Books, 1976, 2000. A novel about a little girl with amazing insights. Truly a heartwarming and illuminating experience.

Germann, Sr., Douglas D. *Simplifying our lives: Insights to living fully now.* Mishawaka, IN: Learning Works, 1999. A collection of insights to help you build a simpler life.

Gibran, Kahlil, *The Prophet.* New York: Alfred A. Knopf, 1923, 1996. 1999 New York: Viking Penguin. This is a classic in-depth sharing of a man's search and discoveries into his deepest spiritual truths.

Girzone, Joseph F. *Joshua, A Parable for Today.* New York: Macmillan Publishing Company, 1987. 1994 New York: Doubleday. When the news of the day gets to be so discouraging that you fear losing your spirit, pick up this book and be renewed.

Gordon, Arthur. *A Touch of Wonder: Staying in Love with Life.* Carmel, New York: Guideposts Associate, Inc., 1975. 1996 Grand Rapids, MI: Fleming H. Revell Publishing. Ah! Refreshing. Comforting.

Graham, Billy. *Angels: God's Secret Agents.* Carmel, New York: Guideposts Associate, Inc., 1975. 1995 Revised edition, Dallas, Texas: Word Publishing. Yes, there really are angels, and they are blessing us right now.

The Editors of *Guideposts.* *His Mysterious Ways.* Carmel, New York: Guideposts Associates. This is a series of books taken from the monthly feature in *Guideposts* magazine. Every story is a true extraordinary experience with ordinary persons.

Harris, Thomas A. *I'm OK--You're OK: A Practical Guide to Transactional Analysis.* New York: Avon Books, 1973. 1999 Galahad Books. This book and workshops based on the book brought a major change to my marriage.

Hay, Louise L. *You Can Heal Your Life.* Santa Monica, CA: Hay House, 1987. 1994 Hay House. Another book I reference often.

_____. *Gratitude: A Way of Life.* Santa Monica, CA: Hay House, 1998.

Heavilin, Marilyn Willett. *When Your Dreams Die: Finding Strength and Hope Through Life's Disappointments.* San Bernardino, CA: Here's Life Publishers, 1990. In these pages you will learn how others have managed to begin again after experiencing the death of their dreams, whatever they may be.

Higgs, Liz Curtis. *Only Angels Can Wing It.* Nashville, TN: Thomas Nelson, 1995. Liz is an encourager with a great sense of humor. Humor heals.

_____. *One Size Fits All.* Nashville, TN: Thomas Nelson, 1993. More wit and wisdom.

Hill, Napoleon. *Think and Grow Rich.* New York: B. C. Forbes & Sons, 1953. One of those classics that keeps on showing the way to the richness of life, as well as financial gain.

Holmes, Marjorie. *Hold Me Up a Little Longer.* New York: Doubleday, 1977. A little book with a big heart, one I've turned to often through the years.

_____. *I've Got to Talk to Somebody, God.* New York: Doubleday, 1968. A God-incident brought this one into my life, just when I needed it most. And I thought no one was listening, not even God!

_____. *Love and Laughter.* New York: Bantam Books, 1972.

_____. *To Help You Through The Hurting: A Loving Guide to Faith, Hope and Healing.* New York: Doubleday, 1983. 1984, New York: Bantam Books.

_____. *Still by Your Side: A True Story of Love & Grief, Faith & Miracles.* New York: Crossroad, 1996.

Hurnard, Hannah. *Hind's Feet on High Places.* Wheaton, IL: Tyndale Publishers, 1975. 1986. Original publication by The Church's Ministry Among the Jews (Olive Press, London, England. n.d.). Another magical experience of spirit working in our lives written in novel form.

Jampolsky, Gerald G. *Good-Bye To Guilt: Releasing Fear Through Forgiveness.* New York: Bantam Books, 1985. You can feel the love as you read Jampolsky's books.

_____. *Love is Letting Go of Fear.* Putnam Valley, NY: Cogent, 1989.

_____. *Teach Only Love: The Twelve Principles of Attitudinal Healing.* New York: Bantam Books, 1983.

Jeffers, Susan. *Feel the Fear And Do It Anyway.* New York: Ballantine Books, 1988. Here are some dynamic techniques for turning disabling fear and anger into powerful love in action.

Johnson, Barbara. *Stick a Geranium in Your Hat and Be Happy!* Dallas, Texas: Word Publishing, 1990. Writers who see life from the flip side help us keep a healthy perspective. Johnson is one who can find a bit of joy in anything.

_____. *Splashes of Joy in the Cesspools of Life.* Dallas, Texas: Word Publishing, 1992.

Johnson, Spencer. *The Precious Present.* New York: Doubleday, n.d. Touching the spirit at all times of the year. Great gift to give or receive.

_____. *One Minute For Myself.* New York, William Morrow and Co., Inc. 1985. Small book, quick read, big message.

Jozefowski, Joanne T. *The Phoenix Phenomenon: Rising from the Ashes of Grief.* Northvale, NJ: Jason Aronson Inc., 1999. This book has many real-life examples of how people have overcome their grief, and the commonalities in how they did it.

Kaufman, Barry Neil. *Son-Rise — a beautiful and moving love story of a family's devotion, dedication, understanding and caring for their autistic son.* New York: Warner Books, 1977. This book came to teach me nothing is hopeless — somewhere there is an answer, if we'll but look.

Keen, Sam. *Learning to Fly: Trapeze — Reflection on Fear, Trust, and the Joy of Letting Go.* New York: Broadway Books, 1999. Something more than just the excitement of flying through the air; an experiential flight to freedom.

Kellor, Phillip. *Lessons from a Sheep Dog.* Waco, Texas: Word Books, 1983. When we open our hearts and minds, lessons are everywhere.

King, Barbara. *How to Have a Flood and Not Drown: Essays on Stress-Free Living.* Marina Del Ray, CA: DeVorss & Co., 1990. King's essays are life savers for those who feel they are drowning in troubles.

Kinkaid, Thomas. *Lightposts for Living: The Art of Choosing a Joyful Life.* New York: Warner Books, Inc., 1999. This famous author puts light into his words, just as he does in his paintings. Keep handy for those times when your spirit needs lifting.

Kübler-Ross, Elisabeth. *To Live Until We Say Goodbye.* Englewood Cliffs, NJ: Prentice-Hall. Photography by Mal Warshaw. 1978. True stories of counseling work with terminally ill patients.

_____. *On Death and Dying: What the dying have to teach doctors, nurses, clergy and their own families.* New York: Macmillian, 1979.

Kushner, Harold S. *When Bad Things Happen To Good People*. New York: Avon Books, 1983. 1989 New York: Schocken. This book is not about why (for often there is no explanation), but how people cope with the most difficult of burdens.

Lawson, Douglas M. *Give to Live: How Giving Can Change Your Life*. La Jolla, CA: ALTI Publishing, 1991. This is a thought provoking and inspiring book filled with a multitude of ideas for changing our lives and our world.

Levoy, Gregg. *Callings: Finding and Following an Authentic Life*. New York: Harmony Books, 1997. 1998, Paperback New York: Three Rivers Press. Within each person are many kinds of callings. In this book you will learn how to recognize them, evaluate and choose the ones best for you.

Lewis, C. S. *A Grief Observed*. New York: Seabury Press, 1963. 1976 New York: Bantam Books. This journal of Lewis's passage through his grief after his wife's death touched my heart deeply after my husband's death.

Lindbergh, Anne Morrow. *Gift from the Sea*. New York: Pantheon Books, 1955. A friend's gift that came in time to bring life back into a dried-out spirit.

Littauer, Florence. *Blow Away the Black Clouds: A Woman's Answer to Depression*. Irvine, CA: Harvest House, 1979, 1986. 1987, New York: Walker & Co. Another one of those books that came into my life at just the right time.

Maltz, Maxwell. *Psycho-Cybernetics*. New York: Warner Books, 1976. This book brought The Reverend Amalie Frank into my life and new meaning to my life.

Maltz, Maxwell and Charles Schreiber. *Live and Be Free Through Psycho-Cybernetics: A 21-day Do-It-Yourself Course.* New York: Warner Books, 1976.

Mandino, Og. *The Choice.* New York: Bantam Books, 1984. We all face choices, some easy, some seemingly impossible. This is a book about the seemingly impossible. Mandino's books are fast becoming classics of inspiration. Spellbinding, awesome and life-changing for me.

_____. *The Greatest Miracle in the World.* New York: Bantam Books, 1996.

_____. *University of Success.* New York: Bantam Books, 1982. A collection of stories about successful people and what made them successful.

Mandino, Og and Buddy Kaye. *The Gift of Acabar: The Touching story of a boy who does indeed capture a star — and learns from that star that heavenly secrets are to be found right here on earth.* New York: Bantam Books,1979. A marvelous story for every age.

Marshall, Catherine. *Meeting God at Every Turn.* Carmel, NY: Guideposts, 1990. 1995, Fairfax, VA: Chosen Books Publishing. Catherine Marshall's books have become my mainstay for getting through stormy times.

_____. *The Helper.* Carmel, NY: Guideposts, 1990. This is about the Holy Spirit.

_____. *Something More.* New York: Avon Books 1976. All of it is good, but the chapter on "Aughts and Anys" is life changing. A must read.

_____. *To Live Again: The Inspiring Story of Catherine Marshall's Triumph Over Grief.* Fairfax, VA: Chosen Books Publishing, 1996.

Millman, Dan. *The Life You Were Born To Live: A Guide to Finding Your Life Purpose.* Tiburon, CA: H J Kramer Inc., 1993. Once you find and begin cooperating with your purpose, life becomes one grand adventure.

Mitchell, W. *It's Not What Happens To You, It's What You Do About it.* Arvada, CO: Phoenix Press, 1999. The story of incredible determination by a man who refused to be stopped after being severely burned and, later, paralyzed from the waist down.

Moody, Jr., Raymond A. *Life After Life: The Investigation of a Phenomenon Survival of Bodily Death.* New York: Bantam Books 1975. Meet the people who have seen the other side and you'll never fear death again.

_____. *Reflections on Life After Life.* Covington, GA: Mockingbird Books, 1977.

Moore, Thomas. *Care of the Soul: A Guide for Cultivating Depth and Sacredness in Everyday Life.* New York: HarperCollins, 1994. This book gave me a deeper understanding of my soul, filling a void I did not know existed.

Muller, Wayne. *How, Then, Shall We Live? Four Simple Questions That Reveal the Beauty and Meaning of Our Lives.* New York: Bantam, 1996. Truly a book of inspiration for meaningful living, opening vistas of beauty and peace.

Needleman, Jacob. *Money and the Meaning of Life.* New York: Doubleday/Currency Books, 1991. This is a fascinating look into the relationship between money and the spiritual life — a real eye-opening experience.

Nemeth, Maria. *The Energy of Money: A Spiritual Guide to Financial and Personal Fulfillment.* New York: Ballantine, 1999. Learn this concept and never feel poor again.

Pace, G. Eric with Dorothy Lois Lissner. *Don't Just Sit There-LIVE!* New York: Perennial Library, Harper & Row. 1977. This book gives many techniques for using the mind to change your life.

Peale, Norman Vincent. *The Power of Positive Living.* New York: Bantam Doubleday Dell for Peale Center for Christian Living, 1990. 1996, New York: Fawcett Juniper. Peale's books provided the foundation for all that followed in my life. Little did I know how valuable these early lessons would be.

_____. *The Power of Positive Thinking.* New York: Prentice-Hall, Inc. 1952. 1985, New York: Fawcett Juniper.

_____. *Stay Alive All Your Life.* New York: Prentice-Hall, Inc. 1957. 1997, New York: Simon & Schuster.

Pearsall, Paul. *Making Miracles: Finding Meaning in Life's Chaos.* New York: Prentice Hall Press, 1991. 1993, New York: Avon Books. An incredible story of one man's journey into the shadows of death and how he helped make the miracles that brought him back to a rich, fulfilling life.

Ponder, Catherine. *The Dynamic Laws of Healing.* Marina del Rey, CA: DeVorss & Company, 1976. Here are some interesting viewpoints of healing to ponder.

Porter, Eleanor H. *Pollyanna*. New York: Baronet Books, n.d. Many children's books have influenced my thinking, giving me hope, courage and truth.

Progoff, Ira. *At a Journal Workshop: Writing to Access the Power of the Unconscious & Evoke Creative Ability*. New York: Dialogue House Library, ©1975 Ira Progoff. 1992, New York: Putnam Publishing Group. Progoff's journaling method has become a daily habit for me in my search for answers to life's daily and toughest questions. It works!

Pryor, Karen. *Don't Shoot the Dog! The New Art of Teaching and Training*. New York: Bantam Books/Simon & Schuster, 1985. An insightful and humorous book about behavioral training for all relationships, from animal to human, between parent and child or just for your own self.

Redfield, James. *The Celestine Prophecy*. Hoover, AL: Satori Publishing, 1993. 1993, New York: Warner Books. Another novel that brings many insights, particularly into the realm of serendipitous experiences and how they connect us to the Source of all that is.

Remen, Naomi. *Kitchen Table Wisdom*. New York: Riverhead Books, 1996. This is a book filled with healing stories written by a very wise and loving doctor. Comforting and enlightening.

Rhode, Naomi. *The Gift of Family: A Legacy of Love*. Nashville, TN: Thomas Nelson, 1991. A treasure of insights about families.

Robbins, Anthony. *Awaken the Giant Within*. New York: Summit Books, 1991. 1992, New York: Fireside. Robbins tells how to take immediate control of your mental, emotional, physical and financial destiny.

Roberts, Monty. *The Man Who Listens To Horses.* New York: Ballantine Publishing, 1999. Although this autobiography focuses most on Robert's lovingly respectful manner of training horses, you'll gain a whole new perception for personal relationships. A fascinating story.

Ruiz, Miguel. *The Four Agreements: A Practical Guide to Personal Freedom.* San Rafael, CA: 1997. If everyone pledged themselves to these four agreements, the whole world would be free of fear and full of love.

Schachter-Shalomi, Zalman and Ronald S. Miller. *From Age-ing to Sage-ing: A Profound New Vision of Growing Older.* New York: Warner Books, 1997. For everyone who plans to grow older, here is a book filled with insight and wonderment of the ageing process.

Schuller, Robert H. *Self-Love.* New York: Jove Publications, Inc., 1978. 1986, New York: Berkeley Publishing Group. Schuller's "Crystal Cathedral" broadcasts helped my husband, Ken, through his recovery from his first heart attack. I shall always be grateful.

_____. *If It's Going to Be, It's Up to Me: The Eight Principles of Possibility Thinking.* New York, HarperCollins, 1998.

_____. *Life's not Fair but God is Good.* New York: Bantam Books, 1997.

Seaward, Brian Luke. *Stand Like Mountain Flow Like Water: Reflections on Stress and Human Spirituality.* Deerfield Beach, FL: Health Communications, 1997. Simple, fun and delightfully visual guide for finding our spirit in a stressful world.

Seuss, Dr. *Oh, the Places You'll Go!* New York: Random House, 1990. When I started out on my first solo journey in the Hummingbird (RV), a friend and neighbor gave me this book as a Bon Voyage gift. What a treat!

Sher, Barbara, with Annie Gottlieb. Wishcraft: *How to Get What You Really Want.* New York: Viking Press, 1979. In this book you'll find ways to uncover your strengths, skills, dreams and how to make them work for you.

Sher, Barbara, with Barbara Smith. *I Could Do Anything If I Only Knew What It Was: How to Discover What You Really Want and How to Get It.* New York: Delacorte Press, 1994. 1995, New York: Dell.

Siebert, Al. *The Survivor Personality.* New York: The Berkley Publishing Group, 1996. Siebert's book is a practical guide to understanding what makes a person a survivor, and teaches how to become one.

Siebert, Al, As told to Sam Kimball. *Peaking Out: How My Mind Broke Free from the Delusions in Psychiatry.* Portland, OR: Practical Psychology Press, 1995.This is Siebert's personal story of how he discovered the survivor personality. A hero's journey.

Siegel, Bernie S. *How to Live Between Office Visits: A Guide to Life, Love & Health.* New York, HarperCollins, 1993. Siegel is a doctor who understands the spiritual heart as well as the one in our bodies. His words become powerful medicine for the soul as it helps to heal the body.

_____. *Love, Medicine & Miracles: Lessons Learned about Self-Healing from a Surgeon's Experience with Exceptional Patients.* New York: Harper & Row, 1986. 1998, New York: Harper Perennial.

_____. *Peace, Love & Healing: Body Mind Communication, the Path to Self-Healing: An Exploration.* 1998, New York: Harper Perennial.

Sinetar, Marsha. *Do What You Love and the Money Will Follow.* New York/Mahwah: Paulist Press, 1987. Why settle for just a job when you can make a living doing something you really love?

_____. *To Build the Life You Want, Create the Work You Love: The Spiritual Dimension of Entrepreneuring.* New York: St. Martin's Press, 1995.

Stearns, Ann Kaiser. *Living Through Personal Crisis.* New York: Ballantine Books, 1985. 1990. I first read this book while looking for ways to help others, never thinking how helpful it would be in meeting my own crises.

_____. *Coming Back: Rebuilding Lives After Crisis and Loss.* New York: Random House, 1988. 1989, First Ballantine Books Edition.

Stephan, Naomi. *Find Your Life Mission.* Walpole, NH: Stillpoint Publishing, 1989. Finding your life mission will put passion into your life.

Stephan, Naomi with Sue More. *Find Your Life Mission Workbook: A Guide for Self Study.* Walpole, NH: Life Mission, 1991.

Swindoll, Charles R. *Three Steps Forward, Two Steps Back.* Nashville, TN: Thomas Nelson Publishers, 1980. Swindoll teaches how to keep on keeping on, to persevere through pressure and to be grateful for even small accomplishments.

Tate, David A. *Health, Hope & Healing.* New York: M. Evans and Company, 1989. 1998, DIANNE Publishers. When Tate combined holistic and traditional medicine to heal his cancer and a heart attack, he also healed his spirit.

Taylor, Susan L. *Lessons In Living.* New York: Anchor Books/Doubleday, 1995, 1998. Taylor takes us on a journey through her life, sharing insights that have come through her challenges. Another encouraging story from someone who has been there.

Ten Boom, Carrie. *The Hiding Place.* Fairfax, VA: Chosen Books Publishing. ©1971 Carrie Ten Boom and John and Elizabeth Sherrill. 2000 Uhrichsville, Ohio: Barbour Publishing. The story of two Christian sisters imprisoned in a Nazi death camp for helping their Jewish friends and neighbors.

Wakefield, Dan. *The Story of Your Life: Writing a Spiritual Autobiography.* Boston, MA: Beacon Press, 1990. Journaling is a basic tool for finding answers to life's mysteries.

West, Marion Bond. *The Nevertheless Principle.* Grand Rapids, MI: Fleming H. Revell Publishing, 1986. This is a heart-lifting story of survival as West learns to surrender her fears, doubts and worries through the "Nevertheless Principle."

Wezeman, Phyllis Vos & Kenneth R. Wezeman. *Finding Your Way After Your Child Dies.* Notre Dame, IN: Ave Maria Press, 2001. A beautiful book covering fifty-two themes, ranging from weekly allowances to birthday, to graduations, to help parents acknowledge their loss and grow through the experience.

Wezeman, Phyllis Vos, Jude Dennis Fournier & Kenneth R. Wezeman. *Guiding Children Through Life's Losses: Prayers, Rituals and Activities*. Mystic, CT: Twenty-Third Publications, 1998. This book offers many ways to express and release losses from losing face or friends, or coping with disease or death.

Williamson, Marianne. *A Return to Love: Reflections on the Principles of A Course in Miracles*. New York: HarperCollins, 1992. Witty and wise, a book that will give you a new perspective on the meaning of unconditional love.

Yancey, Philip. *Disappointment With God*. New York: HarperCollins, 1991. Answers three questions: "Is God Unfair?" "Is God Silent?" "Is God Hidden?"

_____. *Where is God When It Hurts*. Grand Rapids, MI: Zondervan, 1977.

Young, Pam and Peggy Jones. *Get Your Act Together*. New York: HarperCollins, 1993. An organization program that gets the overworked, overbooked and overwhelmed back on track. This book helped me to get my house in order for the first time in my life!

Ziglar, Zig. *See You at the Top*. Gretna, LA: Pelican Publishing Co., Inc., 1975, 1994. This is a "how to" book that helps you eliminate "stinkin' thinkin'" and avoid "hardening of the attitudes."

Zukav, Gary. *The Seat of the Soul*. New York: Fireside, 1990. In this book Zukav teaches us how to live life with reverence, compassion and trust.

A number of these authors have web sites which offer further information as well as workshops. Check the internet or publisher.

Order Form

☏ **Phone orders:**   (866) 289-1539 (toll-free)

☐ **Fax orders:**   (219) 289-2823

✉ **Mail orders:**   Moorhill Communications
Joanne Hill
PO Box 4114
South Bend, IN 46634-4114

Name _____

Address _____

City _____ State _____ Zip _____

Phone _____

....

Please send _____ copies of *Rainbow Remedies*
    for Life's Stormy Times at $19.95 each $_____

Sales Tax (Indiana residents only)   x .05   _____

Shipping ($4 for first book, $2 each add'l book)   _____

Total Payment Enclosed $_____

....

Payment Type:

☐ Check (made out to Moorhill Communications)

☐ Credit Card (circle one):   VISA   MasterCard

    Number _____ Exp Date _____

    Name as it appears on card _____

    Signature _____

Marriage Encounter (Weekends to help couples with good marriages strengthen and keep alive the love in their relationships.)

National Committee for Youth Suicide Prevention

National Federation of Parents for Drug-Free Youth

National Organization for Victim Assistance Project COPE (A support group for parents experiencing stillbirth and infant death.)

Recovery Headquarters (A support agency for agoraphobics.)

Retrouville: A Lifeline for Troubled Marriages. www.retrouville.org

The Spirit of Freedom (A Christian support agency for alcoholics.)

Upward Bound

Yellow Ribbon Program, www.yellowribbonmn.org (for teens — to prevent suicide.)

12-Step Groups
   Al-Anon/Alateen
   Alcoholics Anonymous
   Co-Dependents Anonymous
   Debtors Anonymous
   Emotions Anonymous
   Gamblers Anonymous
   Narcotics Anonymous
   Overeaters Anonymous
   Sexaholics Anonymous

Order Form

Phone orders: (866) 289-1539 (toll-free)

Fax orders: (219) 289-2823

Mail orders: Moorhill Communications
Joanne Hill
PO Box 4114
South Bend, IN 46634-4114

Name _____

Address _____

City_____ State _____ Zip_____

Phone _____

....

Please send _____ copies of *Rainbow Remedies
for Life's Stormy Times* at $19.95 each $_____

Sales Tax (Indiana residents only)   x .05   _____

Shipping ($4 for first book, $2 each add'l book)   _____

Total Payment Enclosed $_____

....

Payment Type:

☐ Check (made out to Moorhill Communications)

☐ Credit Card (circle one):   VISA   MasterCard

   Number _____ Exp Date _____

   Name as it appears on card _____

   Signature _____

About the Author

Joanne Hill's mission in life is to help others help themselves. She led her community in the organization of crisis intervention services, earning her the title of "Crisis Intervention Specialist" and recognition from WGN Radio, Chicago. She organized neighborhood action groups to preserve wetlands and prevent air and water pollution.

Joanne has written numerous problem solving, motivation and business articles, and human interest stories. In workshops, retreats and Elderhostels, Joanne shares her seven remedies for surviving crises and finding the joy in living. She is a graduate of Bethel College.

Joanne Hill is available for retreats and workshops based on this book.

For details write:

> Moorhill Communications
> Programs
> PO Box 4114
> South Bend, IN 46635-4114
> (866) 289-1539
> E-mail: rainbowremedies@hotmail.com

Inspiring Magazines

Angels On Earth®, c/o Guideposts, P.O. Box 1803, Vernon, CT 06066-9874. Here you will find true stories about God's messengers at work in today's world.

Guideposts® magazine, P.O. Box 856, Carmel, NY 10512-0856. This is an inspirational monthly magazine for people of all faiths. A small magazine with a powerful message told through true stories of how people, from all walks of life, overcame obstacles, rose above failure, handled sorrow and learned to master themselves through faith in God. This magazine has been my rock and my refuge.

Guideposts for Kids c/o Guideposts, P.O. Box 1419, Carmel, NY 10512. This is a bimonthly children's magazine for all faiths that focuses on fun-to-read articles and stories that are value-centered, but not preachy.

Guideposts for Teens, PO Box 1404, Carmel, NY 10512-9923.

Learn more about the Guideposts family of magazines and books, along with daily inspiration at www.dailyguideposts.com.

Additionally, there are many other good magazines on the newsstand with a positive emphasis, as well as those that speak to a particular faith. I urge you to check with your favorite librarian or place of worship. No matter what your problem, someone, somewhere has encountered it and probably written about it. The list of possibilities is so huge, I cannot put them all into this resource section. I suggest you treat yourself to a day at the library perusing the magazines where I'm certain you will find something that fits your needs.

Music, Music, Music

Music soothes the soul, lifts the spirit, motivates and empowers. Here's a few of my favorite inspirational musicians:

Jana Stanfield • 1-888-530-JANA • www.janastanfield.com. My favorite recording is "I'm Not Lost, I'm Exploring." In addition to programs, Jana has a series of distinctive original CDs.

Ken Medema • 1-888-KEN-KEN-KEN • www.KENMEDEMA.COM. Ken's songs are also originals, written on the spot from stories that people share from the audience.

Carmen Moshier, 100 Quartz Street, Hot Springs, AR 71901. Carmen has over 100 positive, motivating and uplifting songs. Many are in her songbook, *Let's Be! Today*, as well as musicians copies. She also has a marvelous cassette tape for children called "Attitoad's Attitude."

Helping Others & Support Systems

Today many support systems are available for those in need. This is a way of helping us help ourselves. The Twelve-Step Groups lead the field in this arena. Contact your local telephone directory, Crisis Center, Volunteer Resource Center, United Way or the World Wide Web for help in locating a support group for your particular situation. Because information can become outdated quickly, I will list only the names of some self-help groups that have been beneficial to me or people I've known.

Beginning Experience (A weekend experience for divorced and widowed to help them release the grief and move on in life.)

Compassionate Friends, Inc. (For parents who have lost a child.)